Radclyffe Hall
at the Well of Loneliness

Radclyffe Hall
at the Well of Loneliness

A Sapphic Chronicle

LOVAT DICKSON

CHARLES SCRIBNER'S SONS
New York

Illustrations

For Harold Rubinstein

Foreword

Although she never made any secret of her own deviant nature, Radclyffe Hall's decision to expose it in a novel which would show the trials, turmoils and tortures of homosexual love was the outcome of what she felt to have been a succession of public humiliations. The fictional form of *The Well of Loneliness* is the thinnest of disguises, with her own birth and upbringing romanticized, and the end transmogrified by a sacrifice in the tradition of the Victorian novels on which her imagination had fed when she was young.

There are only two ways for a biographer to treat this. To laugh about it in the enlightened sexual atmosphere of our times; or to try to illuminate by facts and records in the biographer's hands the background of painful personal experiences the novelist describes.

The latter alternative is likely to get the biographer into trouble with some readers who will resent what they may suspect to be a pejorative tone taken towards the sexual acts of the past, and will feel the references to John's and Una's pathology, the genetic effects of their association and other references of that sort out of tune with today's approach to this subject.

But I am reflecting only what the documents and records which fell into my hands reveal. The 'Twenties and 'Thirties were decades in which daring attempts to establish a sexual freedom we have come to take for granted clashed continually with repressive restrictions inherited from a Victorian past. Radclyffe Hall took very seriously her self-appointed role to have sexual inversion accepted as a trick of nature, deserving sympathy and understanding, not condemnation. I try to show her as the unique personality she was, part of a 'twentyish scene now vanished in the clearer if harsher light of our times.

9

Una Troubridge's diaries cover the years 1911 to 1933, with the exception of 1915 and 1922, the volumes for these years being missing. For the period of Radclyffe Hall's life up to 1915, I have relied largely on the account given in Una's *The Life and Death of Radclyffe Hall*, on the five volumes of poetry which Radclyffe Hall published before 1915, and on the evidence given in the communications with the discarnate Mabel Batten, reported at length in Volumes 30 and 32 of the *Proceedings* of the Society for Psychical Research.

For the naval events which culminated in Admiral Troubridge's request for a court-martial, I have drawn chiefly on the excellent account given in Barbara Tuchman's *The Guns of August*. I have supplemented this with the entries in Una's diaries. For much of this period there are the letter files belonging to Una, which include the correspondence with Admiral Lord Fisher, the letters from the Board of Admiralty, and the extensive correspondence with Baroness Massola concerning both the court-martial and her meeting with Radclyffe Hall. An unpublished and untitled manuscript of sketches and essays, autobiographical in intent, which Una left on her death, includes the account I give of the Admiral's interview with Winston Churchill and the story of her sculpturing of Nijinsky.

The background of the events described in Chapter six is taken almost wholly from the diary, except for the trial for slander which was reported at considerable length in the London *Times*. The account of the sittings with Mrs Osborne Leonard is taken largely from the diary, and from the subsequent papers printed in the *Proceedings*. I owe a great deal for background information on E.S.P. to Rosalind Heywood's masterly *The Sixth Sense* (Pan Books).

The encounter with Havelock Ellis is well-documented in the continuing exchange of letters between them which are in my possession. The part played by Jonathan Cape in the affair of *The Well of Loneliness* is documented in the correspondence with her agent and friend, Audrey Heath, and in verbal reports noted down in Una's diary almost daily. But the best and most amusing account of this baffling business is to be found in *Jonathan Cape*,

Publisher, by the firm's historian, the late Michael Howard. I am obliged to the firm of Jonathan Cape Ltd for permission to quote from this. The simultaneous *imbroglio* with Knopf in America is reflected in the correspondence between Blanche Knopf and Radclyffe Hall. For permission to reproduce these letters I am obliged to Mr Alfred Knopf. I acknowledge gratefully the permission of Michael and Anne Yeats to reproduce the two unpublished letters from W. B. Yeats. The account of the last affair with Evguenia Souline is taken with permission from the collection of Radclyffe Hall's letters held by the Humanities Research Center at the University of Texas at Austin.

I have been greatly helped in writing this book by the memories of those who attended the trial as witnesses; above all by the account given me by Harold Rubinstein, who was in the confidence of the chief figures in the defence throughout. One of the many benefits to me from our long friendship has been the fascinating glimpses he has provided of a literary London and its figures long before I became attached to it. For the account of the American trial, I am indebted, as anyone who writes about censorship in America must be, to Mr Morris Ernst.

I also owe thanks for some stimulating recollections of the period and of the figures of whom I have written here to Patience Ross of the Heath Agency, and to Joan Saunders of Writer's and Speaker's Research in London, my stay and help still, as in past years.

Toronto   LOVAT DICKSON

Chapter One

In London one day just after the Second War, I was lunching with Harold Rubinstein, an able lawyer who is also a good writer and an excellent playwright, when he suddenly asked me if I would be joint-executor with him in a will he was at that time preparing.

'You will be wondering why I, instead of the testator, should be asking you this,' he said. 'That is because you don't know her yet. But she knows all about you, and she has made up her mind that she wants you.'

I was then general editor and a director of an old-established family publishing business, presided over almost invisibly by a classical scholar-publisher of the old school, a man of great sweetness of character which he kept aggressively concealed from the world, uncovering it only in the company of a few trusted friends of whom I was fortunate to be one. Publishing he loved, but authors with their unceasing demands and misconceived notions of what could be done for their books, he could not abide. It fell to me to have most of the dealings with authors and agents. As a consequence, I appeared to be much more prominent and influential in the firm's councils than I really was. In a time of paper famine my opinions were listened to, and my pronouncements received, with a respect they were quite unworthy of.

So that when Harold Rubinstein told me that it was Lady Troubridge whose will he was drawing up, and I remembered that she had been the lover and companion of Radclyffe Hall, the author of a number of novels, including the notorious *The Well of Loneliness*, all of which were no doubt out of print, I immediately assumed that it was not my wisdom and steadiness that were being solicited, but my ability to allocate some paper to these forgotten books.

Although I had not seen them during the war, and had never

met either of them, I could remember Una Troubridge and Radclyffe Hall quite clearly. When I first came to London in 1929, they were well-known public figures, frequently to be seen lunching and dining at fashionable restaurants in London, or at the opening of a new play, when they customarily had seats in the front row. In the foyer between the acts they seemed to flaunt their unnatural connection, but this may have been my youthful imagination at work. Certainly they were very unusual-looking, Una with her monocle, and both of them smoking little green cigars. I wasn't the only one impressed. An early water-colour of Evelyn Waugh's, done in the 'twenties, catches what they looked like perfectly.*

Radclyffe Hall had been a successful writer, who had published several volumes of verse before turning to novels. She had scored a considerable *succès d'estime* with *Adam's Breed*, which in 1926 carried off the two great literary prizes in England, a feat accomplished only once before, with E. M. Forster's *Passage to India*. She had followed this up with *The Well of Loneliness*, an outspoken appeal for an understanding and acceptance of sexual inversion. The magistrates had promptly suppressed the book, but an English edition flourished in Paris, and most Britons returning from a holiday on the Continent brought back a copy in their suitcases.

Radclyffe Hall was a slender handsome woman with a marvellously clear-cut profile. She wore her fine hair close-cropped. In the evenings she wore a man's dinner-jacket above a short black pleated skirt. She was much given to diamonds, and these in her shirt, her cuff-links, and on her fingers made her seem to flash with light. Una Troubridge was fair and extremely pretty. She too looked masculine, but like an effeminate young man. Staring at them both with the eyes of youth, they seemed alluring and attractive figures, and I wondered to myself, as young men do, what the heat of their strange passion did to those mask-like beautiful faces, those slender limbs, dressed now so oddly.

Then they disappeared from the scene. I heard that they were living in Rye. I read during the war of Radclyffe Hall's death in

* See p. 64, *Evelyn Waugh and his World*, edited by David Pryce-Jones, London, 1973.

London. Then I did not think of them again until Harold raised this curious proposal.

He went on to tell me that Radclyffe Hall had left over £100,000 to Una Troubridge, and this sum she was disposing of in the will. No problem there. They had both been Catholics, and Una was leaving it all to the Order of Poor Clares.

The joint-executor was required for another and higher purpose, to guard from defilement the copyright of her friend's books. They were all out-of-print, as was so much else, but she was convinced that they would soon be asked for again. Una Troubridge lived in terror of *The Well of Loneliness* being tricked out in a gaudy jacket and sold as a sex book. There must be someone to exercise control when she was gone. She had just had a great row with a publisher whose interest in the 'works' had seemed to be genuine. But he had turned out to have very different ideas. She wanted someone who had experience of handling literary property, and was honest. I was that paragon.

At first I demurred. I had enough to do. But Harold urged me to meet her before dismissing the proposal. He would be very much obliged if I would agree as a friend to that, particularly as he had spoken so highly to her of my judgement and good taste. The books *were* very good, had been much praised by the critics. The verse was highly thought of, and a lot of it had been set to music. The royalties that came in were really quite substantial, and the copyrights would be left to me on Una's death. She did not expect my firm to reprint the books; she wanted only advice, and the satisfaction of knowing that they would be in good hands after her death.

His gentle urgings, as always, prevailed. A luncheon date was discussed. He was not to appear himself. We were to get to know one another.

I thought I knew what to expect: an older version of the attractive woman with the monocle I used occasionally to see in the distance fifteen years before. I rose from the table at the Caprice to greet instead a shrunken little lady in her mid-sixties, dressed in a coat and skirt of that sub-fusc pattern, worn in the old days by governesses who might be suddenly summoned to appear if the children were called down to the drawing-room. Her white hair was screwed back into a bun, and on top of it she wore an unbecoming blue beret. Her whole appearance demonstrated a lack of interest in herself, and in the impression she made on others. Remembering her daintiness, her *soigné* appearance in the theatre, I could hardly believe that this was the same woman.

Out of this colourless background looked a face still quite handsome. It was innocent of powder and make-up of any kind, and this gave the very pale and unblemished skin an ivory glow which was becoming. Her eyes were a washed-out blue, but they came to life as she talked of the past and of John, which was the name she called Radclyffe Hall. Her voice surprised me. It was so much at odds with her pale, unanimated expression. There was a tonal variety, a warmth and a depth to it which I have observed usually goes with strongly-sexed women.

I don't know what course I had expected our conversation to take, but I suppose that I expected to be persuaded, and I was ready to resist. She seemed to assume that I had already agreed to act as executor, and that I was now one of the party, so to speak, who had been absent and needed to be caught up on the news. She was very easy to talk to. I began to get a picture of what their life had been like together; she made enquiries about mine and my family; and small exchanges of this sort began to flow back and forth between us.

I had been curious as to what kind of confidences would be given and even wondered whether these would be embarrassing. I need not have worried. I was talking as to a widow, one who thought she was separated only by an impalpable veil from re-union with her adored one. I was emboldened to ask her about the social embarrassments and difficulties that went along with their condition. Did female homosexuals keep company only with other inverts? Una's Admiral-husband had been said to have been the handsomest officer in the Royal Navy. What did it feel like if you had been the much-admired and envied wife of such a man to be swept off your feet by love for another woman

'The best friend a woman ever had,' she said, as though

Marguerite were of the opposite sex. Yes, Una had loved men, but had never felt any inclination towards them after she had fallen in love with Marguerite. She had discovered then for the first time what sexual rapture felt like. The primness was only in her appearance. Talking quietly and closely, our heads together, in order not to be overheard, I could see that she had been very beautiful. It was not difficult to imagine her suffused with that hot content that burns away the flesh; and to imagine this flame lit by someone other than a man. She seemed to have absolutely no sense of embarrassment in talking about it all to me. She wished, she said, 'to dwell in the palace of truth', and although such phrases always sound spurious when spoken, it was obvious that she was sincere in saying that she had no wish to hide this love from the world.

Once it was established that there was no hope of my firm issuing the books, she seemed perfectly happy to have me just as a friend and confidant. We lunched and dined often in the next few years. I found her company more engaging all the time, and she melted with me and I could see that she must have been flirtatious when she was young, when the Admiral, so to speak, was in ownership. She was very good with men, pandered to their appetites, vanities and emotions, and once I had shown that I did not like the mood lugubrious about her departed lover, she kept off that tack, and we had many laughs together. A publisher was found* who was willing to issue all the books, including *The Well*, which would be a challenge to the Director of Public Prosecutions. When in due course it appeared, the publication excited no official move against the book, as Una had correctly anticipated. It sells today steadily in paperback editions in many languages, and what I rather squirmed about accepting as a responsibility has turned out, since I inherited it, to be a valuable literary property.

There remained wanting only an official biography, which she was most anxious I should undertake. The intimate relationship which Una could not describe except with a wealth of metaphor is set out quite frankly in *The Well of Loneliness* which is in effect,

* The Falcon Press, later taken over by Hammond & Hammond.

with some romantical trappings, an autobiographical account of Radclyffe Hall's life. But I refused on the plea that I had too much work to do.

That was not the true reason. Something in the middle-class consciousness, and I was exemplifying it, still took instant alarm at the plea *The Well of Loneliness* explicitly makes for an understanding and acceptance of inversion. Sex, that unavoidable subject of adolescent dreams, had been so hedged about with prohibitions that instant alarm bells rang at the slightest deviation from the accepted and sanctified myth. Helpless infantile responses to the throb of nature were condemned with the passion of missionaries exorcising the devil. Headmasters, and housemasters, faces sombre with the awful message, had varied the prohibition from the persuasive 'gentlemen don't do such things', to the admonitory, that prison and madness lay at the end of that road.

At 45 my mind still harboured those early inhibitions. Una was able to help to shake me free of them before there was a general discarding of them everywhere. She began by awakening my interest in Radclyffe Hall. As we talked I began to see the slender girl with all her raging passions who was the sapling from which grew the middle-aged, mannish-looking woman smoking green cigars whom I remembered from before the war. Una once showed me a picture of them both, taken at a dog show. They wore men's Fedora hats, bought at Lock's in St James's Street, and knickerbockers and golf stockings, suitable apparel for a dog show, and each is holding round her midriff a dog, their entries for that particular show. Who could mistake them for anything but 'queers'?

From such flamboyancy I shrank, until Una patiently explained that it is inseparable from homosexual love. The lovers know that their thoughts are pure, but they are aware that others regard inversion as impure. They do not want to be accepted as abnormal heterosexuals, but as normal homosexuals. There is a burning sincerity in establishing themselves as apart, but worthy. They send out in unusual clothes, mannerisms, gestures, signals of a difference they are aware may incite anger in the human pack, but which they are as incapable of hiding as an animal its scent.

Radclyffe Hall was a congenital invert. She had taught others to be brave about this. I was beginning to catch the glow of the embers that had stirred into flame between these two, but I was not yet ready to write the biography, which would demand complete sympathy, even partisanship.

In the end Una herself wrote the life in 1961.* She inscribed a copy to me, and I read it with a growing disappointment. It rang with reticence, which had been absent in her talks with me. She had been a successful translator, and had first introduced Colette to English readers, but she had no gift of characterization, and she had an unreserved admiration for her subject which puts off readers who prefer to make their own judgements.

Una does not mean to hide, she really wants to present a truthful portrait. But she was first and foremost a lady in the old-fashioned sense of the word, and there were Rules. These included not talking about oneself to comparative strangers, which is right for ladies, but not for biographers. I could not help but be rather luke-warm in my comments. This did not offend her; in fact my guarded frankness and mild criticism seemed quite to please her, as though they demonstrated my trustworthiness.

Soon after, she went to live in Florence. I saw her only once after that, when our paths happened to cross in Milan. But we kept up an intermittent correspondence, and exchanged gifts at Christmas. With absence, the early warmth and confidences of our first meetings died away, and I expected nothing more than these seasonal greetings for the future.

Suddenly word came through Harold Rubinstein in November, 1963, that she had died. She had not even told me that she was ill. She died in Rome of cancer, and she must have been in hospital waiting for death when she wrote her last letter to me.

She had not changed her will. The Poor Clares were enriched by something over £100,000, and the copyrights came to me. The only charge laid upon me was that I should care for the upkeep of the vault in Highgate Cemetery where Radclyffe

* *The Life and Death of Radclyffe Hall* by Una Troubridge, London, Hammond & Hammond, 1961.

19

Hall's coffin lay, and her own was eventually to be placed.

Nothing seemed to go right in this affair. Una's Italian lawyer had arranged for her burial in a Roman cemetery before the English will was read and probate received. There did not seem at that stage any point in exhuming these poor remains and transporting them to Highgate.

It was two years after Una's death before my conscience prompted me to visit the grave in Highgate Cemetery. I had never been in that historic necropolis before. It is a forest of stone carved into the fantastic shapes that funerary splendour reached in the nineteenth century. Karl Marx's tomb is the most famous, and the one most visited. For a man of his modest fortune and revolutionary ideas, it is ornate, but not more so than hundreds of others that lie half-concealed, overgrown, deserted, in the lush jungle of cultivated trees and horticultural marvels that weave fantastic arbours about the grottos, vaults and tombs.

It took me a little time to find the one in which the remains of Mabel Batten and Radclyffe Hall lie together. I came upon it at last unexpectedly. I could identify it from the name of Mabel Veronica Batten painted in gold, now rather faded, on a black board above. The tomb was in the form of a Greek temple set back about twelve feet into the side of a hill. A stone doorway with a heavy pediment above gave entrance to the chamber. To the left wall holding the door a marble plaque was affixed, bearing the name Radclyffe Hall, and an inscription: 'And if God choose I shall but Love thee better after Death – Una'. It was as though I had happened suddenly on a private room where people lay sleeping and where a wall was missing. I looked through a grille of iron bars reaching from roof to the floor. On a stone bench set longitudinally to me one of the coffins lay. A table on which there was a lamp and some ornaments separated the two coffins, the second of which lay broadside to my view. An iron gate gave entrance to the tomb. The lock had rusted, and so had one of the iron hinges that held it to the stone pillar, and the gate stood askew as though pushed aside by a hasty and thoughtless visitor. It would have been the easiest thing in the world for me to enter this sleeping chamber, and gaze down at these coffins, even perhaps to have lifted their lids if I had the strength, for the hinges were as rusted as those of the gate. Everything was open to the weather. Before leaving for Canada, I reported these dilapidations to the Poor Clares, and they undertook to make the necessary repairs.

It was curious and rather eerie that on a subsequent visit to England six years later, I should have been reminded of the 'unfinished business' with which my legacy of the copyrights under Una's will had implicitly charged me. A record of their lives together remained to be written. I had dodged it with the excuse that there was little evidence to make a book beyond a few letters and the memories of some of their friends. Such an unusual and long relationship, so secret in its intimacies, needed more than the bare account of their goings and comings and the passage of their days.

Harold Rubinstein had a surprise for me. A file of letters, and nineteen volumes of Una's diaries had turned up. They had been in the possession of John Holroyd-Reece, the publisher in Paris of the English edition of *The Well*. They had been returned to Harold Rubinstein by Reece's widow after his death in 1969. So there is no longer an excuse, but only an explanation to offer.

Why do I feel that I should tell it now, when I was so supercilious about it before? An eerie feeling that beyond this veil of life some insistence is being bent upon me. Also because, of course, homosexuality has now become an open subject freely discussed, and is no longer something to snigger over, or condemn as criminal. For that enlightened attitude, books among other causes have to be thanked. It was Radclyffe Hall's urgent desire to have the subject dragged into the open light of day that made her write *The Well of Loneliness*. It isn't a great literary work, but it is a book of importance in the history of the unending struggle with censorship. It was the stone that loosened the avalanche. No one would say that *Uncle Tom's Cabin* awoke the world to the horrors of slavery, but its wide circulation did much to hasten the American Civil War, and the outcome of this was to bring about the end of slavery in America.

The Well of Loneliness, promptly stamped out by authority, seemed at the time to have failed in its aim. But the story is too vividly told to be quenched by throwing over it the cold water of magisterial disapproval. In the United States, as well as in many foreign languages, it seized the imagination of readers, not for its erotic element, which is practically non-existent, but because it appealed to the reader's sense of justice and his conscience.

Like *Uncle Tom's Cabin*, to force the comparison that would otherwise seem ridiculous, it appeared just at the right moment, when the immediate past (meaning late Victorian and Edwardian times) had still not entirely been cast off, and the future (meaning the Second World War and the complete social revolution which accompanied it) had not yet been entered into. What the apocryphal writers call the time between the times. It always seems to need a book to spark the explosion which uncouples society like a train of freight cars from one age and joins it on to a new one.

One does not expect a romantic novelist to remind us that life is harsh and mercenary, but that is what the story of the publication of *The Well of Loneliness* does. One sees the busy greedy world like bees about a hive, the publishers and booksellers and agents on to a good thing, the red-faced judges and magistrates intemperate in condemnation. The diaries and letters now in my hands show us not only the view from the inside of the hive, but something of the sound and temper of life within it. Una was no natural diarist, but she was a young woman in love, I think for the first time in her life. Even her prose comes alight in the glow, and we can sense the furious consuming passion, knowing climaxes and joys, some psychologists say, often beyond the experience of heterosexual lovers. Yet with its bitter aftertaste of barrenness, always to mock the high moments. This is mentioned again and again. In heterosexual unions children come to bind the parents together when the first raptures are over. In homosexual unions there is nothing.

What prodigious love it must have taken to keep these two together through thick and thin. The diary shows the frequent and passionate domestic rows. It may have been an unholy love, but it had some element which survived the white heat of passion and the cold deadness, the non-feeling which is so often the consequence of unnatural union.

The Well of Loneliness does not set out to glorify the joys of deviant sex, and legitimacy wins out all along the line. In the end, Stephen sacrifices her Mary to Martin, and Stephen Gordon is left alone, crying out to God 'Give us also the right to our existence'.

The answer was then an outraged 'No' from authority. Nearly fifty years after the trial which condemned *The Well of Loneliness*, we would seem to have reached the goal at which she aimed. But Radclyffe Hall asked for sympathy and understanding, not for indifference, which is all we have brought ourselves so far to offer. And from that Other Life, with which while they were here these two tried so persistently to communicate, that low, urgent voice of Una's sometimes seemed to reach me with an echo of the same cry.

Chapter Two

Where did the lives that ended in these neglected graves begin? And what drove them to the course they followed? One turns first for an explanation to writers on the psychology of sex, Krafft-Ebing, Havelock Ellis, Moll, Hirschfeld, Clifford Allen and the rest. Only to find that there is no general agreement as to whether inversion is a congenital characteristic, or simply a caprice of sexual appetite which becomes a habit generating its own satisfaction and, automatically, a distaste for normal sex. One devours book after book on this subject – noting, with surprise, how well-written they are – to find that the only matter on which the experts seem united is that inversion is an anomaly and not a disease or degradation, a fundamental point on which they are at issue with the law-makers.

To take two views: Havelock Ellis thinks that there is an infinite gradation of sexuality between a complete male at one extreme and a complete female at the other, with bisexuality hovering at some stage between; while Moll recognizes only bi-sexuality and complete inversion, with none of the many stages in between that Havelock Ellis allows for.

Radclyffe Hall always stated emphatically that she was a congenital invert, by which she meant that no other aspect than homosexuality had ever presented itself to her. This is almost certainly true. Una Troubridge would by this definition have been bisexual, for she was already married and the mother of a child when she fell in love with Radclyffe Hall. But she was also then a neurasthenic wreck, and even the non-expert can see that, while her husband adored her and she thought that she loved him, she used every excuse to get away from him, or to postpone joining him wherever he was stationed. One might have explained this merely as frigidity, except that she was a very passionate lover when she fell in love with a woman. Bisexuality seems hardly the term to describe a *volte-face* of this kind.*

The technicians are not therefore really of much help. One has to fall back on the old methods that writers use, intuitive rather than scientific. Look into the past, see what traits these characters inherited, examine their childhood for clues. All human beings leave tracks, from the moment they first rise shakily to their legs as infants, until as adults governing their own lives they delude themselves into believing that they can hide their traces. One does not have to be a psychologist, only a close observer, taking care, however, not to force parallels and seek neat solutions from insufficient evidence.

Both Radclyffe Hall and Una Taylor, as she was born, came of upper middle-class families. Both their fathers had been at Eton and Oxford, and the paternal grandfathers of both of them had come to fame in different ways but almost at the same time.

Dr Charles Radclyffe Hall, Marguerite's grandfather, was a vigorous and ambitious man, although he appears in his photograph† to have been bilious and disillusioned in appearance. He had begun his career by contributing to the *Lancet* in the year he qualified, 1845, a series of nine articles on the new phenomenon of Mesmerism. At that time he had been attached to the Manchester Royal Infirmary, but contracting tuberculosis he moved south for the sake of a milder climate and settled in Bristol. Here he began to specialize in the disease from which he periodically suffered, writing papers on the subject for the medical journal, and addressing the British Medical Association at its annual meeting on 'Nature's Method of Arresting Tuberculous Disease in the Lungs'.

He did not pause or relax in his steady climb towards wealth and fame until the end of his life. Una tells a curious story of an unhealthy affection he had for a young step-daughter brought to

---

* e.g. Edith Lees, Havelock Ellis's wife, with his agreement, continued to have affairs with women, while living with him. And we have lately had the example of Harold Nicolson and his wife. (See Havelock Ellis, *My Life*, and Nigel Nicolson, *Portrait of a Marriage*.)

† Photographs of Eminent Medical Men Vol. 1. Churchill 1857.

him by his marriage to a widow. The early death of this child turned him socially into a bitter recluse.

But he seems to have remained concerned enough with worldly ambition, and after opening a sanatorium for chest diseases in Torquay in the middle of Queen Victoria's reign, making that town fashionable as a spa, earning him a knighthood and making himself rich in the process, he hyphenated his name and took out armorial bearings, which traced his descent back to no less than William Shakespeare, by the marriage of Dr John Hall of Stratford-on-Avon to Susannah, Shakespeare's daughter.*

Una says that he was not on good terms with his only son who, unlike his ambitious and industrious father, never did a day's work in his life. Christened Radclyffe Radclyffe-Hall, but known by the affectionate diminutive of 'Rat', he was entered at St John's College, Oxford, where he matriculated in 1869. The bracketed indication after his name in the College records as 'arm' presumably means that he was the son of a squire, not of a peer or pleb. He appears not to have taken his degree, and to have left before his time. Probably he was too lazy to do the necessary work. The Reverend Walter Begley, who had tutored him for Oxford, remained his friend all through his life, and was suitably rewarded with quite a substantial legacy on Rat's death.

Rat had had a passion for music, which Walter Begley encouraged in him. He had learnt to play the mandolin, and in the course of his life was to make quite a valuable collection of these instruments, which at that time were coming very much into vogue. He had composed innumerable pieces of music for the mandolin, some of which had been published, and these, as well as his unpublished compositions, he left in his will to his teacher and loving friend, Miss Victoria Holloway, of Battersea Park Road, listing them after his jewellery as the most precious and disposable items in his estate.

No daughter was ever more like her father in appearance and

---

* Confirmation of the possible correctness of this claim can be found in *Shakespeare's Son-In-Law*, a Life of Dr John Hall, by C. Martin Mitchell, Birmingham: Cornish Bros, with a preface dated 1947. See also Fripp: *Shakespeare, Man and Artist*, 2 vols. C.U.P. 1938.

tastes. Marguerite was to inherit Rat's passion for music, and his liking for wearing expensive jewellery. Writing the lyrics to his compositions had afforded him as much pleasure as scoring the music. He liked to think of himself as a 'poet-fellow'. He looked the part with his slender, elegant figure, his handsome head and taste for dress, the diamonds that flashed in his shirt-front and cuffs, the cats-eye stud set in a circle of diamonds which he usually wore in his cravat. The slender, diamond-studded figure of his daughter, whom forty years later I was to watch with interest from the theatre stalls, really brought him back to life.

One was not then morally obliged to have an occupation or appear to be busy about something, and as Rat had inherited from his father a weak chest, he took to spending the winters abroad and his summers sailing off the English and French coasts in a ten-ton yacht, accompanied by his valet. He seems to have been of an unambiguously amorous disposition, his will which was proved in 1898 providing for two mistresses and an illegitimate child who survived him. But he resisted matrimony until on a visit to America he fell in love with an American widow, a Mrs Sanger, who had been born Mary Diehl of Philadelphia. She was to become the mother of Marguerite Radclyffe-Hall.

The new Mrs Radclyffe-Hall proved to be a silly woman, a prey to jealousy, and to have a vile temper. Rat soon found that he could not stand her, and although she was seven months pregnant with his child, he left her within two years of the marriage. Soon after the birth of the little girl on 12 August, 1880, at Surrey Lawn, West Cliff, near Bournemouth, he obtained a divorce. He made a trust settlement through Messrs Hastie, the well-known London solicitors, to provide for the education and care of his daughter, whom he was to see for only an hour or so on two occasions in the rest of his life.

Mrs Radclyffe-Hall could not abide country life in England, and as soon as the divorce settled matters financially, she left the house near Bournemouth where her daughter had been born, and came to London. She took a furnished house at first, and was soon happily involved in the social life which an attractive divorcée with a comfortable allowance could command for herself. No doubt there were several proposals of marriage, but she had tried it twice and it had not worked, and she was in no hurry to make a third attempt. She had brought her mother, Mrs Diehl, over from America to live with her, and act as chaperone. Mrs Diehl became devoted to her little grand-daughter.

Mrs Radclyffe-Hall was pursued to Belgium by one ardent suitor, Alberto Visetti, a Professor of Singing at the Royal College of Music. One of Marguerite's earliest memories was to be the excitement of his arrival at their hotel in Bruges. His enterprise was rewarded. Mrs Radclyffe-Hall became Mrs Visetti.

Soon they were all established in a large house in Addison Road. In the walled garden which surrounded the house, Mr Visetti built a studio where he could take singing pupils, some of whom came to lodge in the house. As they were young and attractive girls, as Mrs Visetti was consumed by jealousy, and as Mr Visetti had an explosive temper, the resulting rows were frequent and noisy, her mother's silliness and helplessness and Alberto's Italian temperament and robust, musical voice combining to make such occasions seem like scenes from an opera. Mrs Diehl did her best to protect her grand-daughter from these displays, but it was difficult to escape the storm. Objects were hurled, doors slammed viciously, the house rocked. A little girl with thin legs, a white face and light blonde hair which already grew down below her shoulders watched and listened, absorbed.

The child led a solitary life in the large walled garden that surrounded the house. I do not know why she had no friends. Perhaps Mrs Visetti did not welcome them. It may be that Kensington parents looked down on a divorcée married to a singing-master. The Royal Borough took itself with immense seriousness socially.

The house and the money were her daughter's as Mrs Visetti frequently told her when confiding in the child that she would never speak to Mr Visetti again. And that impression was confirmed by Mr Hastie, the solicitor, who came to call once a quarter, and had a private conversation with Mrs Visetti anent accounts, from which Mrs Visetti always emerged flushed, angry and tearful to call her daughter to the drawing-room where Mr

Hastie insisted on speaking to the child alone. He would ask her if she were happy, and she would usually say that she supposed so, not knowing what other answer to give. He would enquire about her schooling and her friends, what books she had read, what she did with her spare time – which, he would say, should be given to improving herself by visits to the famous museums and galleries so conveniently near to hand where she lived. She soon came to know, being a sharp child, able to pry information from a silly and garrulous mother, that he was the emissary of her father to whom her mother had been married before incomprehensibly she exchanged him for fat Alberto. She added bit by bit to her stock of information; learnt from her mother that her father was rich, owned a yacht, and lived abroad; built fantasies from this. Saw herself as an unfairly-held prisoner of these middle-class circumstances, awaiting rescue by the coming of a rich and handsome father. As she grew older she asked Mr Hastie why her father did not come to see her. 'He will be coming one of these days,' said Mr Hastie, 'the next time he is in England.'

And suddenly one day in her fifteenth year, he did come, romantically on horseback. He rang the doorbell, told the parlour-maid to send someone to hold his horse, and asked to see his daughter. In the drawing-room he looked her up and down, and asked a few questions. He was just as she knew he would be, tall, trim-bearded, slender, pale, and interesting-looking. He had evidently liked what he saw in her too – perhaps an image of himself when younger, for he told her abruptly that he wished that he had seen more of her. After half-an-hour's conversation he had left. But before going he had said, putting his hand on her head and looking seriously at her: 'I came here to look at you because I am making a new will. I will tell you now that I am going to leave you all my property.'

He left as quickly as he had come, and she did not see him again for three years. Then in 1898, just when she had finished school, and was on the point of entering King's College, London, she was summoned to a hotel in Folkestone where her father was gravely ill. He had been living in the South of France for some years, and slowly dying of consumption, which was to kill Una's father, Harry Taylor, too. When the end was very near Rat had had himself sailed back to England in his own yacht. He had to be carried ashore to the Lord Warden Hotel at Folkestone on a stretcher. He had sent for his child and his solicitor.

Her father's death released part of her inheritance to her. For the remainder, her grandfather's money, she had to wait until she was twenty-one. But when she returned from the hotel in Folkestone where her father had died, she was an independent young woman financially, and an extraordinarily difficult one, for which the Visettis were not altogether to blame. Although, if they had been sensible people and not so absorbed in their quarrels with each other, they might have given her a chance of a more normal life. Clifford Allen states unequivocally, 'I don't believe there is such a thing as inborn homosexuality, or if it does occur I have never been privileged to see such a case.'* To him it is the resistance power to the demand which determines the psychosexual inclination. There was nothing in Marguerite's upbringing to encourage or fortify resistance to the inclination, but everything to sharpen the temptation.

Now that she was financially independent she left the Visetti household, and took a house of her own in Church Street, Kensington, taking along her grandmother, old Mrs Diehl, as chaperone. The old lady was merely a figurehead. Once installed in the house, Marguerite – or John as she now insisted on being called – had begun to dress like a man, to smoke and swagger, and keep strange company. After King's College, she went to Dresden for a year with the object of learning German, but really to allow herself adventures outside England. Then she went to America to discover her mother's family, took up with one of her cousins, female of course, and together they spent a winter touring the southern states.

She had by now come into the balance of her money, and was a rich young woman. She was also growing into an extremely handsome one. Her predilection for men's clothes added to her physical attractiveness, for when her ash-blonde hair, which came down to her knees, and was as fine as silk, and worn at this stage

* *Textbook of Psychosexual Disorders,* p. 179.

coiled neatly round her small head, was covered by a man's hat, she looked like an extremely handsome, slim young man. The mask had a stimulating effect upon some young women, and her conquests were frequent.

But at the same time these triumphs were at war with the struggle to become a poet, to be able to express all these passions and tempests that stormed through her mind, leaving her body intoxicated with joy, or sunk in lassitude and dejection. The fantasies of our childhood shape our personality. Hers were sending her in a direction from which there could be no withdrawing.

Very different was the atmosphere of the home, not more than a mile or two away from the establishment in Kensington where Una Taylor, born seven years after Marguerite Radclyffe-Hall, was brought up.

Harry Ashworth Taylor, Una's father, was the only and much loved son of Sir Henry Taylor, a senior civil servant at the Colonial Office, who had married the youngest daughter of Lord Monteagle. Sir Henry was an author of some note, his line being historical dramas in blank verse, at least one of his compositions, *Philip van Artefelde*, being translated into several other languages, and earning him a place in the *Dictionary of National Biography*.

Sir Henry had not much money but he had plenty of influential friends with whom he kept up a perpetual and gossipy correspondence. When his son Harry, on coming down from Oxford, had gone into the army as a career, it was confidently expected that he would marry a fortune, and letters went out to Sir Henry's friends in foreign stations to which Harry's regiment was sent, beseeching their hospitality. When his correspondents complained that he never came to call, Sir Henry had to confess that the boy had fallen in love, and could think of nothing but the prospect of marriage to his loved one.

Sir Henry could only put a brave face on it. The girl had no fortune, and was not fitted to be a poor man's wife. But she was Irish, like his wife, and Irish girls can be happy without what money brings. Rueful, but making a joke of it, Sir Henry wrote

to a friend: 'She is all Irish. Harry is half Irish, and Irish temperament has a great deal of helter-skelter happiness in it – as Ben
Jonson expresses it (with his usual refinement of language):
Helter-skelter, hang sorrow, care'll kill a cat, up-tails all, and a
louse for the hangman.'

But bills had to be met, and so Sir Henry cast about among his
influential friends for a more rewarding occupation for his son
than the army. There was no question of going into trade. These
were the 1880s. The Consular Service, refuge for many an
unskilled, charming, under-endowed son offered possibilities, and
Sir Henry addressed himself to no less than the Foreign Secretary,
Lord Granville.

> When I told him (he confided to a friend) of my difficulty, he
> said that there was no one he should desire more to get out of
> a difficulty than myself, and that he would take the first
> opportunity he could to find Harry a place in the Consular
> Service when one or two prior claims had been disposed of,
> and I have no doubt that he will do so if he does not forget
> about it.

Lord Granville did not forget, as Sir Henry had known quite
well he would not. An opening conveniently occurred in the
King's Messenger Service, and Harry was easily able to meet the
not very exacting requirements for entry – a sufficient knowledge
of the first four rules of arithmetic to enable him to make out his
accounts in the simplest form, and enough command of either
French, German or Italian to make himself understood while on
his duties on the road. The stipend upon entering was com-
mensurable with these modest requirements, £250 per annum.
A few long-service messengers, men at the top, got £400 per
annum.

On this income, added to by a small army pension, and
frequent 'tips' from his grandfather, Lord Monteagle, and his
'governor', Sir Henry, young Harry entered confidently upon
matrimony. In a note dashed off to his parents from the United
Services Club on his wedding day he thanks them for all they
have done for him, writing: 'I shall have taken over charge of

Minna in an hour or so, and I am perfectly confident that she is the purest and most true little soul in the world.' It was a blissfully happy marriage, though money worries were ever present. In due course there were two little girls, Viola and Una. Captain Harry Taylor had a house in Montpelier Square, staffed by three servants, was a member of the St James's Club, and entertained and was entertained in return. Minna Taylor was lovely, his children were charming and clever. There must often have been financial crises in the bosom of the family; not only there, in the back of the mind of Harry Taylor as he whistled the latest tune; crises nearly as convulsive as those Mr Micawber had to meet when disappointed of some hope fondly relied on. But these worries were never allowed to appear. The family life was built on beauty, wit, and style. Even to each other they did not betray their anxieties.

Harry Taylor's duties kept him away from home for long stretches at a time. From the Orient Express, from clubs in Istanbul and Moscow, he wrote to his children letters that demanded answers as amusing and clever. Only gradually does one begin to sense, reading these faded letters, what a constant strain the family lived under, perhaps without always being aware of it themselves. They were gifted, but never for a moment allowed to forget it. Too much grandeur and fame, Firsts at Oxford, literary talent, important friends: too much of this high level of achievement had gone before, and had become the standard which one had to live up to. Success became something to be striven for even when one was fainting; social success first and foremost but, as money became more important, the need to command that commodity too. There were ghastly worries, especially after the governor and grandfather died. It was vulgar to talk about money, but the voices of rude creditors kept breaking in, as the pay of a King's Messenger failed more and more to keep pace with the steadily increasing cost of living.

Harry Taylor contracted tuberculosis in 1906, and died in January, 1907. For the last six months of his life he and his wife had had to live abroad. The Foreign Office magnanimously kept up his wretched pay until the end, even though he could not work for the last year. Foreign hotels were expensive; sanatoriums even more so. There being no longer parental 'tips' to be looked for, Minna Taylor had to accept 'loans' from friends, and tears of thanksgiving when the arrival of one of these loans meant that Harry could keep on a room with a balcony, replaced those which used to come when they were helpless with laughter at one of their sustained family jokes. Harry wrote to Una: 'I know there is this money question, and how that darling Min. has kept from me all worrying letters, wants, etc., and borne the whole herself. That Min. is a crownèd saint. Ireland is not: he has a black heart.' (A reference to the Lord Monteagle who succeeded Harry's grandfather, but did not assume his obligations.)

The compulsion to succeed was in both of Harry Taylor's daughters, and necessity drove them now. In the last year of her father's life, Una, who had been a pupil at the Royal College of Art, and had been much encouraged by friends of the family like Sir Edward Poynter, the President of the Royal Academy, G. F. Watts and Rudyard Kipling, had set up on graduating a studio of her own. She had taken to sculpture. Her figurines had been exhibited and had won some favourable notice from the critics. She had been busy in this year executing commissions from her numerous friends.

But suddenly there was nothing more to laugh at. They were in debt, and alone in the world. Her father's death and the break-up of the home, made marriage essential, little taste though Una had for it. Her sister had spoiled the family hopes by marrying a journalist, Maurice Woods. In place of any of her young admirers, with several of whom she had sufficiently deep attachments, Una accepted, within a few months of her father's death, a captain in the Royal Navy, a widower twenty-five years older than herself with a grown-up family of his own. Captain Troubridge had everything to recommend him except that he had entered the Navy before Una had been born. He was in fact only ten years younger than her father, but he was a vital and vigorous man, extremely good-looking, and with a reputation for bravery which spread a sort of halo about him, and together with his handsomeness excited her enough to drive her in the direction which necessity was pushing her. Someone had to support her. Could she do better than this?

Troubridge came of a distinguished fighting family. His great-grandfather, Sir Thomas Troubridge, had been a brother-officer of Nelson's. His grandfather had been a flag-officer. His father had lost his right leg and left foot at Inkerman. Troubridge himself, while a sub-lieutenant on a destroyer, had dived into shark-infested waters in the China seas at night while his ship was travelling at full speed to rescue a signalman who had fallen overboard, an act of bravery for which he had been awarded the Albert Medal. He had been Naval Attaché in Tokyo at the out-break of the Russo-Japanese War, and had been with the Japanese fleet during the sea engagements that had decided the outcome of that conflict. The demonstration of what superior fire power could do when the enemy had been engaged at sea impressed him sharply and his reports to the Admiralty on the subject were considered so valuable that he was made a Commander of the Royal Victorian Order, the citation noting that it was conferred 'as a mark of the King's personal appreciation of his services in the Far East'. Coming under the favourable notice of his political and naval masters, Troubridge seemed destined for the highest rank in the Navy.

Harry Taylor had extravagantly admired 'your Captain' as he always called Troubridge to Una. Harry Taylor died in February 1907. In November Una and her Captain were married. In the same month Troubridge was appointed Flag-Captain to the Commander-in-Chief of the Mediterranean.

Una had to give up her studio, her portraits and sculptures, the hard but satisfying and exciting free life she had lived ever since she graduated from the Royal College of Art: all this for the life of the leading lady in the most fashionable station abroad. There are no indications that she then felt any regret at the prospect of leaving England. She felt herself swept along by the tide of her own feelings, and Zyp, the familiar name she used for her husband, assumed the place her father had had in her affections, with the added privileges of a lover.

Chapter Three

That same year, 1907, was the one in which Radclyffe Hall entered into her first long-lasting love-affair, as well as the year in which she published her first book of poems. She was twenty-seven, and since returning from the United States, she had been dividing her time between her house in London and the home she had made in the country. First she had taken a cottage at Malvern Wells, and had joined the local hunt. Then as she grew more interested in hunting and wanted stabling and quarters for a groom, she had bought a larger house in the district, and had begun hunting with three packs, which kept her in the saddle several days a week. The hunting scenes in *The Well of Loneliness* are founded on this experience.

She had inherited her father's taste for music, and Alberto Visetti had seen to it that she had learnt to play well. The frustrated emotions stirring within her drove her to fierce exercise and to poetry, which was meant no more at first than to provide the words for songs she wanted to compose at the piano. By 1907 she had enough of these poems collected to make a small volume, and it was at her grandmother's suggestion that she approached Bumpus to publish them. Bumpus was ready and willing, provided she paid for the production, and in January, 1907, appeared '*Twixt Earth and Stars* by Marguerite Radclyffe-Hall.

The poems in this first volume are not remarkable for the originality of their subjects or the depth of their thought, but they do have a musical quality which attracted the song-writers of the time, ever on the look-out for lyrics to satisfy the incessant demand for songs for the piano. No less than twenty-one of the poems in this little volume were set to music before the end of the year by Mr Hubert Bath, Mr Cuthbert Wynne and Mr Easthope Martin, all well-known composers of accompaniments for songs, published by such firms as Chappell & Co. and Boosey & Co.

What gives this little collection a touch of its own is the sequence which closes it called 'A Sea Cycle'. These sixteen poems describe the beginning and end of a love-affair on a sea voyage. The poetry romps. The language is rhetorical, Swinburnian in emphasis and ardour, but curiously false to our ears. That is not the way contemporary lovers talk.

> I have striven for three whole years to forget;
> I have prayed, ay, grovelled to God; and yet
> At the glimpse of a pictured face, or a form
> That suggested yours – like a blighting storm
> The past rose up, and in anguish cried
> 'Oh, fool . . . I live. It was you who died.'

We can hardly bear it. And yet, reading these sixteen poems at a gulp, one has the impression that the emotions described in this fantastic language were actually felt and that the parting was pain. If not a poet there is someone here who feels deeply, memorializing a rapture that has fled.

It was the publication of this little sheaf of verses, and particularly their success as songs, that first brought John into contact with Mrs Mabel Batten, a well-known beauty of the time, whose portrait by Sargent hangs in the Tate Gallery. Mabel Batten, known to everyone as Ladye, and her sister Lady Clarendon, were two striking Irish beauties who, though a generation older, were cousins of Una Troubridge's through her mother. Mabel Batten had a beautiful and well-trained mezzo-soprano voice, and was a much admired amateur singer of German *lieder*. She had married George Batten, a man much older than herself, who had ended an army career as Secretary to the Viceroy of India. His wealth enabled Mabel Batten to give practical help to young musicians of promise, and both Percy Grainger and Mischa Elman, among others, owed something to her patronage.

Besides being beautiful and hospitable and kind to young artists, there was something else in Mabel Batten's life even before Radclyffe Hall came into it. Years later when Radclyffe Hall was forced to sue a well-known scientist for slander, the defendant, seeking to justify his indiscriminate use of vigorous statements about her moral depravity, had declared in court that Mabel Batten had been a thoroughly immoral woman, and that for years Radclyffe Hall had lived with her.

He left no doubt in the court's mind that he meant that their association had been a sexual one, and that Radclyffe Hall had become as notoriously depraved as Mabel Batten had been. The scientist in question, who will appear later in this narrative, was a man of considerable gifts but narrow views. The glint of vice always aroused his strongest emotions and most intemperate language.

Mabel Batten's interest at first was simply that of an older patron in a promising young writer. She saw that John had an ear for words, and a strong sense of rhythm, and she probably soon guessed that, while the turmoil of her emotions supplied the necessary source for the imaginative quality of '*Twixt Earth and Stars*, the young poet had not come to terms with her condition, and was not yet fit to write poetry about love.

John knew the homosexual thrust of her nature by now. But the affairs in which she had found herself involved had given her an unrequited feeling. She continually came up against the shock of remorse in her lover, just when her own passion was growing with what it was feeding upon. Even worse than remorse, the discovery that what was to her a deep and throbbing ardour, which enveloped the mind, the body, the whole spirit, could be to others a sensation that provided a momentary thrill because it was forbidden. She was seeking, as all young lovers seek, for perfect union. But like Stephen in *The Well of Loneliness* she was finding only Angela Crossbys. Grandmother Diehl had to put up with her tantrums, as Puddle in *The Well* has to do with Stephen's. The portraiture here is an exact reflection of what occurred in London in 1907, and it makes these pages in *The Well of Loneliness* some of the most vivid and moving in the book.

In Mabel Batten John found for the first time someone who must have responded as ardently to her as her imagination had always pictured. Afterwards there was no remorse, but the deep satisfaction of a shared fulfilment. For too long she had had to be defensive. Mabel Batten was a woman of great sophistication. What had been the shy awkward thrusts of a nature twisted by desire became under her gentle hands and whispered teaching smooth and accomplished love-making. John learnt not to make the wry self-deprecating jokes about her small compact breasts, her muscular shoulders, the narrow slender flanks of an athlete which seemed a parody of womanly form, but to see these things through the eyes of her adorer as beauty, and take pride in them. Love requires understanding if it is not to wither and die, most of all a love like this that must be secret. Mabel Batten created that understanding, and her young lover responded with all the pent-up feelings that had been driving her since she had set up a home of her own, with Grandmother Diehl as chaperone, and escaped abroad to rough anonymous adventures.

Since these all ended unsatisfactorily, she had come home each time and assuaged her blind seeking for the only solution which nature would accept, with hard physical exercise in the hunting field, and the outpouring of her poetry. But although Mrs Diehl encouraged her in this, John knew that something was missing. In *The Well* Stephen blurts out to Puddle:

> It's unfair! It's unfair! Why should I live in this great isolation of spirit and body – why should I, why? Why have I been afflicted with a body that must never be indulged, that must always be repressed until it grows much stronger than my spirit because of this unnatural repression? What have I done to be so cursed? And now it's attacking my holy of holies, my work. I shall never be a great writer because of my maimed and insufferable body.

It was this tragic sense of being shut out by her warped nature, not only from the pleasures life afforded normal people, but even from proper fulfilment of the anodyne she had made to replace it, her work, which Mabel Batten taught her not to weep about but to accept with pride, as a subtle distinction, not an ugly affliction. For the first time she could take delight in love. Never had she felt so deeply before.

George Batten, then aged 75, took himself off quietly, and John moved in to take his place at 59 Cadogan Mansions, an address which was to figure much in these lives in the next ten years. Then suddenly the vigorous tomboy, more man than girl, that John had become since leaving Addison Road, happier in the hunting-field than in the drawing-room, softened and became a real poet. The manners in the Visetti household had been vigorous, abrupt and unrefined. The several years of wanderlust she had experienced had done nothing to subdue her. Ladye detested hunting, and persuaded John to give it up after she had had a bad fall in the hunting-field in which she damaged a vertebra. At this stage John was very much in love with Ladye and desirous of doing anything that would please her. She gave up hunting, but retained her horses to ride in the beautiful country where three counties of England meet, Worcester, Hereford and Gloucester.

She was fascinated by Ladye's soft speaking voice, her delicate ways and powerful social instincts, a faculty which she had never seen in play before. The same qualities, even more marked in Una, were to attract her. She could be mesmerized by this social ease, her assertive tomboyish manner suddenly surprised into quietude under this feminine dominance in one field. One imagines her unaccustomedly silent in the drawing-room while poets read their compositions, musicians played, and trained voices rang out in song. Ladye encouraged her to go on with her writing, and soon John had another volume of verse ready for publication.

A Sheaf Of Verses, published in 1908, a little more than a year after they had become lovers, shows a considerable advance in technique over the first book, and is more interesting to anyone who knows about the author for its now often quite explicit description of lesbian love. The conventions had not changed so much as the author had done. Ladye had drawn her out, pulled her from behind the poetic diction which had covered her shyness and uncertainty in the first book. There are still dewdrops and rosebuds; breezes are still tender. But now for the first time Sapphic love is celebrated.

and for the first time, with increasing confidence and power, the passion of those first years of their association is struck for all to hear:

> Come with me, sweetheart, into Italy...

to the last passionate declaration,

> And then drink in my love; the whole of me,
> In one deep breath, one vast impassioned kiss,
> That come what may, thou canst remember this:
> That thou hast lived and loved in Italy.

A still further collection, *Poems of The Past and Present*, was ready in 1910, and this time it was issued by a publishing firm, Chapman & Hall, at their own risk. Here the assurance has grown marked, the variety of the metre is exhilarating, the images no longer conventional and stiff. The love poems are even more explicit, in some cases openly revealing to their friends who knew where they had been, for they were travelling much at this period. A pleasing note of detached irony gives both a lightness and a new depth to the verse. 'Non Omnis Moriar' looks forward without self-pity or any false emotion to the day when

> ... all your beauty that has fed on love,
> and all my ardour that has fed on you
> Will count for less than nothing when we two
> Are lying with the cold earth up above.

Passion will be lost in death,

> And none shall speak of us with bated breath
> Because we risked our souls' eternity ...

But, like Horace, she may hope *nom omnis moriar.*

> Perhaps some day when men shall speak of fame
> And then remember you, a man will say,
> 'She had yet one more lover in her day,
> A poet fellow, I forget his name.'

The nispero tree, with its fruit gleaming gold from afar but bitter to the taste, is taken as a symbol of lesbian love. The wounded cries of the lovers at the barrenness which is the inevitable end of their passion is echoed again and again.

Strip her until she weepeth
(From all her ruined branches)
Tears that contain the life-blood
And very sap of summer.

For what is all her ardour,
Whose fruitfulness doth mock us,
To our enduring passion,
That yet remaineth barren?

Three years were to pass before in 1913 she had yet another collection ready for publication. *Songs of Three Counties* was the title she chose for the book. It was again issued by Chapman & Hall, with an introduction this time by R. B. Cunninghame Graham, and pages of praiseful quotations of her previous books by eminent authors and musicians. She was by now becoming something of a figure, for her songs were being taken up by well-known concert singers in France and Germany as well as England, and were being reprinted profitably as sheet-music. Cunninghame Graham in the idiom of the time praised her work as being that of a writer 'not striving to be modern or filled with strange conceits; but with a love and trust of the brown earth, from which all poets take their birth, and into which they all return'. And now Robert Coningsby Clarke, Coleridge Taylor and Liza Lehmann set these poems to music.

The new volume was more deliberately rustic in note, and suggests the influence of A. E. Housman's *A Shropshire Lad*. This is perhaps because it commences with a series called 'Rustic Country', and ends with one of her most accomplished lyrics, 'The Blind Ploughman'.

Set my hands upon the plough,
My feet upon the sod;

Turn my face towards the East,
And praise be to God.

Every year the rains do fall,
The seeds they stir and spring;
Every year the spreading trees
Shelter birds that sing.

From the shelter of your heart,
Brother, drive out sin.
Let the little birds of faith
Come and nest therein.

God has made his sun to shine
On both you and me;
God who took away my eyes
That my *soul* might see.

A religious note has entered her poetry. Ladye had been born
a Catholic, and John had recently been received into the Catholic
Church, and much of the verse in this volume reflects not only
the lover of earth but the lover of a God newly found.

If I should pray my prayer would be
For gratitude unlimited . . .

Then would I kneel before my God
Whose matchless genius made the earth;
The Poet-God who sows the hours
With all the scented hosts of flowers,
Who gives the little winds their birth,
Who doth unloose the sea song's might,
And fling the foam-flakes high in mirth . . .

From Swinburne's influence through Housman's; to that of
Bridges' perhaps, with her next book, *The Forgotten Island*: this
seems to be the chart of her course. No, not Bridges, except for
the classical allusions, but the author of the *Indian Love Lyrics*
which were the rage of 1913, and which, put to music, throbbed

forth from the open windows of English homes all through that summer before the outbreak of war. *The Forgotten Island* was to have appeared in the autumn of 1914, but delayed by the war, it did not come out until 1915. From this point on she was to turn to prose, encouraged to do so by Ladye who perhaps was sensitive to the autobiographical element which could not be kept out of so individual a poet's celebrations of love.

John had already turned her hand to short stories, a number of which Ladye had sent to Mr William Heinemann, the publisher. Mr Heinemann, accustomed to showing encouragement where he felt it was deserved, had found it expedient in dealing with authors, especially beginning ones, not to overpraise. He invited Ladye and John to lunch, and over lunch waxed so enthusiastic about these stories that John trembled with joy and fear lest their publication might not meet with the success which this experienced literary judge evidently anticipated for them, and in case she might not be able to write others to make up a book which would please him as much. One of the stories in particular, *The Career of Mark Anthony Brakes*, he declared to be the best short story ever submitted for his approval. When after an interval of this copious flow of praise, Mr Heinemann had said nothing about the matter of publication John directly enquired: 'Then you are going to publish my stories, Mr Heinemann?' He was as direct in his answer:

> I will certainly do nothing of the kind. I am not going to present you to the public as the writer of a few short stories, however good they may be, and what is more, I do not want you to offer them to any periodical. You will set to work at once and write me a novel, and when it is finished I will publish it.

But eleven years were to pass before in 1924 John's first novel *The Unlit Lamp* was ready, and by that time both Ladye and Mr Heinemann had disappeared from the scene. They were years tumultuous with the events of her love-life, and they did not provide the detachment necessary to undertake a long sustained work like a novel. The poetry dried up because after 1915 the

Georgian love lyric was crushed beneath the tremendous events of the World War. From Rupert Brooke to Wilfred Owen and Robert Graves was only a year in time, but it was a year that shook the world. The whinny of the *Indian Love Lyrics* died in the rushing wind that swept up from Flanders, and the void was temporarily filled by the sound of *The Trumpeter*, and yes, of Radclyffe Hall's 'The Blind Ploughman', set to Coningsby Clarke's music. In 1918 an audience of over 3000 in the Usher Hall in Edinburgh rose when the singer, a blinded officer, Captain MacRobert, invited them to join him in the chorus. The description of the uncanny atmosphere in the Hall on that evening reached Radclyffe Hall from a famous singer, Mignon Nevada, who was clairvoyant, and who was present.

> Over the audience's head a grey haze that as it ascended higher gradually went from blue to violet, then to pink, then to a dazzling yellow-white which seemed to be full of moving forms. Some looked like spirits, some like stars with five or seven points to them, and these were constantly vibrating and over the whole building there seemed a wonderful feeling of Peace and Harmony.

> From the shelter of your heart,
> Brother, drive out sin.
> Let the little birds of faith
> Come and rest therein.
>
> God has made his sun to shine
> On both you and me
> God, who took away my eyes
> That my *soul* might see.

From this song which swept the country in that year Radclyffe Hall received no royalties. As the Chairman of Chappell & Co., the music publishers, explained to her when she complained about this:

Dear Miss Radclyffe Hall,
   I yield to no one in my admiration of your words for 'The Blind Ploughman'. They are a big contributing factor to the

success of the song. Unfortunately, we cannot afford to pay royalties to lyric writers. One or two other publishers may, but if we were to once introduce the principle, there would be no end to it. Many lyrics are merely a repetition of the same words in a different order and almost always with the same ideas. Hardly any of them, frankly, are worth a royalty, although once in a way they may be. It is difficult to differentiate, however. What I do feel is that you are quite entitled to have an extra payment for these particular words, and I have much pleasure in enclosing you, from Messrs Chappell, a cheque for twenty guineas.

Yours sincerely,
William Davey.

With which for the moment she had to be content. It was her first argument with a publisher, a tribe for whom she was to come to have a lasting suspicion.

But in early 1915, before the battle of the Aisne had given a forewarning of what the casualty lists were to be like; and when it was still thought that the men who had marched away would be back before Christmas, there was interest in what had only temporarily to be laid aside, the romantic dream of a forgotten island somewhere, where love could play undisturbed. *The Forgotten Island* is the most revealing of all her early books of poems. The forty-three lyrics constitute one long and passionate love-poem addressed to a young girl, plainly not Ladye, and so deeply felt and painfully remembered that there could be no doubt that it reflected something that had actually happened.

> Oh! what a wonder is this month of loving,
> And with what rapture stirs the springing garden!
> Behold! sweet goddess, how the blossoms tremble,
> While flowing sap makes music in their branches.
>
> Now is the wandering swallow winging homeward,
> And turning wayward thoughts to happy mating.
> And these mine arms, that winter left forsaken,
> See how they clasp the well-beloved being!

The emphasis is continually upon the youth of the loved one:

> What shall I liken thee unto, O maiden?
> Unto a reed by the side of the water,
> Supple and green with the sap of the springtime.
> Bent with the wind of an infinite longing.
> Unto a reed that awaiteth the master,
> He who shall pluck it, and tenderly fashion
> Out of its slimness a pipe for sweet music!

And later:

> Slim is thy form as the delicate cypress,
> Youth has most tenderly fashioned thy beauty,
> How shall I praise one beloved of the goddess
> I – who am only the maker of small songs.

Not before has her verse risen to such a pitch of passion:

> When thy hands touch me, all the world is compassed
> Within the limits of their slender whiteness
> Where may I hide from this destroying rapture,
> From the swift longing that engulfs my being?

We know from Una Troubridge's memoir that at one time John's fancy did stray. There was an interlude, no doubt referred to in the poem of that title in *A Sheaf of Verses*, but it is briskly dismissed by Una as 'a trivial passing lapse, it broke no bones and left no aftermath . . . Ladye dismissed the incident with a tolerant smile, and no one but John, scourging herself for infidelity, gave it any great importance'.

Yet every stage in the arc of this interlude, from the invocation to Aphrodite:

> O Aphrodite, goddess of the world
> Bless thou my little pipes that I may play
> A magic melody, and thus beguile
> My love across the field of asphodel

through:

> Thy beauty burns me as a breath of fire

to the awareness that this response she awakens is not love:

> As a lamp of fine crystal, wonderfully wrought,
> Is the soul of the woman I love.
> Behold the oil and the wick for the burning,
> Yet the light of the lamp is absent.
>
> How may I kindle the soul of this woman,
> With what torch may I touch it to flame?
> Since love himself hath no part in her beauty
> Nor findeth abode in her spirit.

Too soon, regret enters, and then comes the final sad realization of the barrenness of love to an invert. Here she is addressing herself –

> Hot with love and cold with passion,
> Knowing in thy swift fulfilments
> All thy longings unfulfilled . . .
>
> O thou mortal weary-minded,
> Thou who wert alone created
> As a pastime for the gods –
> When thou treadest thy sad measure
> Making songs to ease thy spirit,
> With the laughter on Olympus
> Mingles falling tears!

After that, silence. But a new and lasting love was in the year of the publication of *The Forgotten Island* to open up to her. She was passing through a crisis in her physical love-life. In 1915 she was 35 and Ladye was 58. With the war she could not escape to Europe. There was this little circle of homosexually inclined women of fashion in London, but this gave her only intermittent satisfaction. The quick temper, the recklessness, the frustration of her sexual life, and her instincts as a creative artist, all combined to make her difficult to live with. Ladye's great calm and serenity, and John's unswerving devotion to her, mitigated much of the awkwardness of the situation. But Ladye's health was failing in this year, and she was forced to live very quietly. John was at the height of her physical powers and her physical attractiveness. She had cut her long silver-blonde hair, and looked more than ever like a handsome man. She was alive and vibrant to the very core of her being, a rich, adventurous, thwarted young woman, aching for life. And just at this moment, one afternoon in Lady Clarendon's drawing-room, she met an attractive young woman seven years younger than herself whose expression bore marks of grief and tension, and who ignited to life the moment she talked to her. The familiar physical tremors over her skin she always felt at such a moment of recognition made her own features light up. She knew that another lover had approached her.

> I am the lover.
> I call thee, O thou maiden,
> Forsake all else thou lovest
> And shelter in my arms.

Chapter Four

By 1915 both Admiral Troubridge and his wife knew that their marriage had not been a success. After eight years the Admiral, as the Captain had become in 1914, whose career before hostilities had seemed so full of promise, no longer had a sea-command, but was at the head of a mixed international brigade on the Danube.

What had gone wrong? Mrs Troubridge had been perhaps a bit young at twenty to marry a middle-aged widower. But she was extremely attractive, artistic and clever, and came from a good family. She had seemed the ideal wife for an officer who enjoyed the confidence of his superiors, both political and naval, and who seemed marked out for high command.

For the first year or two all was well. Captain Troubridge was Flag-Captain to the Commander-in-Chief of the Mediterranean, Sir Berkeley Milne, who was a bachelor. It was a great asset to the C.-in-C. that his chief executive officer had such a charming wife who could act as hostess for both of them. Malta was an island at which nearly all foreign potentates on state visits which took them through the Mediterranean, or on private cruises, paused and expected to be entertained. Princes of the church, members of both the British and the Italian parliaments, paid visits to the island. Even the *Enchantress*, the Admiralty yacht, bearing exalted figures like the First Lord or the Prime Minister, on visits to the Fleet, dropped anchor at Malta for a week or more. Mrs Troubridge charmed them all. If her marriage was not entirely happy not a soul knew of it. In 1907 ladies kept such disappointments to themselves, shattered dreams being glazed over with exquisite politeness. Mrs Troubridge was so witty and pretty, so daring and clever, did sculptures and painted and sang like a bird, by jove, and elderly statesmen and sea lords, confident of Troubridge's qualities and safe future, allowed themselves the pleasure of mild flirtations with her. She drew them out, made them remember poetry they had once learnt, recalled to them things of beauty they had glimpsed at some time or other through their hard naval or politically experienced eyes. She was a great letter-writer, and some commanders' quarters on ships, and great country houses in England, saw their masters bent over their writing desks answering her stimulating, saucy letters.

She was a delicate little thing, and seemed often to be ill. No one ever said what the illness was, and delicacy forbade asking questions. She would grow very pale and hollow-eyed and inaudible when one of these attacks was coming on. Then for a few days she would not be seen. At last she would re-appear, a little chastened and quiet, but so beautiful in her white linen dress and big floppy hat, a parasol shading her face from the sun.

Admiral Lord Fisher, the First Sea Lord and the great man of the Navy, was one of those who fell head over heels in love with her. He was forty-six years older than she was, and happily married still to the daughter of T. Delves Broughton, but he could not resist the charms of little Mrs Troubridge. He met her in 1910 when Troubridge was appointed Private Secretary to the First Lord, Reginald McKenna. Fisher had just been retired, much against his will, from being First Sea Lord, a post to which he was recalled when the Great War broke out in 1914. It was then, by an unhappy chance, that Troubridge had to face a court-martial, and Fisher, as First Sea Lord and head of the Navy, had to confirm the Court's findings. A painful time.

But in 1910 he was enraptured with the Troubridges, and particularly with Troubridge's pretty missus. Always indiscreet in his letters, urging his correspondents to burn them once they had read the dangerous matter included often in them, Admiral Fisher's letters to Una convey chiefly an elderly man's warm response to the sympathy of someone who had captivated his imagination. 'I am so glad I met you', he writes in a p.s. to his first letter to her. 'We have another bond', he exults in his next letter, 'You hate a fool. At least you write me you love brains.'

'Yours till the angels smile on us' or 'Yours till the angels arrange our meeting', or 'Yours till we meet at the Pearly Gates

(You'll get in – I shan't)' are his simple parting salutations. Touring the Mediterranean in *Enchantress* with Winston Churchill, who had succeeded McKenna as First Lord, Fisher writes from Naples: 'I think you ought to send me one of your lovely letters soon and your photograph – considering I haven't seen you since Westminster Abbey when I was godfather to St Michael, and I quite forget if I ever told you that I pointed you out to the Dean of Westminster as one of the angels in St Faith's Chapel.'

All this was harmless and meant nothing, although Fisher was careful to head the letter 'Burn this!', but this was because he was reporting to his pretty correspondent on the trials of travelling with that restless individual, Churchill, his political chief. 'Winston intimated another pilgrimage and I said I'd see him d . . . d first. (This I need hardly tell you is "entre nous"!!!) and you had better burn this at once.'

Only an old sea-dog basking in the warmth of remembered fires. But she did create the glow, not only with this correspondent but with several others. There was something strongly sexual about her, and it was not just her looks or her cleverness, both of which she rather paraded, which attracted all sorts of men, but that subtle emanation of sexuality which I noticed in London when she was in her mid-sixties, when she was neglecting her appearance to the point of caricature.

With this quality, and with such a vigorous, handsome husband, why on earth was she unhappy? She was bored. The relentless round of social calls, dinner-parties, operas, polo matches, prize-givings, imposed by custom on the wife of a senior naval officer in a fashionable naval station, gave her no time to herself. She thought back with longing to the year in London with a studio of her own. She had been making a name for herself, and it had all had to be put aside when she married and came to live here. She realized that she had sacrificed a career for a marriage which had not aroused her physically and which was a meaningless round of social duties. She missed the warmth, the flow of good humour and love which made her parents' home such a wonderful place. She missed her friends who were artists, and she thought the intellectual level of naval society dreadfully low. When she became pregnant at the beginning of 1910, one of the compensating factors to an event to which she did not look forward, was that the baby's birth would take her back to London for three months at least.

Troubridge's appointment to the Admiralty just at this time was to take them back to London for three years instead of three months. The baby girl was born in London on 5th November 1910 and was christened Andrea. From the beginning, Troubridge called the child the Cub, affectionately transformed to the diminutive 'Cubby'. They went on to lead an active social life, many of their engagements being official ones connected with Troubridge's position at the Admiralty. But they always tried to keep 'Cubby-time' free, the child's bath-hour at night when they played with her and talked intimately to each other.

Una was continually ill. At first there was just a question of being 'seedy', not up to the mark, feeling listless rather than physically ill. But then physical symptoms of a distressing nature did develop, a painful nausea, sleeplessness, vertigo, and a terrible sense of depression. Troubridge did his best to be sympathetic, but he had no sick-bed manner and his efforts did more harm than good. She consulted doctors, but none of them could find the cause for such physical distress. Psychoanalysis was in its infancy in England.

One day early in January, 1913, her sister Viola was lunching with her. Viola told her of an Edinburgh doctor named Crichton-Miller who had written a book on hypnotism, and had recently set up a practice in Harley Street and opened a nursing home at Harrow-On-The-Hill.* Troubridge had just been promoted Rear-Admiral, and appointed to command the Cruiser Squadron in the Mediterranean. Her sister urged her to see Crichton-Miller before going off to Malta, and find out if through hypnotism and psychoanalysis she could overcome the recurrent nausea that was making life barely tolerable for her in London, and would be insupportable when she was in Malta, and had official duties to perform on the station.

* Dr Hugh Crichton-Miller, the founder of the Tavistock Clinic for functional nervous disorders, who had ahead of him at this time a career of great distinction.

The examination took place. Crichton-Miller said he could cure her if she would submit to psychoanalysis, and give herself up to an extended treatment which was to include hypnosis. Admiral Troubridge was taken along to have all this explained to him by the doctor, and he agreed that his wife should remain in London and have the treatment.

His letters show Troubridge to have been the nicest possible kind of man, sympathetic, loving, anxious that his wife and the Cub should be happy. They also show that he was a simple-hearted, simple-minded person, doing his best to understand the quirks and vagaries of other people, while being wholly free of them himself. He did not want a seedy, tired wife, too listless to respond to him. He was all for her consulting this 'nerve chap'. But he little guessed the ultimate consequences. Crichton-Miller must have explained the facts of the situation, the nature of which one can only guess from the guarded terms used even in the diary to be connected with a sexual antipathy, which psychoanalysis might cure. But the Admiral was perhaps too embarrassed, or too excited by his new command, to take it in. Off he went to Malta alone on 18 January, and on the 23rd Una notes an 'epoch-making visit' to Crichton-Miller. This must have been the occasion when the doctor explained to her in full terms what inversion meant. She wrote to her husband all about it, and she notes on 3rd February: 'Two letters from Malta and made me so, so happy.'

Almost immediately she felt some benefit from the treatment. As the truth came pouring out of herself she discovered what it was that she had been repressing, which had resulted in these constant attacks of nausea, and had made her life a misery ever since her marriage. She wrote almost daily to Zyp (her pet name for the Admiral), reporting these startling developments, with all an egoist's certainty that he must be as interested as she was with such news, which cannot have been very cheering to him. Dr Miller taught her how to induce self-hypnosis, and her experiments were alarmingly successful:

> suggested to myself that I should become completely un-conscious, and found myself fighting it just like chloroform – still very lightheaded, though I have woken up.

But by March, the Admiral's patience was wearing a little thin. His wife seemed to have no plans for returning to him, and he sent her an unhappy letter begging her to come home. By this time Dr Miller had become her confidant, and the Admiral's plea was taken to him for his consideration.

Miller must have recommended completing the cure, but the Admiral was not satisfied, and continued now to insist on her return. By the middle of the month she had decided to go, and had wired Zyp to expect her. But when she got to the station she had to turn back: 'Tried to leave England tonight. No go.' is the entry in her diary. Finally she summoned up the will to leave, and at the end of March arrived in Malta where she was met by the Admiral in his barge, a foretaste of the officialdom in store for her.

There followed what she had come to hate, now that she knew what was wrong with her, the relentless round of social affairs.* It would have been an exacting enough life for a woman who liked society, and had the stamina which it demands. But to this nerve-shattered wreck who in a few years of marriage had turned from a beautiful laughing girl – '*Du bist wie eine Blume*', wrote one of her admirers – to a pale, tragic-looking beauty, terrified of life, it was torture. She was an artist, and when she could work

---

* 'Now that she knew what was wrong with her.' Long afterwards Una told several friends that her husband had had syphilis, and that her continual ill-health was due to this. At the time when she was receiving treatment from Dr Crichton-Miller, and was so reluctant to return to Malta, Admiral Troubridge had been given what was expected to be a key command on the outbreak of war.

It seems extraordinary that senior officers in the Services, especially those placed in commands expected to be of great responsibility, should not be subjected to a rigorous medical examination before the command is confirmed. But as the answer to an enquiry to the Minister of Defence on this point makes clear, medical examinations, now obligatory every four years, were not required during the period 1914-1924.

The prescription which Dr Sachs, the well-known gynaecologist to whom Dr Miller referred Una, gave her is noted down in the diary. Medical opinion confirms that this is not for the grave disease of syphilis, but for a gynaecological irregularity. Crichton-Miller would surely have made a thorough physical examination of Una when she became his patient. He said that he could cure her by the use of psychoanalysis and hypnosis. The conclusion to which one is regretfully drawn is that this was a fantasy conjured up by Una's need to justify to herself and her friends her action in leaving the Admiral for Radclyffe Hall.

with her hands at a drawing or an etching, she knew the peace that came from total concentration on a task that utterly absorbs. Without that, and without Crichton-Miller to build up her shattered ego, she was driven on the island to the edge of a breakdown.

She returned to London for the summer of 1913. It was the summer when London first fully realized the beauties of Serge Diaghilev's Russian ballet, and above everything, the genius of Vaslav Nijinsky. She felt herself drawn back again and again to Covent Garden and Drury Lane, haunting the theatre and the stage door, making drypoints and etchings of the unforgettable figure of Nijinsky, so expressive of the spirit of life.

A chance came for her to meet him. Enrico Cecchetti, Nijinsky's instructor, was known to General Sir Ian Hamilton, one of her father's friends. Nijinksy agreed that she might attend and watch his rehearsals and daily exercises in the Drill Hall in Goodge Street.

She sketched him first in his part as the Faun in Debussy's classical composition. Soon he consented to sit for her, and they became friends. '*Tiens*', he would say in mock surprise, when he found her waiting for him on his arrival at Goodge Street, '*le faune*'. But something unlocked his shyness when he was with her. He even allowed her to stand in the wings with him while he was waiting for his entrance, a privilege he would permit to no one else. He would not speak. She remembered him as rocking from his heels to his toes, with his eyes tightly shut, and finally muttering '*un, deux, trois; hoop-la*', fling himself on to the stage as the unforgettable, broken puppet in *Petrouchka*, propelled by the kick of his cruel master. She saw that he had the rarest of stage qualities, the power of transfiguration before an audience, his almost squat body dissolving into the leaping figure with the apparent faculty of remaining stationary in the air.

She too, as she worked, was transfigured from the pale, sick woman with the sad heart, to the artist burning with passion. At such hours she forgot Malta; she forgot even her pain. The marble bust, when it was shown at a gallery in London late in the summer, attracted wide attention. It was shown at the International Exhibition in Venice in the following year, and was then bought by the Theatrical Museum at La Scala, in Milan.

Through Dr Crichton-Miller she had taken the house, vacant for the summer holidays, of one of the French masters at Harrow School, so as to be near him for her treatments, fifty-seven in all that summer. She was a profitable patient to Crichton-Miller. Yet she was not with her husband, and still she was not cured.

She had to return to Malta in October, and another winter of utter boredom passed by, with its rounds of dinner-parties – sixty guests sat down one night at Admiralty House. Nearly every day the entry in her diary begins '*Mal di capo*', and she has to stay in bed for days at a time.

Once again in June 1914 she could escape to the mainland, using Cubby as an excuse. They went to Levanto where she met May Massola, the young English wife of the Baron Massola who was to become a very good friend to her.

As the tension leading to the war mounted, she records only sea bathes and operas and evenings spent with the Massolas. There is no mention of Zyp, no hint that the dramatic events in Europe in July might shortly affect her, and would certainly involve her husband. The first reference appears in her diary on 29th July when she records that the papers are full of talk about the war declared the day before by Austria against Serbia. She might have been writing of some conflict in Ruritania. On the 2nd of August, she merely notes without comment 'Declaration of War against Russia by Germany'. Then she began to think it might be serious, but she had heard nothing from Zyp, who by this time had put to sea on the mission that was going to alter the whole course of their lives, and that of many others besides. Even when she records England's ultimatum to Germany she has had no word from Malta, and she stays at Levanto irresolute, until suddenly she receives a telegram from Captain Cardin, the Naval Secretary at Malta, urging her return.

The mission on which Admiral Troubridge had put to sea two days before the declaration of war in 1914 was part of a movement by the Mediterranean Fleet to take up battle stations for the coming conflict, and in particular to shadow two German cruisers, the *Goeben* and the *Breslau*, which were loose in the Mediterranean and threatened the French troop transports then assembling to move French colonial troops to France. Admiral Troubridge was in command of the Second Squadron composed of four armoured cruisers, four light cruisers and fourteen destroyers. Early on August 2nd, Sir Berkeley Milne, the Commander-in-Chief of the Mediterranean, received a signal from Churchill: 'Watch on the mouth of the Adriatic should be maintained, but *Goeben* is your objective. Follow her and shadow her wherever she goes and be ready upon declaration of war which appears probable and imminent.' 'Winston with his warpaint on', as Asquith the Premier said to a cabinet colleague, 'is longing for a sea-fight to sink the *Goeben*.' But Winston was restrained by the Cabinet until the British ultimatum to Germany expired.

The German declaration of war against France had occurred the evening before, and Admiral Souchon, the German commander, working under a different rule book than the British, had already, even before that declaration, run up the Russian flag on his German cruiser, closed in on Philipville and Bone and bombarded these ports. All the British could do under the rules of war was to stand by, bursting with impatience, and longing for the taste of blood, an overpowering desire felt by the whole service from the tempestuous First Lord in London down to the youngest officer in the Fleet.

It was a moment of intense excitement, and everything depended on Troubridge whose fast cruisers, although their armaments were less powerful, were the only ones capable of keeping up with the new German cruisers. Troubridge's four armoured cruisers had 9·2 inch guns while the *Goeben* had 11 inch guns. The German admiral's task was to keep the pursuing British cruisers outside the range of their guns, but inside the range of his; the British admiral's task was to close with the enemy in darkness so that at first light his four cruisers, with the Germans within range, could destroy them with the superior fire-power four vessels offered against two.

By midnight on the 4th August the British ultimatum to

Germany expired, and the British were free to sink the Germans if they could find them, and bring them within range in darkness. There began a chase which lasted for three days, while unknown to the British command Turkey, which had been expected to come in on the allied side but was still neutral, was busy negotiating a treaty with the Central Powers. But Admiral Souchon had been told of what was happening, and on instructions from Berlin was making for the safety of the Dardanelles, while British ships kept watch on the haven offered by the Austrian ports in the Adriatic, and the exit into the Atlantic by which it was thought the Germans might try to escape.

It was soon evident that the Germans were heading east, not west, and Troubridge's ships cruising at the mouth of the Adriatic to prevent the Germans coming in and the Austrians getting out, were the only ones that could catch them. Troubridge set off in pursuit. It was now the night of 6th August, and the German vessels were reported to the south of him on a westerly course. His aim was to intercept them before 6 a.m., when morning light would put his ships at too great a disadvantage. When by 4 a.m. he had not closed with them, instead of dropping back and continuing the pursuit at a distance, he gave up the fight and returned with his ships to the Adriatic. The Germans were free. A Turkish haven awaited them. By one commander's misjudgement at a critical moment in battle the whole tide of the subsequent conflict swung in a new direction.

For the German ships, entering the Dardanelles as Turkey declared war against the allies, sealed off the Black Sea, and Russia was dealt a blow which added immensely to the difficulties she had in waging war. It left her dependent on the ports of Archangel, ice-bound half the year, and Vladivostok, which was 8000 miles from the battlefront.

Much of what flowed from this miscalculation was mercifully then still hidden in the future, the disastrous Gallipoli campaign, and the campaigns in Mesopotamia and the Middle East. Turkey's neighbours, Bulgaria, Roumania, Italy and Greece were now drawn into the conflict, so that there is harsh truth in Winston Churchill's sombre and eloquent account in parliament of the direful effect that flowed from the entry of these ships into the Dardanelles that evening in August 1914 – 'bringing with them more slaughter, more misery and ruin than has ever before been borne within the compass of a ship.'

The taste of defeat was bitter to a First Lord as belligerent and bold in his ideas as Winston Churchill, and to a proud service like the Royal Navy on which the outcome of this European War had seemed to depend.

Troubridge, of course, had been unaware of the political implications of his decision. He believed himself under instructions not to risk his forces needlessly. Yet his instructions were also to sink those ships, and by giving up the chase – 'he did forbear to chase H.I.G.M.'s ship *Goeben*, being an enemy then flying' in the archaic and doomful words of the charge eventually brought against him – he brought down on himself a fearful personal disaster.

So strong was the criticism that he was forced to apply for a court-martial in order that his honour might be cleared. Leaving his ship, and hurrying home by a Greek steamer, he met Una in Naples, and they went on together to London. Una's diary gives a sense of the urgency and strain they were both under. On 22nd October, the day after their arrival in London, he had to spend $11\frac{1}{2}$ hours at the Admiralty under question by his superiors. Then they had to wait until 5th November – the Cub's birthday, as it happened – for the court-martial, which convened and sat at Weymouth. The hearing lasted until 9th November, when at 8 p.m., Admiral Troubridge was fully and honourably acquitted.

But it was a hollow triumph. Neither the Navy nor its fiery civil head could forgive him. Three or four months passed while Troubridge waited round in London for instructions for further duty. Then just as Lord Curzon gave notice that he proposed at Question Time to ask why a distinguished Flag Officer, tried and fully exonerated and acquitted of any error by a court-martial, was not being employed in time of war, Troubridge received a summons to see the First Lord.

Admiral Troubridge found the man who had been his chief and his intimate friend during the three years of planning the

Naval strategy for this war, writing at his desk when he was ushered into his room. Churchill did not look up as the Admiral came to attention before his desk. Several minutes of great embarrassment for Troubridge passed, and then Churchill, without rising or greeting him, looked up and said, 'Troubridge, I have an appointment to offer you, but as it is in the forefront of the battle, I think you may not care to accept it.'

Troubridge was an intelligent and sensitive man, and was not likely to miss the insult. But he was also a man harassed by his domestic afflictions and the experiences of the past year. He knew that what he had done had been correct according to a literal reading of the orders, but that it was not in the naval tradition established by Nelson. No First Lord could have been more sensitive to that point than Churchill, and Troubridge did not protest at the cutting rebuke. Instead with eagerness he told the First Lord that he was ready to accept any appointment that might be useful to the country in time of war. When the details of the appointment were disclosed, to command several batteries of naval and marine guns being sent to Belgrade to keep the Danube open for the Allies, he knew that his career as a sea-going officer was done.

Una, who had stood by her husband during the cruel public exposure of the court-martial proceedings, could not abandon him now, when by this appointment an officer of his seniority was being publicly censured by the Naval High Command. She accompanied him to Belgrade. Then she returned to London, ostensibly to raise money for a British hospital for naval ratings in Belgrade.

One cannot resist the conclusion that Troubridge's unhappy marriage had something to do with the failure of his career at this particular point. No one had ever doubted his courage or ability, especially his presence of mind in any situation requiring immediate decision. But he had had two unhappy years on the island since the days when he worked in the war-room with Winston Churchill, making strategic plans for instant action on the outbreak of hostilities, and they had made him a different man.

This simple, loyal, courageous officer was up against a force of nature with which he did not know how to deal. Of his love for his young wife, and his child, there cannot be the slightest doubt. But that he treated as tantrums, or the eccentricities of an artistic type of young woman, what were really symptoms of a disturbed psyche, not only did nothing to cure the differences; it aggravated them.

His frustrating marriage must also have worn hardly on his own temperament. Breezy, bluff, but brainy and courageous, he had all the right qualities for command, as he was to demonstrate again when the Navy banished him to the obscurity of the Danube. He 'believed in seamanship as a soldier of Cromwell believed in the bible' in the words of one of his younger officers.* The Royal Navy is a closed and secret service, much more so than the British Army where each regiment has its own tradition and reputation. The Navy stands together, and Troubridge at a crucial moment had failed to apply the telescope to his blind eye. Technically nothing could be held against him, but his career was as smashed as though he had handed over his ships to the enemy. Brought up in the naval tradition, Troubridge must have known this, and understood his brother-officers' attitude. Nineteen-fifteen must have been a terrible year for him.

In London the Admiralty gave only grudging support to Una's plans for the naval hospital. For two unhappy months during which her naval friends cut her, she was reduced to writing to ship commanders, former brother-officers of her husband whom she knew, for personal contributions. Admiral Lord Fisher, the architect of the modern Navy, with whom for a long time she had kept up such a flirtatious and amusing correspondence, wrote from the Ritz in pencil in very brisk terms:

> Dear Mrs Troubridge,
> So happy to get your letter. Forgive haste and pencil for I am *exceedingly* busy. When I can I will come and see you.
>
> Yrs
> Fisher.

* Commander J. N. Kenworthy: '*Soldiers, Statesmen and Some Others*' quoted by Barbara Tuchman in *The Guns of August* from which my own account is largely taken.

Finally the Admiralty relented, but only slightly. They refused a grant to the unit, but the Admiralty's anonymous scribe wrote to Una:

> My Lords have, however, been pleased to approve payment from Admiralty Funds of a daily rate of 6 shillings for any Hospital accommodation that has been given in the past or may be given in the future to any member of the British forces in Serbia, and it is hoped such payments will be of assistance to your Unit.
>
> I am to add that, provided the expression *Naval* Hospital is not used, and no reference is made to the fact of Naval Officers and Naval Ratings serving in Serbia, their Lordships have no objection to the issue by you of a public appeal for funds.

With that she had to be content. Depressed beyond measure at the prospect of returning to Belgrade with the Hospital Unit, she went one warm Sunday afternoon in August to call on her cousin Lady Clarendon. She found in the drawing-room another cousin, Lady Clarendon's sister, Mabel Batten, and a third woman, a girl near her own age whom she had met once briefly before at a garden party in Chelsea, during the two years Troubridge had been attached to the Admiralty as Naval Chief of Staff. On that occasion she had been momentarily struck by this young woman's unusual face and piercing gaze. She knew from gossip that this was Marguerite Radclyffe-Hall, the young poet and song-composer whom Mabel Batten had taken to live with her.

Una was suddenly overcome on that August afternoon in Lady Clarendon's drawing-room by Radclyffe Hall's searching look. Her own neurotic condition made her ready to respond. She knew all about John, and was perfectly well aware of what was conveyed in the current that almost immediately began flowing between them. Her nervous troubles of the last few years had imposed a severe strain on her, and this had touched breaking-point in the court-martial and all the attendant publicity. She felt that Troubridge's failure had been at least partly her fault. She recognized that she owed him some loyalty, but like all neurotics she was an egomaniac. She longed now to be taken into somebody's arms and kissed and comforted, and she yearned to pour out to someone the great reservoir of passionate love stored up in her which her marriage had not succeeded in tapping. The right or wrong of homosexual love hardly occurred to her. She could feel the intensity of John's desire for her grow, and this aroused in her feelings that nothing except the solace of John's arms about her could assuage. Looking back to that meeting many years afterwards, she wrote:

> I could not, once having come to know her, imagine life without her. I had, at twenty-eight, as much consideration for Ladye or for anyone else as a child of six.

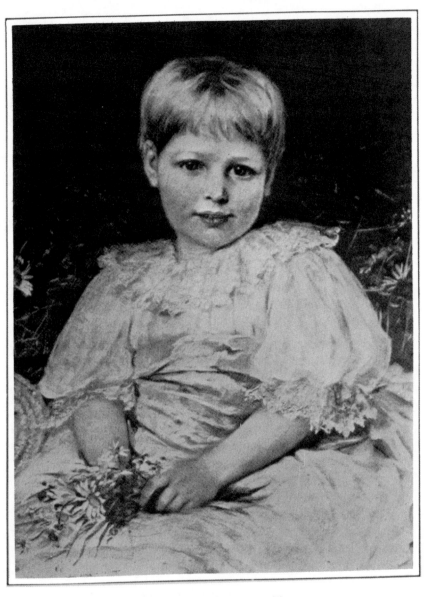

Radclyffe Hall at the age of five.
An oil painting by Katinka Amyat.

Una Troubridge in 1915
at the time of her first meeting with Radclyffe Hall.

Chapter Five

Radclyffe Hall would have known all about the pretty young woman whose appearance stirred her feelings that afternoon, for Admiral Troubridge's sad history had focused attention on his wife as well, and as Una was Ladye's and Emmy Clarendon's cousin, she would have known that husband and wife were now separated by the war. She would certainly have known of Una's paintings and sculpture. Una had exhibited at the Fine Arts, and her 'heads' were fetching good prices. She was an artist, not an amateur of the arts, and John, as a practising poet, felt that this established a bond between them. When they had met before no sparks had been struck between them. Now the changed circumstances of both their lives altered the case. At this afternoon meeting in 1915, John saw a very attractive, slim young girl, with an admirable figure, and clear blue eyes and fair skin. Her blonde hair was cut into an Eton crop, a style that was new in 1915, and she wore an expensively-tailored coat and skirt, with a white linen blouse. The figure was totally feminine, but the clothes and the set of the head, the neat shoes and stockings, and the page-boy cut of the hair, suggested something boyish. Only the sadness of the face did not sustain that impression. She did not look strong; she seemed fragile and melancholy. Radclyffe Hall's interest was immediately and violently aroused.

Una, of course, knew all about the relationship between her cousin, Mabel Batten, and Radclyffe Hall, for that was common knowledge in the family. She had been so busy organizing the hospital unit, getting for it official recognition and raising the money for its support, that she had not seen her cousins since her return to London. May Massola was doing the same thing in Levanto for Italian troops, but she had not had the disillusioning and chastening experiences which Una had had to suffer. It had been brought home to her for the first time how deeply naval pride had been hurt by the *Goeben* incident.

Depressed by this, and by her commitment to sail with the unit in September, Una's spirits were very low when she came to take tea with her cousins that afternoon, and it was with a shock of surprise that she came face to face with this slim, odd-looking but beautiful young woman who took her hand and looked at her in such a piercing way. She could remember their earlier meeting and thought that she would have recognized Radclyffe Hall easily. She was mistaken. She had remembered a masculine-looking figure, a face marked by a strong nose, and an expression that was withdrawn and uninterested; she had only a colourless memory of Mabel Batten's curious friend.

She must have been blind that afternoon two years before, or half asleep and dreaming of something else. Thirty-five years later she was to recall this present meeting:

> I can still see John as I saw her on that day, as clearly as if she stood before me now. She was then thirty-four years of age, and very good indeed to look upon. At that time short hair in a woman was almost unknown and she had not yet cut hers. Ladye would have been horrified at the mere suggestion! It was silver-blonde, and she ruthlessly disposed of its great length and abundance (it reached nearly to her knees and its growth defied frequent pruning) by wearing it in tight plaits closely twisted round her small and admirably shaped head. Her complexion was clear and pale, her eyebrows and very long lashes nearly as golden as her hair and her eyes a clear grey-blue, beautifully set and with a curiously fierce, noble expression that reminded me of certain caged eagles at the Zoological Gardens! Her mouth was sensitive and not small. It could look very determined; indeed in those days it sometimes looked hard, but was liable to break into the most infectious, engaging and rather raffish smile that would spread to her eyes and banish the caged eagle. Her face and the line of her jaw were an unusually pure oval. From her great-grandfather, John Hall, she had inherited an aquiline nose with delicate, tempered wings to the nostrils. From her mother's side, unusually high cheekbones. In any case it was

66

not the countenance of a young woman but of a very handsome young man. Like her father she was only of medium height but so well-proportioned that she looked taller than she was, and the very simple tailor-made clothes which she wore, even in those days, fostered the illusion. Her hands, and here again they were not feminine hands, were quite beautiful and so were her feet. Altogether her appearance was calculated to arouse interest. It aroused mine, and for reasons less obvious that interest was returned.

But although the signals were perfectly clear to one another they had to be hidden. John's relationship with Ladye had become much more that of mother and daughter than lover and loved one. But any attempt of John's to escape aroused jealous rages, bitter quarrels and reproaches, which plainly added to the distress of Ladye's illness. They had to be careful, and as the summer died, and Una allowed the unit to sail without her, it was the predator who hung back, and the victim who longed to be sacrificed.

The rest of that summer was taken up with a courtship dance. No other phrase so well describes the slow, stately but relentless seduction of one of the species by another. Una had taken rooms in Brighton for the Cub's sake, and was there established with a nurse for the child, within easy reach of London. 'Brighton,' wrote May Massola from Levanto, 'I always thought it was a horrid, noisy place.'

Ladye and John came to stay at the hotel. They all then moved on to Watergate Bay in Cornwall. The child had its nurse, and the pleasures of the beach to occupy its day. Ladye could take no exercise and was confined to the hotel. In that warm August and September, 1915, while the battle for Paris was raging just across the channel, and the battle for Serbia raging seven hundred miles to the East, these two walked and talked together in quiet Cornish lanes. Ever increasingly Una came under the spell of this beautiful man-like creature, who wore short-skirted tweed suits, a collar and tie, unusual on a woman, and man-like Heath hats with pot-shaped crowns.

She was so intensely alive, she could be so kind and so tender, and she was also so wilful, so humorous, and in those days so intolerant! Her temper was so violent, and so quickly spent, and her penitence, if she thought she had given pain, so extreme.

We are at our most attractive when we are in love, and are trying to draw to ourselves and hold the love of the loved one. This was a wooing that could lead only to one end, towards physical surrender, and it followed the same time-honoured steps, the shared laughter and the shared serious thoughts of life and death, the touching of one another gently, fearfully and exploratively, the kisses, the swift, trembling embraces. It would go no further at this stage. But it had gone far enough to make any thought of returning to Belgrade impossible for Una, and luckily she had the excuse that the attack on Belgrade now made a retreat towards the mountains of Albania probable. A separate passage back for her would have been difficult to procure. With relief she put the thought of it out of her mind.

The holiday-makers all returned to London in the autumn with nothing resolved, Una to a little house she had taken in Bryanston Street, Ladye and John to their flat in Cadogan Place. During this long winter they were forced to act like guilty lovers, for the first Zeppelin raids were occurring, and Ladye objected to being left alone in darkened London. They could not abandon the intimate talks they had been having in Cornwall, and they could not carry these on in the presence of someone else, particularly someone like Ladye sensitive to the threat of impending loss.

Three times during the course of the winter they manufactured excuses and got away alone, each time to a hotel, twice to Malvern, and once to Tunbridge Wells. John had decided to dispose of Highfield House, her place in the country. The first time she had gone down there with Ladye on their return from Cornwall, driven by their own chauffeur, they had been hit by another car emerging from a side road. Their car had been turned over on its side in the ditch from the force of the impact. It had fallen over on Ladye's side, and she had been quite seriously shaken. The injuries had seemed superficial but they were deeper than at first suspected and were to hasten her death, and thus to add to John's sense of guilt.

Having decided to sell Highfield House, they had the excuse for two further visits on which Ladye could not accompany them. Thus, at last, was their love committed, and there was now no turning back.

A fourth time in May they left her alone in order to go to Maidenhead to buy a bull-terrier puppy which John was giving Una as a present. It was a lovely day. The river looked inviting. They lunched at Skindles Hotel, and debated manufacturing some excuse to stay the night, but the thought of Ladye's distress alone in the flat, if there should be a raid, drove John unwillingly back to London. They parted at Paddington Station. It was only a five-minute taxi drive for Una to Bryanston Street; ten minutes longer for John, who had to cross the Park. As Una entered her house the phone was ringing. It was Ladye, asking if John had returned. She sounded perfectly normal to Una, only anxious that John should get home before darkness fell.

An hour later Una's phone rang again. At the other end was John, speaking in an urgent and subdued voice, asking her for the name and address of her doctor. She went on to tell her in a few hurried sentences, of what had happened on her return. They had had an argument over dinner. Ladye had risen from the table to leave the room and had fallen to the floor. They had managed to get her to her bed but she was breathing harshly, and seemed to be losing consciousness.

Una, the born organizer, had telephoned her doctor, ordered a taxi and gone to the flat. The doctor had arrived at the same moment. By then Ladye had already lapsed into unconsciousness from a massive cerebral stroke. She was to linger on for nine days, and although her eyes sometimes opened, she had lost all powers of speech. She seemed to them to be trying to say something, but the effort was unavailing, and several days before the end she lapsed into total unconsciousness and seemed scarcely to be breathing.

What John was to remember always was that the discussion at the dinner table had concerned Una. Ladye had previously made it plain that she resented John's growing interest in Una, but she had not before expressed it so hysterically. With the selfishness of someone in love, and blind to another's pain, John had been as hard as steel towards her. What John was always to remember were those last bitter words they had exchanged, Ladye's attempt to rise from the dining-table and leave the room, then her hand clutching her head as she sank to the floor.

John scourged herself with grief. She reproached herself with having neglected Ladye in the last months of her life. She could not get over the feeling that at the moment when she was bereft of speech Ladye had wanted to say something to her, to give her some important parting message, and that she had died with this unspoken. She strained now to hear it across the void, and only momentarily and guiltily gave way to that new love waiting to inherit its place, to grasp and consume her. In her remorse she almost turned from her new lover, as though the sacrifice of her own happiness would be an expiation of her sin. But she kept turning back to Una, the only source from which she could now derive comfort.

Chapter Six

John found it impossible to live on alone in the flat she had shared with Ladye. She could not ask Una to join her there, nor go and share Una's house which Una urged her to do. Instead she went to stay as a paying guest with her cousin, Dorothy Clarke, at 1 Swan Walk, Chelsea. Una thereupon gave up her house in Bryanston Street, which was across the Park, and took another small house in Royal Hospital Road which was just round the corner from Swan Walk. They were together for a few hours at least every day, and Una's diary faithfully and lovingly records these meetings and their moods.

Reading about this protracted wooing one is reminded of Stephen Gordon and Mary Henderson in *The Well of Loneliness*. There the congenital invert, Stephen, holds herself back from taking the young girl who so plainly adores her because she wants the younger woman to know what her decision involves, and it is Mary Henderson who finally precipitates matters. One cannot resist suspecting that the intensity of John's grief may in part have been a sexual ploy to entrap this young woman who had a solid husband and child with claims upon her. It was necessary to make her appear the pursuer. Then there was an additional reason which gave them an added excuse to be together at least part of every day, something which was forbidden to them as Catholics. This was John's earnest desire to communicate with the spirit of the departed Ladye, and to have her assurance that she was forgiven before she gave herself up to her new love.

The attempt to communicate with spirits by table turning had been a popular pastime in drawing-rooms from Victorian times. In 1916, a few months after Ladye's death, Sir Oliver Lodge had published his account of the experiments he had made to communicate with his only son Raymond who had been killed in the fighting in France on 15th September, 1915. The appearance of this book coincided with a great increase of public interest in the possibility of communication with the dead, when so many were mourners, and the departed were those who had been tragically cut off from life at the moment of its flowering.

Sir Oliver Lodge's standing as a scientist drew attention to the work of The Society for Psychical Research which had been in existence since 1880, and had applied itself to the scientific study of such psychical phenomena as thought transference, foretelling the future, the alleged appearances of ghosts, the movement of objects, and the investigation of messages purporting to be received through mediums from the spirits of the dead. The Council members of The Society for Psychical Research, of whom Sir Oliver Lodge was one, were all distinguished and earnest, and the literature on the subject contributed by them, for example such books as F. W. H. Myers' *Human Personality And Its Survival of Bodily Death*, and now Sir Oliver Lodge's *Raymond*, impressed even the sceptical.

It did not take Una long to discover that a decree of the Holy Office of the Roman Catholic Church, while it condemned spiritistic practices by the ignorant, permitted legitimate scientific investigation of phenomena. If therefore in the guise of investigators they could legitimatize their approach to the subject, all would be well.

Without more ado, Una wrote to Sir Oliver Lodge, with the satisfactory result that always followed Una's appeal to older men. The great man himself responded, and put them in touch with a professional medium, probably the best-known in England at the time, Mrs Osborne Leonard, whose 'Feda' – the 'control' which 'possessed' Mrs Leonard in her trances – had been the control in all the seances reported by Sir Oliver in *Raymond*. Mrs Leonard seems to have taken greatly to them, and before long they were having sittings one or more times each week with her, one or other of them keeping careful notes, or taking photographs of the phenomena which manifested themselves, and writing it all up at considerable length.

An interesting study of Mrs Leonard's mediumship* reveals to the uninitiated what occurred in these serious attempts to communicate. Four agencies are involved, the sitter who is seeking to establish communication; the medium, who is the mainly passive 'switchboard', who is in a trance during the seance, and through whose inert body the lines of communication seem to pass; the *Control*, merely a voice, who 'possesses' the medium's consciousness; and on the other side the *Ostensible Communicator*. In time the *Control* can give way to the *Ostensible Communicator*, the discarnate spirit, who then momentarily possesses the medium's consciousness, and communicates directly with the sitter. There is then dialogue, question and answer between the two.

The key to communication is the *Control* who plays the most important part in the proceedings, who constantly interrupts, urges, persuades – acts as mistress of the puppets, as it were – so that the perception of a human figure irresistibly stamps itself in the imagination. Feda, Mrs Osborne Leonard's control, has a childish, rather squeaky, female voice with some idiosyncrasies of pronunciation, although it is otherwise the voice of a well-educated English woman. But suddenly it changes, words are fumbled for, she speaks like a foreigner with an imperfect command of English, leaving out definite or indefinite articles, or syllables of words. She is petulant at times, irritable at others, sometimes with the spirit who is communicating, sometimes with the sitter. Garbled messages make her quite testy. Lack of experience in the communicator is spoken of disparagingly. She likes her little jokes, some of them rather macabre. She treats her communicators and sitters alike, much as Mary Poppins treated her charges, as often wilfully naughty but always lovable. Feda did not have a high opinion of Mrs Leonard. In Una's words, she 'speaks of her as a not very satisfactory and distinctly inferior instrument who must be protected and humoured merely because, such as she is, there is none better to hand'.

How deeply sitters, even highly-trained scientists, could become attached to controls like Feda is illustrated in letters

* *The Phenomenology of Mrs Leonard's Mediumship*. Proceedings S.P.R.

exchanged between Una and Dr Prince, the Principal Research Officer of the American Society for Psychical Research, who was later invited to become President of the S.P.R. in London. Dr Prince's familiar, in a case he recorded which received wide publicity,* was Margaret. It was Margaret who took possession of the body of Doris Fischer.

'Yes', Dr Prince writes to Una, 'there is something bizarre in being so fond of a Feda or a Margaret with the view that we at least conservatively, or provisionally, have to entertain at present in regard to their nature. But it is a fact that we are, and that deserves two exclamation points!! I shall never cease to feel a pang whenever I think of Margaret, and the pang is precisely as poignant as if Margaret had been a separate individual, body and all.'

In the second letter he continues:

I was pleased with your little confession that you love 'Feda', and you were perfectly right in saying that I loved 'Margaret' and I do not care who knows it. She was the most winsome, humorous and ingratiating fay . . . and I am not able to think of her to this day without the pain of her loss. It is even difficult for me to read a few pages of my record of the case, specially those parts which relate to Margaret, because it recalls to my mind with such poignancy the indescribably charming entity who is gone forever. The small articles of her property, paper dolls and other childish articles which she 'bequeathed' to me, are kept in the drawer which was hers, there to remain as long as I shall live.

So it is with Feda. She calls Radclyffe Hall 'Mrs Twonnie', and Una, 'Mrs Una'. The sittings are conducted behind drawn curtains, Mrs Leonard inert in a trance has her face illuminated by firelight and the light of the lamp. Inert is hardly the word. Only her body is this. Her lips move, her hands make gestures. Usually Una is the recorder, sitting a few feet away and writing all the evidence down under the light of the lamp. Bent forward, rapt

* *The Doris Fischer Case of Multiple Personality* by Dr Walter Prince, p. 352. Letters dated April 7 and May 27 1922.

74

with concentration, one has to imagine the face of Radclyffe Hall carrying on through Feda – invisible but temporarily 'in control' of Mrs Leonard's body – a conversation with Ladye, the communicator, who now stands on the other shore.

How much of this was fraud, how much some genuine psychical phenomena into which these two neurasthenic women were plunged by the fierce intensity of concentration? Occasionally the responses to questions put by John are so banal it seems incredible that they can issue from the voice of one now in the solemn world of the dead. Much more likely, one would think, that they emanated from the medium, or were reflections of the very things that were in the minds of the sitters. Here is an instance. John had been devoted to horses, and Ladye had feared them. At one of the sittings, the following was recorded. (F is Feda and M.R.H. is Marguerite Radclyffe Hall.)

F.   Feda [who always refers to herself in the third person] sees a horse, how funny! He's looking over her shoulder, he is a brown, sleek horse, she says she is keeping it for when you come over.

M.R.H.   Describe it.

F.   Thin face, slender face, slim horse. Feda knows the difference between this kind and the kind that draws carts. He's got a very soft mouth.

M.R.H.   Is there any colour on his face?

F.   There is some mark on his forehead; the ears are not very big, little ears, a beautiful shiny-looking face. He has large eyes and a beautiful expression. The little ears give him a smart look, but his eyes and mouth have a sweet, kind look. She thinks you will be pleased.

In the following week, Feda is able to report that Ladye is learning to ride, and that 'you will love it when you come. There are plenty of horses that love to be exercised, and the ground is so springy.'

At a subsequent séance, several months later, this matter of horses is referred to again. The recording shows:

F.   She's so glad there are animals in the spirit world. She's not really afraid of horses, and she knows now that they can't hurt her, but when she first passed over she was still a bit wary of them.

Una and John both threw themselves into these investigations with all the ardour and energy of converts. There are almost daily séances with Mrs Leonard, notes are written up at length, tests examined and reported on, and all their findings are passed on to the Society. Soon John is invited to give a paper, a high honour, and there is talk of her possible election to the Council to fill a vacancy. Una, as the 'Lieutenant' in all this, as she styled herself, nearly became a nervous wreck in the process. Her diary is filled with strange inexplicable occurrences: 'At about 6.30 p.m. I felt my hair touched on top of my head, and in the evening, about 10 o'clock, while reading to John, a very cold air in gusts on my hands . . .' '. . . Woke during the night with distinct consciousness of two raps, and felt bedclothes gently drawn down from my face and chin.' These or entries like them are of almost daily occurrence. But she resisted total surrender; she kept her head, and noted just as firmly in her diary: 'Table levitation failed – a "ghazi" materialized fully and knocked against my extended foot. No one came to me whom I recognized. Sister Amy materialized, and a terrier dog. She was heard and felt jumping up, but no "fur" that I felt. Many points for and against.'

There were lighthearted moments too. Una was called 'Squig' by John, an affectionate diminutive. Squig does funny drawings, and some of these appear on the margins of the diary which demonstrate that she still has the ability to laugh at herself and her antics. Although now passionately directed towards John, and incapable of feeling even a spasm of affection for or interest in a man, she is quite aware of her own attractions, and it is noticeable that the poet, W. B. Yeats, himself deeply involved with spiritism at this stage in his life, and even Sir Oliver Lodge cannot resist attempting to get her alone. John was quite obviously the intellectual force in these experiments, but it is hard to keep one's eye off a pretty woman, and Una with her charming ways drew men's attention even when the business was solemn.

Something which was to be called *The Psychic Telegraph*, which never seems to have come to life, was much in the air at this time, and both Yeats and Sir Oliver Lodge were excited about it. Yeats, who was living not far away in Pimlico, called at Una's house several times to discuss this matter, as well as their psychic investigations in which he was taking a great interest. Yeats held séances at his own lodgings from time to time, and invited them to join him. Vout Peters, the medium he mentions in the following letter, was as well known in serious psychical circles as Mrs Leonard.

Royal Societies Club,
3 January, 1917.

Dear Mrs Troubridge,

Vout Peters is coming to my place for his seance on Friday night at 8.30. One or two friends and myself are sharing the expense. Would you and your friend care to join? I find half-a-dozen about the best number for Peters. 8.30 is a horrid hour, and we have to start punctually, or Peters will be upset and get nothing.

Does your letter mean that Feda had got Sir Hugh Lane's name?

Yours,
W. B. Yeats.

P.S. The Peters fee will be at most 3/– or 4/– each.

Yeats's calls at Royal Hospital Road were evidently sudden and frequently unannounced, and were always concerned with spiritualism.

Royal Societies Club,
13 Decr. 1916.

Dear Mrs Troubridge,

I cannot find your letter. It arrived in a whirl of work in this dispute with the National Gallery. I think you asked if I could go and see you on Saturday night. Yes I can, if ask me you did. Please let me know if that is right. I would not perhaps be able to dress as I am going to be busy all day on this Gallery business.

I arrived at 10.30 for the séance, but 10.30 p.m. (You had

not said which), and was shown into a room where there was a young man in bed with a cold. It was very stupid of me not to ask whether it was a.m. or p.m.

Yours ever,
W. B. Yeats.

The plan for setting up *The Psychic Telegraph* involved a man called Wilson, and 'a machine', one presumes a printing machine – Una is sparse on business details – both man and machine being at St Leonards-on-Sea in Sussex. On 10 February, Sir Oliver Lodge came to tea with John, and asked her to go to look at the machine and see what it was like; then to report back to him before he went any further. Two evenings later Yeats and Edmond Dulac came to dinner with them, and they discussed *The Psychic Telegraph* all evening, 'Yeats writhing like an unhappy beetle upon the pin of John's business attitude', Una notes proudly. But they settled all to go to St Leonards on a day the following week. Before this plan could be carried out, it was reported in the press that the police had seized the machine, and arrested a Mr Wilson, its owner.

Their first visit to the Lodges' occurred early in 1917. They arrived in the afternoon at Mariemont, Sir Oliver's home near Birmingham. Sir Oliver came into the drawing-room while they were at tea with Lady Lodge. After dinner Sir Oliver read aloud a report from Oxford of a table-sitting, and there ensued a long discussion regarding their work. 'Such delightful people I have never met, and one could not long be shy,' notes Una that evening.

The next morning Sir Oliver sent for Una and asked her if she would read through for him the manuscript of the French translation of *Raymond*. She notes in her diary several interesting talks with him during the day. That afternoon after tea they all sat with hands linked around a huge oval table until, Una notes, 'we got two faint raps and in the end it tilted right up and moved around'. After dinner Sir Oliver read aloud their report of the sitting with Yeats, and there was much talk. Later in the evening John had a nose-bleed and had to retire upstairs. Una went with her, and at 10.30 came down to say goodnight.

'Instead,' she records in her diary, 'he kept me with him talking until ¼ to 1. So *very* interesting, and a great and adorable man. Took me into his study and gave me Myers's autobiography signed – a memorable evening, and I was sorry for poor John who was so generous when I went up, and said she was glad he appreciated her Squig.'

The next morning they left Mariemont, and Sir Oliver gave John his book *Continuity*.

> When he said goodbye to John, he said 'This isn't the last we shall see of you', and to me he kissed the fingers of his hand and put them to my forehead – a benediction I shall never forget.

Meanwhile, life was not without its troubles. At 1 Swan Walk, Dolly Clarke was being rather snappish about the devoted friendship developing between John and Una, and appeared to be making mischief in letters to mutual friends. John herself was beginning to feel persecuted, and was venting her flaming temper on Una from time to time. Una would dissolve in tears, but would rejoice when everything was made up between them, as it always quickly was. John took to spending an occasional night at Royal Hospital Road, and the Mrs Grundys of the neighbourhood lost no time in passing on such incidents to Mrs Gregory, the owner of the house, who was living in Ireland. Una received notice to quit on 15 February. She took another furnished house at 42 St Leonard's Terrace only a hundred yards away. On the day of her removal Una went over to Swan Walk to use the phone. Then together they moved some of her things to St Leonard's Terrace, meaning to move the rest in the afternoon after a sitting at Mrs Leonard's. But on their return from St Leonard's Terrace they found that Mrs Gregory had given orders to evict Una by noon. After a busy day she notes sadly in her diary: 'Very much depressed at new start in another squalid little lonely abode, but one must do one's best and go on. I am very, very tired.'

The paper on which they had been working was finished in September 1917 and shown to the Council. At first it was scheduled to be given at the November meeting, but then it was postponed. Sir William Barrett, an elderly and very distinguished member of the Council, and a pioneer in drawing the attention of the British Association for the Advancement of Science to the seriousness of the evidence available for discarnate existence, wished to occupy the whole of the time of that meeting with a paper of his own. He might, they thought, have stepped aside with his hastily produced and quite needlessly urgent paper, entitled *Evidence of Supernatural Communications*, because this was precisely what *their* paper was about. It is plain that they suspected this great man of being motivated by anti-feminism. At the same time Sir Oliver Lodge wrote to John asking for money for the cause. Una notes: 'I wrote to him rather a pointed letter anent J.' What she presumably pointed out was the money which John had already spent in sittings with Mrs Leonard, for the next mention of this in the diary is 'a very long letter from Sir Oliver Lodge to me anent my letter to him re the S.P.R. and Mrs Leonard.'

It was agreed by the Society that Mrs Osborne Leonard should become the official and paid medium of the Society for a trial period of six months – a high honour indeed because the Society so far had looked askance at anyone who made money out of spiritualism. This appointment was largely due to Radclyffe Hall's and Una's persistence. They had won over the Secretary of the Society, Miss Newton, and the Editor of the Proceedings, Mrs Salter, and they had got on to their side the only woman member of the Council, Mrs Sidgwick; this revolutionary step was engineered through the Council by these determined women. It was indicative of a division of opinion on the Council which was to become more noticeable later.

The Council of the Society for Psychical Research, to which Radclyffe Hall was in due course to be elected a member, was a very distinguished body. The President was Lord Rayleigh, who was also a past-President of The Royal Society. The Council members included a former prime minister, A. J. Balfour, who was also a Fellow of The Royal Society, and his equally brilliant brother, Gerald. It included men of the intellectual stature of G.

Radclyffe Hall in about 1915, painted by Charles Buchel.

Admiral Troubridge when A.D.C. to the Crown Prince of Serbia.

Lowes Dickinson, Professor Gilbert Murray, the then President of The Royal Society, Sir Joseph Thomson, Sir Oliver Lodge, and two other members of The Royal Society. Several of these famous men held the Order of Merit.

The aims of the Society were scientific and strictly investigatory. They shunned unwelcome publicity, discouraged sensation-seekers, and tried to keep the attention of members firmly fixed on the possibility of establishing communication with discarnate spirits. But the rising tide of public interest in the subject of survival after death which spread throughout England, Europe and the United States in the last years of the First War and particularly in the 'twenties, could not be held back by these great intellects bent on investigations for which some training and skill was needed. Between the men of science and the thrill-seekers there was an important body of intelligent people who simply wanted an answer to the question, did human personality survive death? Great intellectuals, as well as the intelligent majority wanted to know, and the presence of thrill-seekers with their attendant professional mediums who had to make a living and produce tappings and bumpings and unearthly lights and hands glowing in the darkness, all earning the scorn of the sceptics, was something that the serious investigators were being forced to accept.

We see this when we come to the spirit in which Radclyffe Hall and Una Troubridge approached the subject. Their interest was purely an egotistical one; they wanted an assurance that Ladye had not died with great unhappiness while they were immersed in the exciting discovery of their love for each other. As practising and devout Catholics and Christians they must have believed that there was eternal life; that beyond the thick curtain that separates existence on the earthly plane from that on the eternal, Ladye survived in her own personality. Contemplation and intense prayer should have been the means of communication used, but spiritualism offered a short-cut; it was like sending a telegram, you got a quicker response that way than with a letter. Having dabbled with the forbidden (to a Catholic) subject, and elicited through a skilful professional medium a reassuring response, John was drawn on by qualities in her own nature. She was a woman of exceptional intelligence. She was also a sexual invert, and under the strain of repression this factor can lead to exhibitionism.* It was not in her nature to play a passive part in the Society. Tempestuous by nature, she was not an easy person to get along with, though charming Una was able generally to mollify those upset by John's blunt manner. Her painfully unusual dress and mannish manners also put some people off. The women, the secretary, Miss Newton, and the Editor of the Proceedings, Mrs Helen Salter, were soon supporting her, as were some leading members of the Council like Sir Oliver Lodge and Mr Gerald Balfour. But there were others who took a rather masculine view of the propriety of two women like this bashing their way into what was really a man's preserve (the very learned Mrs Henry Sidgwick, D.Litt.LL.D. was the only woman member of the Council). They were disturbed as events were to show, as much by Miss Radclyffe Hall's apparent sexual unusualness, to put it at its mildest, as by her lack of scientific qualifications. In particular, Mr George Fox Pitt,† a friend of Admiral Troubridge, and the Hon Everard Feilding, the second son of the eighth Earl of Denbigh, both members of the Council, were for very different reasons to become enemies of Radclyffe Hall.

Finally 31 January, 1918 was set for the delivery of the paper. It was much too long to be given at one session, and half of it was reserved for a further meeting. The hall was crowded. Mr Gerald Balfour was in the Chair, and Mrs Henry Sidgwick also sat on the platform. The remainder of the Council were in front row seats in the hall.

* Sir Comyn Berkeley, *Ten Teachers.* In the chapter on 'Neurasthenia in Females' (p. 481) he writes: 'Cases in which the symptoms are mainly due to sexual neurosis dependant on repression factors . . . subconscious projection . . . may be reinforced by an element of exhibitionism.'

† St George Lane Fox Pitt was a pioneer of electric lighting. He patented a carbon filament lamp with a platinum iridium 'wick' and a complete system of distributing the current by the aid of electric mains and branch wires with current meters and regulators, which was shown at the Crystal Palace Exhibition. He lost a law suit over patent rights which would have brought him in millions in royalties from his invention.

The paper began with an introduction and a defence of the use of a professional medium. Radclyffe Hall averred that she had remained anonymous to Mrs Leonard until some time after the sittings commenced and until after Mrs Leonard's control, Feda, had described a communicator on the other side, a physical description which bore an unmistakable resemblance to the friend whose life she had shared for many years, and who had 'gone over' to the other side some months before.

There follows a very rapid and skilful description of Ladye's appearance, meant to establish that it was indeed she who was there communicating with the control. Not only her appearance but her mannerisms are clearly indicated. The sceptical observer, years afterwards, sees that the questioner herself, by the direction her questions take, by pleading for more and more information, is really supplying the information which is eventually returned to her. But not altogether. Even to the sceptic either a lot of hard homework has been done by the medium, or a communication of a remarkable kind has been established with someone who in this case has been dead for a year and a half.

Then the paper proceeds with evidence of memory retained by the communicator – the houses where they lived together, Radclyffe Hall's fondness for hunting and Ladye's constant fear of it. Of a visit they took together to Teneriffe, and memories of scenes on the island that could have been gathered only by direct experience. Then a memory of the motor accident in which they were both involved in which Ladye received the injuries that were to lead to her death. Memories are evoked of words and phrases peculiar to Ladye, of John's method of composing her poetry which she often did to the accompaniment of the piano, setting the lines to music as they established themselves in the head. Memories of swimming together. Memories, in short, of a deep and emotional friendship, some of the details of which would have been unknown even to Una, who now sat recording them as through Feda's childish voice this recollection of shared pleasures drifted back from the other side, with only questions coming from the rapt John.

Next the paper passes to a knowledge of contemporary events

shown by Ladye, happenings on the earthly plane long after her departure from it. She describes Una's rented house and particularly the dining-room where John and Una are doing all their investigatory work for Sir Oliver Lodge. This room, of course, was unknown to her in life, and certainly Mrs Leonard had not seen it. She shows a knowledge of incidents shared by John and Una since her death.

The paper concludes with reports from sittings in which Ladye showed a knowledge of matters, which at the time of the séance were completely unknown to the sitters, but which were revealed upon checking to have actually occurred. They are matters unimportant, even in a sense ludicrously so, except to the sitters; and here we suddenly perceive that shouting across the void, so to speak, the sitter gets back a distorted echo of what it is his voice asks to hear. A typical incident concerns Billy, one of Una's innumerable succession of dogs, and the mystery of his death. The mystery is solved because M.V.B. (Mabel Batten) is helped by two people 'over there' who were able to tap Billy's memory of his last fight in which he received the bite that brought about his end. Explaining this through Feda, especially how in a presumably crowded after-world she could have discovered Una's Billy, a dog she had not known on earth, the discarnate voice of Ladye explains: 'I don't know how these things come to one, but they do, and I found myself automatically in touch with Billy. We have a far fuller knowledge of things here than I can ever hope to explain to you through Feda, it's much too big a thing to get through one's brain.'

The first part of this paper – in printed form the whole extends to over two hundred printed pages – was such a success that the second meeting was made open to the public, and the remaining part of the paper was given on 22 March, 1918, at the Steinway Hall. On this occasion Sir Oliver Lodge was in the Chair, and several distinguished members of the Council were present on the platform supporting the Speaker; others were seated in the Hall. But one prominent member was not present: Mr George Fox-Pitt, who had heard the first part of the paper given in the

Society's rooms in Hanover Square in January, but found himself so put out by its contents that he left the room before the discussion began, and almost immediately thereafter began to make himself a nuisance. He complained to the Secretary that the content of the paper was 'scientific rubbish', and went round to other members of the Council muttering that its effect was 'immoral'. It began to be plain that there were differences on the Council as to how its affairs should be conducted and that at least some of the pure scientists, who detested the popular presentation of their researches, were allied with relics of the Victorian world who thought all women ought to be kept at home, and to whom the sight of an abnormal woman like Radclyffe Hall was as infuriating as a red rag to a bull. Against them were the more popular propagators of the doctrine of communication with the dead like Sir Oliver Lodge and Mrs Sidgwick, who saw in Radclyffe Hall's extended and self-financed investigations a form of popular education in psychical science which could only be of benefit to the Society.

Meanwhile it is possible to reconstruct from Una's diary the effect her letters were having on the Admiral. The least articulate of men himself – his own letters might have been written by a schoolboy – he was nevertheless an intelligent and proud man, and he must have begun to believe that there was altogether too much of this spiritualism, and that Radclyffe Hall's company was having an unhealthy effect on his wife. He knew, of course, what the doctors had told him, and at this stage he must have been anxious to comply with their recommendations, to allow her as much happiness and freedom as possible, and as long as she was being his wife in name, looking after their child, and keeping up a home, he had no grounds for saying from a distance of seven hundred miles away that he did not much like her friends.

Then Una wrote so rapturously about John, what a good, affectionate helpful friend she was: the same ecstatic phrases that she was confiding to her diary. The Admiral had never met Radclyffe Hall; he just had to take his wife's word that she was the paragon she said she was.

He became more uneasy when, 42 St Leonard's Terrace not proving a success, she made an offer for a house, 6 Cheltenham Terrace. She wrote Troubridge to tell him what she had done as the house was to be purchased in his name; also to tell him that he had 'appeared' at a séance only a few days before, and there had been some very interesting talk. This was plainly not to the Admiral's liking. He applied for immediate leave, and the ladies were suddenly disturbed by a message received by Olga, the nursemaid, while they were out that the Admiral was coming home and would be there next day. He wanted his 'civvies' out of Taylor's Depository, and that was all that they knew.

Alarmed, they flew in a taxi to the Admiralty to find out the hour of his arrival and the extent of his leave, with no success. They went to see Sir Eyre Crowe at the Foreign Office, with no better success. The next day a telegram from Troubridge from Dover announced the hour of his arrival at Charing Cross that evening. Una dined with John and at nine o'clock met at Charing Cross the husband she had not seen for a year and a half.

It was a strange homecoming. In the few minutes in which she greeted him on the platform she had to tell him that he was not coming home with her, and that she had reserved a room for him at the Charing Cross Hotel. She sat with him there downstairs for an hour and a half, telling him no doubt, although the diary does not mention this, that St Leonard's Terrace was being dismantled, and the house in Cheltenham Terrace not ready to receive him, as it was in the hands of the decorators. As she did not offer to stay with him at the hotel, it must have been plain to the Admiral that his marriage was, in effect, over, and that what his friends had been telling him about Miss Radclyffe Hall was true.

Troubridge remained in London from 29 May to 28 August. He had conferences at the Admiralty to attend, and high officials to see at the Foreign Office, but he had to sleep somewhere, and he had to entertain and be entertained by his friends. Without an open break, which he was anxious to avoid, Una had to share in these engagements, and a curious working arrangement was evolved, which Troubridge seems at first to have accepted. John exercised her charms, which could be considerable, on him, and appealed to his sympathy about his wife's health and 'nerves'. He could not have been so simple a man as not to recognize the true meaning of the relationship between his wife and his hostess. He was, of course, a good deal older than either of them, but not so old that he was immune from sexual interest himself. But he evidently made no claims on Una, and they all three spent much time together. The diary reveals that they all went to Mass together, taking with them the Cub, now a little girl of seven. Several times when they had all gone back to John's flat for a nightcap, Una remained to sleep at John's flat, while the Admiral went back to the Travellers' Club, to which he had moved.

When he lunched with Wickham Steed, then the Editor of *The Times*, she went too. She was his hostess when he entertained his friends at the Travellers' in a private room, or out at restaurants, and there was no sign of a break-up. But if the diary does not confide the terms of the arrangement, it reveals everything else, her passionate love for the woman who has come into her life, her continuous interest in psychic matters because of John's interest in it, and the returning tide of warmth as she gets used to the presence of her husband, and he seems, or so she believes, to accept the situation. One can trace this in her use of the name. At the beginning he is 'Troubridge', but as his two months leave goes on and they see more and more of each other, he becomes 'True', a name which John invented, and eventually he reverts to the old familiar 'Zyp', the fond nickname of their early days together. When he leaves to go back to Greece, and she has not seen him for two weeks, and their relationship is under strain again, he reverts to 'Troubridge'.

But there is no hope of repair of this wrecked marriage, and even this simple man must have seen it. She uses her health as an excuse not to face the finality of the act she is contemplating. She goes with Zyp to see Sir James Mackenzie, the Harley Street specialist. He says her heart trouble is not organic, but is brought on by worry and unhappiness. There is no remedy except being perfectly happy – 'and other impossible circumstances' as she notes to herself. 'Back to Cheltenham Terrace where John is waiting. Bless her – the best friend a woman ever had.' That this strange passion was burningly responded to is evident in the deeply-felt cry, 'my beloved little Squiggie'.

Troubridge did not return to his post until 28th August. Meanwhile at the end of July John went for a holiday to Fittleworth, and on the Cub's return from school on 31st Una and the child, the nurse and two dogs are seen off to Southbourne where Una has taken rooms for the holiday. Three days later John arrived in her car to pick up Una. They were to motor to Paignton in Devon where Mrs Osborne Leonard and her husband were on holiday. They were there only two days, and packed in not only two sittings, Feda appearing, but a visit to the lady palmist operating on the Pier. John remained on, staying with them, but there is no sign of the Admiral. On one occasion during this holiday Una has to go to London to take one of her dogs to the kennels. Her mother and sister came on to dine with her, and at 9 p.m. Troubridge arrived. They all talked to one o'clock, and then Una went to bed and returned to Southbourne next morning.

She was not to see Troubridge again until after the war, when at a disagreeable interview, with John present, the formal separation was agreed to. On the 28th of August, the day of his departure, her diary simply notes: 'True left at 1 p.m. for Greece.' And then, as though this were a signal: 'after luncheon the fly came and John and I to Bournemouth Central and to London. Arrived at 7.30 and we dined Café Royal – then to flat . . . then home and talked till late and to bed.'

At the end of the year Radclyffe Hall's name was proposed for election to the Council, and Mr Fox-Pitt became extremely agitated. He went to Miss Newton, the Secretary of the Society, and told her that he was a friend of Troubridge's, and had just had a conversation with him at the Travellers', from which he learnt that Radclyffe Hall was a grossly immoral woman, and had wrecked the Admiral's home. She ought not to be elected to the Council. The day following he repeated this charge to Mrs Salter, the Editor of the Society's Journal. He extended the detail.

Radclyffe Hall was a thoroughly immoral woman who had lived for years with Mrs Batten, the M.V.B. of the paper who now purported to speak from the other side, and who had been no better in her morals than Radclyffe Hall. The latter had come between Admiral Troubridge and his wife, and broken up the Admiral's home, and if Mrs Sidgwick did not withdraw her nomination of Radclyffe Hall he would make these charges publicly at the meeting of the Council.

Almost immediately thereafter Radclyffe Hall, through Sir George Lewis, her solicitor, issued a writ for slander. More than two years were to elapse before the case came up for trial. It was naturally to attract the widest attention in the press, the combination of spiritualism with suggestions of homosexuality between women, especially women as well known as Radclyffe Hall, whose songs were being sung at this time on concert platforms all over England, and an Admiral's wife, being more than the popular papers could resist. Even *The Times* Law Report of the action ran to eight columns.

Much was to happen in the year before the action came to trial. Admiral Troubridge had indeed come to London in January 1918, just when Radclyffe Hall had been nominated to the Council and Fox-Pitt had in protest resigned from it. Fox-Pitt had encountered Troubridge at the Travellers' just when he had finally broken with his wife.

The Admiral was almost certainly justified in saying, or at least thinking, that Radclyffe Hall's influence on his wife was a baneful one. Not only had she abandoned him, but she had taken to wearing a tortoiseshell monocle, had adopted a long cigarette-holder, and wore breeches at a dog-show, all of which could be regarded as improper in 1918. He could see the change in her appearance. She was still a beautiful young woman of only 32, but he could see in her face the evidence of the hectic life she was leading. Troubridge was an extremely handsome man, and it must have shocked him that Una should prefer to live with this travesty of a woman than with him. He exuded male vitality, and he could not understand how these two women detested that essence. Nor could he possibly have imagined how deep their love for each other had become. It was not a case of sexual love only; it was an absolute awareness of each for the other that made the senses, the very thoughts and anxieties of one as real to the other as though they had occurred to her. Una notes in her diary examples of the constant telepathy between them. When one of them is coming home by train from London unannounced, the other starts out to walk to the station to meet her. When one is ill the other becomes ill; when one is happy, the spirits of the other lift with her. It was an intertwining of soul and body each with the other, and against this the appeal of male vitality had no chance whatsoever.

Disturbed by what he had heard about their paper at The Psychical Society meeting, Admiral Troubridge came over from Paris in January 1918 to demand that his wife leave Radclyffe Hall and rejoin him. He had written ahead to say that he wanted all his clothes packed, and Una had gone up to Cheltenham Terrace to do this from Datchet, where she was staying with the Temples, who were having the Cub, a school friend of their children, as their guest during her school holidays. Returning to Datchet by a late afternoon train she had found Troubridge in the drawing-room, awaiting her. She refused to see him except in John's presence. He stormed about this but could do nothing except eventually agree. In John's presence Una gave her refusal to leave, and Troubridge said that he must have a separation agreement. She was to see him only once more in his lifetime, a meeting which was equally without dignity. He left abruptly, saying that she would hear from his lawyers. When he had gone she threw herself weeping into John's arms, and received the comfort and release from tension that she always felt in them.

John arranged for her own lawyers, Hastie, to represent Una in making the agreement, although Crichton-Miller had to be asked for his views too. All parties agreeing that separation was the only possible arrangement, the draft of the settlement, representing the best terms that Hastie had been able to exact from the Admiral's lawyers, was in Una's hands within a few days. She was outraged by the speed with which this matter was despatched, angered by the clerk who rang up to ask if she would agree to pay half the stamp duty, and incensed by the alacrity with which Troubridge signed his half of the deed. A mere five days after the stormy interview with him saw their marriage of twelve years broken up legally. She was given the custody of the Cub, and her feeling of having been disposed of vanished in 'the great peace and relief which came upon me'.

Radclyffe Hall's slander action against Fox-Pitt came on on 18 November, 1920. Her solicitors, Messrs Lewis & Lewis, had instructed Sir Ellis Hume-Williams, K.C. and Mr St John Field, a brilliant young junior. Fox-Pitt conducted his own defence. This could not have been for lack of means, but was probably out of a desire explicitly to show that he needed no professional legal assistance to prove that this woman was a fraud.

St George Lane Fox had had the name Pitt added unto him when his father had inherited the family property, and had taken the name of Pitt-Rivers for himself and the name Pitt for his heirs. Although a gifted amateur and not a professional scientist, Fox-Pitt was a man of extreme learning whose contribution to the practical uses of electricity had been of great importance. The loss of the millions he might have derived from his patents for incandescent lights, which might have soured the average man, had left Fox-Pitt seemingly unperturbed, for in addition to being very clever he was devoted to the moral uplift of mankind, and thought of money as the root of all evil. Besides being absorbed in the work of the Society for Psychical Research, he was Vice-President and Treasurer of the Moral Education League. Egotism of any sort he detested, as much as he did immorality. He viewed the craving for personal survival after death, that is the persona in its earthly form instead of the discarnate spirit, as supremely egoistic and an offence against reason. That a paper like Radclyffe Hall's should be given by a person of Radclyffe Hall's immoral character under the aegis of the Society for Psychical Research was more than he could stomach. To understand his behaviour in the trial we must think of him not as a scientific crackpot upset by the meddling of amateurs, but as a man of high ethical views defending these against the profanity of the godless.

The account of the case shows the terrible disadvantage at which an amateur, however gifted in his own field, labours in the formal processes by which justice achieves its end. He was the defendant in the action, but in conducting his defence he kept taking the part of the aggressor. What he had to defend was the use of the slanderous terms 'immoral' in relation to Radclyffe Hall. What he sought to prove was that she was a scientific fraud, and that her paper was rubbish.

He was brought to account by the Judge for thus shifting his terms, and he thereupon denied that he had used the word 'immoral', at least not in relation to her character, but only in relation to her paper which was scientific rubbish and quite unworthy of the Society. It was his duty to protect the Society, and he admitted that there were great differences on the Council as to how its affairs should be conducted.

But the Judge reminded him that he had alleged against the Plaintiff unchastity and sexual immorality. Fox-Pitt's answer to his lordship revealed the fanatic.

> This is a senseless kind of stuff which many people who read it will think is the product of scientific minds. It is pure rubbish and only gives evidence of incipient dementia.

After a minute, and an intervening question to the witness he is cross-examining (Radclyffe Hall, who is in the box, and is glaring at him, for she herself is of no more easy temper than he is) Fox-Pitt again addresses an aside to his lordship:

> The Society was founded for scientific research, but it has drifted away from that and attempts are being made to use it for loose purposes. I am fighting against the pernicious craze of spiritism which is the reverse of spiritual. It produces a state of mind which is bringing about a great deal of lunacy.

The Lord Chief Justice, who was hearing the case, took advantage of the opportunity offered him by much of the evidence to make judicial observations which produced 'laughter in court'.

He was particularly hard on the defendant, evidently wishing to demonstrate that he could recognize a crackpot when he saw one. In the end he summed up for the jury, but so confused them as to what they had to satisfy themselves about that they had to troop back into Court for further enlightenment. On their reappearance they found for the plaintiff, Radclyffe Hall, assessing the damages at £500.

It was a verdict with which neither side could really be satisfied. Radclyffe Hall's character had been far from cleared. In addition to the charge of homosexuality there now lay the strong implication of 'nuttiness' about spiritualism. All the verdict finally said was that the words complained of were not intended to apply to the plaintiff's character, but to her work – which to John was even more intolerable.

To Fox-Pitt the verdict brought not only a loss of £500, but the frustrating feeling that he had not made his point clear. He had had to say to the Lord Chief Justice at one stage in the trial 'You don't see my point'. To which his lordship had irritably replied, 'Well, use plain language.'

But that was beyond Fox-Pitt when he got worked up. As he had complained at another point in the trial, when being cross-examined by Sir Ellis Hume-Williams, there was a conspiracy against him. In the words of *The Times* reporter (those of Fox-Pitt were indubitably more extensive):

> 'Conspiracy', he explained, to the amusement of the Court, 'was a "breathing together". They had been breathing together with the result that lies came out of their mouths.' He said the ladies who had given evidence did not know what was true or false. Their statements were confused and contrary. The conspiracy against him he called 'the Junta'.

Fox-Pitt could not rest satisfied with a verdict which he was utterly convinced had been arrived at through the Judge's misunderstanding of the nature of the conspiracy, and he lost no time in appealing. This time he hired a lawyer, and the appeal was conducted without some of his interventions. The result was that their lordships ordered a new trial on the ground that the learned judge had not told the jury whether the words complained of had been privileged, in that they had been uttered by the defendant as a member of the Council of the Society to officers of the Society in the discussion of business.

The next day John and Una went to see Sir George Lewis who advised that they should certainly not bring a new trial. Sir George spoke as a man who could not go through all that again. He told Radclyffe Hall what she wanted to hear, 'that her character had been more than cleared, and it would be futile spending much money and having more odious publicity when Fox-Pitt will never pay a penny.'

'Home exhausted', notes Una in her diary, 'but it is all *over* and the vital issues attained – so early to bed – both of us very pleased.'

Chapter Seven

John was much too intelligent not to be aware that although Fox-Pitt had lost the verdict, he had in effect won the day. The brief bursts of uneasy laughter which the Judge's remarks had elicited at his expense had been followed, she knew, by an increased sense of respect for him and what he stood for. Appearing without Counsel, stumblingly earnest in his presentation of what he was defending, he managed to give the impression of a man who had devoted his life to science, and had not enriched himself in the process, who had simply complained on what he conceived to be a privileged occasion that a paper read before the Society had not been worthy of members' attention. When the Judge had reminded him that he had not only criticized the paper, but had said that the author of it was an immoral woman, he had corrected himself. But he had made his point.

He knew, and Radclyffe Hall knew, that in the minds of the jury there was a built-in case for regarding him and the Society which he was defending respectfully, just as there was a built-in bias against sexual deviants. So when he had shifted his attack and claimed that his remarks had been directed against her scientific qualifications, not her moral reputation, Fox-Pitt, the defendant, had put her, the plaintiff, in the position of having to justify the scientific nature of her investigations without having a chance to defend the grievance which had led her to bring the case. She had made the same mistake that Oscar Wilde had made. Egotism is a symptom of the disturbed psyche, and the invert, as Havelock Ellis had shown, finds an irresistible attraction in taking risks.

Like Lord Queensberry, whose son-in-law he happened by a coincidence to be, Fox-Pitt was quite ready to be the defendant in a trial in which the plaintiff was bound to show up badly. He must have been confident, as his father-in-law had been with

95

Oscar Wilde, that his victim would betray herself, and that her position on the Council would be weakened even though his was entirely lost. He was right. When the appeal judges in March 1921 ordered a new trial, she withdrew.

Murmurs arose in the Society, and the Council found it necessary to announce in the Journal:

> In view of certain reflections made on the Secretary, and the Editor of the *Journal* and of the *Proceedings*, in the course of the trial, the Council wish to put on record their unabated confidence in these two ladies, and their refutation of the suggestions made against them.

Feelings had been running high before the trial, and well-meant proposals for getting John and Una out of the way had been advanced under cover. Dr Wooley, a member of the Council, and perhaps speaking on behalf of it, had wanted them to go to Belfast for a year on a salary to succeed Dr Crawford in some investigations being undertaken there, but they refused. After the trial, Mrs Leonard, who wanted herself to go to India for the next winter, asked them to accompany her. Again they refused.

That Radclyffe Hall should have won support from such a distinguished body of men and women as those on the Council is a tribute to her strong and compelling personality. She had caught the Society at a moment when the vast increase of public interest in spiritualism made certain influential members ambitious to widen its scope, and they saw in her the means of doing that. Without her brains, and incidentally her private means to pursue research, she could not in so short a time have obtained a seat on the Council, or occupied with her discoveries so many pages of the *Proceedings*.

Some members of the Council who respected Fox-Pitt for his selfless work in the early days of the Society, had felt some regret that it had to be either one or the other. But Fox-Pitt had left them in no doubt on that score, and they co-opted Marguerite Radclyffe Hall, knowing full well that this meant Fox-Pitt's resignation. Even so, the election was not without a last-minute hitch. When the agenda for the Annual General Meeting was circulated the name of Radclyffe Hall was not listed as a candidate for election to the Council, and Una had to ring up and threaten resignation. Rectification was hastily made, and Fox-Pitt simultaneously resigned.

Soon after the Armistice, Una, longing for the country where she could exercise the growing tribe of dogs she was accumulating with the ambition of breeding pedigree strains, had persuaded John that country air was what they both needed. They bought Chip Chase, a turreted house with rough-cast battlements at Hadley Wood, only twelve miles north of Marble Arch, where the rural surroundings promised seclusion, and the quiet John would need to start her novel. The surrounding woods would also provide exercise grounds for the dogs, whose unceasing clamour, constant maladies, and claims on Una's attention, were driving John herself to madness. The house was set in extensive grounds, and it had the advantage of containing a separate cottage which they offered rent-free to Mrs Leonard. At the end of April in 1920 they left London, and took possession of their 'little castle of Winterbourne de St Martin's', as Una rhapsodized in her diary. Una's furniture and effects were moved out of Cheltenham Terrace, which had become the Admiral's home. They were brought down to Chip Chase by van.

They moved in with a secretary, a personal maid, who looked after both of them, a cook and four house servants. On the payroll as well was a gardener and a gardener's boy. It was an extravagant establishment, but it was the first house they had owned, and they were delighted with it. They had got possession in January, but it was April before the decorations were completed, carpets laid, and new curtains cut and fitted.

They were no sooner settled in than Una showed disturbing symptoms of mental strain. The evidence of deep depression is plainly visible in her handwriting in the diary, which became only faintly like her own. She was removed to Bowden House and put under Dr Crichton-Miller's care, and John took up the writing of the diary. The entries between 2 and 19 June – Una returned on the 21st – are all in John's hand, and although self-conscious, as if she were intruding on someone else's private ground, they show her satirical humour, even though no one can hear it but herself. 'Minna (Una's mother) rang up to say that Una is now "Lady", Troubridge having had a "K" added to his threadbare C.M.G.'* And after making in the diary a list of complaints about things going wrong in Squig's absence, the entry is simply, 'Hang everything!' These pages contain some very interesting observations about psychical phenomena she had observed. Much more than Una she gives you the feeling of what it was like to witness these things at séances.

After three weeks, Squig returned from Bowden House like a child released from boarding school. She seemed completely recovered. Her social instincts – traits which were absent altogether from John's make-up – made her want to fill the house constantly with visitors.

Sir Oliver Lodge came and dined and stayed the night. 'He seemed weak and odd in the head', notes Una, 'and rabid against all scientific criticism of spiritualism.' A few days later, the Hon. Everard Feilding, a member of the Council, and at the time a Research Officer of the Society for Psychical Research, came to dine and told them about a Miss Tomcygk, who had second sight, and who he thought could be helped by them. He asked them to invite her to stay at Chip Chase, and he and the girl, a pretty one, arrived together on Saturday afternoon.

It was soon made plain that Everard Feilding's interest in Miss Tomcygk was not purely scientific: she was, in fact, later to become his wife. But she was suffering physically from the effects of some harsh experiences she had had in Eastern Europe during the war, and this, Feilding had confided to John and Una, was threatening her sanity. He believed that if she would agree to let him hypnotize her, she might under trance be able to tell her story, and thus cleanse herself of this perilous stuff in her bosom.

Hypnotism was simply mesmerism grown older, the subject on which John's grandfather had written so copiously in *The*

* In the Birthday Honours List in 1921 Admiral Troubridge was made Knight-Commander of The Order of St George.

Lancet in 1845. Anton Mesmer, a Viennese physician in the early 19th century, had made many cures of obstinate diseases by inducing a flow of what he called 'animal magnetism' from doctor to patient. Young Dr Radclyffe-Hall had examined the report of these cases closely, and had concluded that, while they demonstrated some striking phenomena in the physiology of the nervous system, there was nothing to prove that 'mesmeric phrenology', the submission of the nervous system to the control of the manipulator, and the dissolving of impure, chaotic or troublesome thoughts by the release of tensions, was due to hypnotic control. Dr Radclyffe-Hall did not condemn mesmerism. He would have known that hypnosis had lately been used in one or two cases to anaesthetize pain in amputations. But he thought that its indiscriminate use could result in a dangerous tinkering with the nervous system, and his conclusion was that there was insufficient evidence to recommend its general adoption at that time. Hypnosis was in fact to remain under the shadow of being quackery until quite recent times. Now, as Rosalind Heywood points out in her invaluable *The Sixth Sense*, it is one of the official benefits of the National Health Service in Britain.

By the 1920s, in the world at large, hypnotism had become quite a fashionable cure for a host of ailments from eye-strain to constipation. It was used to strengthen the memory, to eliminate nervousness, banish phobias, even to cure blushing and stammering. In the sleep or trance induced by hypnotism the patient was said to feel a release from inhibitions, and a heightened sense of suggestibility.

While it was now beginning to be used medically in cases of childbirth, and other cases where physical stresses needed to be eliminated, it had become at this time something of a drawing-room trick, and was frequently demonstrated by individuals with no medical qualification at all, for purely frivolous reasons. *A Manual of Hypnotism* gave any general reader the knowledge of how to do it. Una had been shown by Crichton-Miller how to hypnotize herself. She had become quite adept now at hypnotizing others. Feilding, as a research officer and member of the Council of the Society for Psychical Research, knew the technique.

But he would also have been aware that as a practice, it would have been frowned on by a serious body like the Society for Psychical Research, still dominated by eminent scientists, who would even in the 1920s have subscribed to the forceful view of Lord Kelvin who had dismissed 'that wretched superstition of animal magnetism' as so much rubbish. This may have been why he wanted to conduct this experiment in the seclusion of Chip Chase.

That night after dinner Everard Feilding in the presence of the others hypnotized Miss Tomcygk, now called Stasie by them all, in an effort to get her to rid herself of this dark cloud of oppression. But the experiment did not work.

The following weekend Stasie, but not Feilding, came down again on the Friday, and it was Una who put Stasie to sleep. This time it did begin to work. The control appeared as a young woman whose name was Mayenne, and something, but not all, of Stasie's troubles, which had to do with her experiences as a child refugee in the war, came to light. Her mesmeric trance lasted from nine in the evening until one-thirty the next morning. While still in the trance, at their prompting, Stasie wrote a letter to Feilding, and they sent it next day.

The next evening, Saturday, Stasie begged Una to put her to sleep again, but Una refused. The following morning, Sunday, they all, including the victim, got up early and went to Mass where they 'become silly and weak over the absurd singing behind us'. One has continually to overcome a sense of shock at the untroubled way in which they turn from these necromantic practices to the old ones of religion without showing any awareness of the suggestion this offers that they were all at least a little mentally deranged.

That evening again Stasie begged to be hypnotized, but again Una refused, and the diary goes on: 'so she told us her troubles – very real, poor child – in the normal!' The next day Feilding came down to Chip Chase, and asked Stasie to marry him. The marriage took place some months later, but by the time it did, they had learnt from Mrs Sidgwick that Feilding had become an enemy of theirs on the Council, and the mention of his name in the diary is followed by the word swine doubly underlined.

It must have been a strange house, lost in its large garden, and shielded from the outside world by the deep woods that surrounded it on three sides. It was efficiently and comfortably run, Una having a genius for household management, and now as 'Milady' getting from domestic staff that extra measure of willing service which even a threadbare title used to induce. The food was delicious, the wine was beyond suspicion, the beds were comfortable, and fires burned in the many fireplaces.

Only the dogs were a nuisance, if one did not care for them underfoot, or found their constant barking and yapping a distraction. There must have been at least twenty in the kennels, with the superior ones and those in a delicate state, usually suffering from diarrhoea, living in the house.

Behind the closed library door the sound of the typewriter hardly ceased, and laborious work went on. The filing cabinets were full, and new ones were from time to time added. The 'reports' circulated from other investigators were long and involved, and very wordy. Both John and Una, after breakfast upstairs together in their room, descended to the 'office', where the secretary would already have been at work since nine o'clock. Una would emerge from time to time on household errands, but John usually remained secluded until just before lunch. The guests entertained themselves with strolls and chats and gossip, with motor car excursions to the neighbouring shops, and other diversions, until sherry before lunch meant the babble of voices rose in pitch and volume, and the rest of the day was free for fun.

And it seemed almost constant fun. They were all girls together, none of them over forty, all handsome and intelligent, witty and conscious of being daring. Their names float through the diary – Honey and Susan and Gabrielle, Brother and Julia and Alice and Claude. Gales of laughter reduce them to helplessness as Brother, a well-born and immensely large woman, with a passion for slim young girls, tells the story of 'his' life in two volumes. The masculine pronoun is invariably applied to Brother even in the diary, as though she actually were the man she longed to be.

They dance, often until the early hours of the morning, and little jealous spats and quarrels spring up and die down. Their loneliness, for they are lonely in spite of all the fun and laughter, makes their grief and their joys go always to extremes. But they would be more lonely still if they did not share these intensities. Brother appears, immense in fencing breeches, choked with tears, and they listen to the facts of Alice's naughtiness. They swear they will never see one another again, and an hour later fling their arms around each other in a passion of remorse, swearing never to be divided.

The ugly world intrudes from time to time. Troubridge, now in Paris, sends letters which upset Una, and have to be taken to her solicitors in London after close dissection and general discussion at Chip Chase. Or one of the dogs gets ill, and the gloom when Pipe of Peace or Athos or Fitzjohn Little Redskin, or the bearer of some other great pedigree name, 'passes over', although not shared by everybody, lowers the spirits of the party. Or the ladies become ill, and have to go and consult specialists. Pain intrudes on the fantasy world, and the joy is temporarily hushed.

None of this had appeared in the diary before they bought Chip Chase. Nor does it after they sold the house and returned to London. Although these girls are frequently mentioned, the visitors who get the attention are more serious, most of them women writers. It is as though the seclusion of Chip Chase, and its queer battlemented façade, supported and sustained an illusory world where they could be natural amongst themselves, and this was no longer possible when they returned to London, and met these friends at nightclubs, or came home in the early hours of the morning with them, to put on the gramophone and dance.

In the end the disadvantages of Chip Chase seemed to outweigh its advantages. The drive down to it after dinner on foggy winter nights was excessively trying. It was far from Harley Street specialists whom they needed constantly to consult, and now that John had been elected to the Council of the Society for Psychical Research she had many evening meetings to attend. The plain rusticity of Chip Chase and earnest days and nights suddenly seemed dull and unrewarding.

So in one splendid sweep most of the dogs were disposed of, the files disbanded, the secretary dismissed, Chip Chase sold and the furniture put into storage, and they came up to London and took a furnished house at 7 Trevor Square in Knightsbridge, while they looked about for a suitable freehold to buy in town.

Brooding upon the unsatisfactory outcome of the trial had had the predictable effect of hardening John's defence of her inversion. It was nothing to be ashamed of; it was a trick of nature. Why should she and others like her be condemned because the balance of their genes made in their case the need to find physical satisfaction in sexual love drive them instinctively towards someone of their own sex, instead of the opposite sex? Love for another human being was a holy thing, whatever the sex. But the inverts had to hide their love, to live in the twilight. John knew that flamboyancy was the natural, but a completely ineffective form of protest, and that her kind were too often driven to it out of exasperation, thereby increasing the hostility directed at them. She believed that the time was coming when she and her afflicted sisters and brothers would not have to hang their heads in shame, and already she was beginning to talk to Una and others of making this the theme of the novel for which Mr Heinemann had said he was waiting.

During this spring they still had occasional séances with Mrs Leonard. John dutifully attended Council meetings, and Una joined her there for the dinners which always followed. But they seemed glad enough to get away early, and slip off to a night club, either with one or two other friends, or in larger parties to indulge in dancing, the new craze that was hitting everyone in London.

These parties were all of girls. Only on some occasions was a man with them. The sight of women dancing together at the Cave of Harmony or the Orange Tree Club or the Hambone aroused neither amusement nor alarm. Dancing in night-clubs, and even in hotels, did not go back much earlier than ten years before. In the relaxed atmosphere after the war anything was accepted, and the sight of rather mannish-looking women, some of them wearing monocles, some of them smoking cigars and jewelled pipes, wearing short hair-cuts, and black dinner-jackets and bow ties, dancing with other girls aroused no moral tremors such as were to be felt a few years later when Joynson-Hicks became Home Secretary, and typified the growing public reaction to the pendulum swinging too far.

They were all known by their first names, and often as in the case of Radclyffe Hall ('John') and Toupie Lowther ('Brother') by male names. They all seem in this particular circle well-enough equipped with funds to be lunching or dining at the Savoy every day, to be always buying new cars, tinkering with them, going for wild drives, selling them and buying others. They stay up until four or five or six in the morning, reluctant to leave each other. Everywhere there is a beautiful face to gaze into with rapture, dreaming of love. The wit is as sharp as the standard of talent is high, and amongst this crowd the number of self-exiled American artists is noticeable. Tallulah Bankhead seems to prefer an evening or a Sunday with them to one spent in the company of men, and the adorable little Teddie Gerard writes to them from New York, complaining of the favourable notices her play has had, which will keep her absent from them for six months at least. She begs them to use her car, her chauffeur, her butler and her country cottage. The striking-looking artist Romaine Brooks falls for Una and wants to separate her from John and take her off to Capri.

It was a relief from the tensions of their long months of psychical investigations, from the intrigues on the Council and the High Court trial, and from the worry of Admiral Troubridge who, though legally separated, would not stop sending blustering, offensive letters and threatening legal action to recover his child; it was as a relief from these things that John and Una threw themselves, on coming up from Chip Chase, into this never-ceasing round of pleasure and dissipation. Their physical love for each other had reached at this moment a passionate momentum, and the legal separation from the Admiral had, to Una's imagination at least, carried with it the dedication of herself, body and soul forever to John.

The late hours, the rich food, the unaccustomed cocktails, the acceleration of passionate embraces brought retribution in the form of colitis and unseemlier ailments which disposed of one or other of them to bed for several days at a time, but when this happened the other never left her side. Sometimes they lay ill in bed together, talking, talking all the time. One cannot imagine a normal marriage which could support such unremitting intimacy without rows or sulks or a feeling of claustrophobia attacking both victims. John had a very touchy temper, and Una was extremely sensitive to any imagined affront or coldness, so of course there were occasional outbursts when, after long discussion, sometimes into the small hours, they would decide that it would be better if they were to separate. But then, that awful decision taken, they had only to look at each other aghast at the very suggestion, to fly into one another's arms, weeping copiously, swearing never, never to part.

This was the famous hot summer of 1921 when all over Europe the temperatures from the beginning of July soared into the 80s and 90s. The company they were keeping at this stage was almost exclusively lesbian. They were busy arranging their first European holiday together, where in Capri and Sicily, and in Paris on the way, they were to be entertained by their European lesbian friends who always came to London for the season in May and June; a tour which one must believe provided Compton Mackenzie with the plot for one of his wittiest novels, *Extraordinary Women*. Una looked forward to introducing her beloved John to Cencio and May Massola. They had written to express delight at her coming, but oddly, the Massolas had not invited them to stay. They recommended instead the best hotel in Levanto. A suspicion that perhaps May Massola would not approve of their relationship floated uneasily between the former friends.

Cubbie had to be disposed of. The child had come home from school, carrying proudly two prizes, and a medal for good conduct, and confidently expecting to be made much of. Instead she was sent to stay with the Temples at Datchet, after the allotted week she was to spend with her father. In floods of tears, she was seen off for her summer holidays.

This child lived the loneliest life imaginable, always in the way in her holidays, alternatively petted and spoilt by being taken to lunch at the Savoy and a matinee afterwards, or forgotten and left to lunch and sup with the cook and the parlourmaid. In the beginning John plainly hoped to win her love, and was indulgent towards her. But as time passed, she resented the Cub's claims on Una's attention, and a certain sadistic element seemed to enter into the judgements and subsequent punishments meted out by them to the Cub when she had erred in any way. She was not neglected so much as disregarded. Una could become very concerned when the child was ill, but unless an alarm-bell like that was ringing she seemed content to swoon her life away with John.

Mostly the Cub was away at boarding schools, the best of their kind. She was an engaging child of attractive appearance and very intelligent, but she was outside the bond that held these two together. She paid occasional visits to the Admiral under the terms of the Deed, but she was always happy when these were over and she could return to the lonely life she led in the town or country during her holidays. She was ten at the time the case for slander came up in the High Court, and eighteen when *The Well of Loneliness* case was tried in the Magistrate's Court and the High Court in 1928. The publicity arising from these *causes célèbres* must have been uncomfortable for a girl in a prep-school, and for a young lady making her debut in London. Yet her odd upbringing never seemed to have hardened her, or turned her into a psychotic. When I met her in London after her mother's death she was the jolliest person imaginable, happily married to a man of great vigour and heartiness. She was killed in a motor accident not long after her mother's death.

But in 1920, more than forty years before that time, she was a child of ten living in her holidays in a house with two sick women. Hardly a day passed that one of them was not ill, the other devotedly nursing the invalid and lunching or dining off a tray in the invalid's bedroom. Aside from the ills that plague all human beings, colds and headaches and constipation and things of that sort, it is clear that the sexual practices of lesbianism induced some gynaecological woes of an unhappy kind for which the medical treatment can be protracted and painful.

At last at the beginning of September Radclyffe Hall and Una were off. After a deliriously happy week in Paris they left by *luxe* train for Levanto. Alas, the meeting confirmed the unhappy suspicion. Una had sung the praises of her friends to John so much, and to her friends the praises of John, and neither of them rose to the occasion. Depressed, Una fell ill and had to take to her bed. When she recovered they were invited up to the Castle, but not frequently enough, and a little coldness sprang up between the hosts and their visitors. The Baron Massola assumed yachtman's gear, and his yacht was summoned to the landing stage and off he went, turning the stern of his ship towards his wife's friends. They stayed another fortnight, then booked rooms in Florence. Cencio miraculously returned from his voyage, but only in time to spend a few minutes seeing his wife's friends off at the station.

If only it had been the idyllic surroundings, even of the catty atmosphere pictured by Compton Mackenzie in *Extraordinary Women*. The reality was more sombre. In Florence they had an unseemly row with a jeweller from whom Una was endeavouring to buy a present for John, and one cannot help feeling that either she came too much her *Inglese* Ladyship or, alternatively, her part as passionate adorer of the he-woman with her was an affront to the virility of the jeweller. Whatever the reason the jeweller was 'unspeakably rude', which is not in the nature of Italian jewellers making their living from Anglo-Saxon tourists.

Then these were tense times in Italy. On their first night in the hotel they heard fifty rifle-shots, and were assured next morning by the concierge that there had been a Fascist-Socialist brawl – dismissed as being of no importance at all.

An autumnal mood of settling down for life in some villa in the hills seized them, Una writes, and they even started negotiating for the purchase of a baby which they could adopt and bring up as their own. They distributed to the boy-beggars who were thick upon the streets five lira notes, and shouts of gratitude pursued them to the hotel like hosannas. But a return of sanity, and a restlessness in John, brought them to their senses.

This restlessness was writer's itch. It was now 1921 and John had written nothing since 1915 when *Songs of Three Counties* was published. Mabel Batten's death, and their work for the Society of Psychical Research, followed by the slander case against Fox-Pitt, had occupied the time between. Una's idea of rusticity with kennels of dogs had only appealed because it enabled her to hide herself while she recovered from the shock of the verdict. A great wound had been opened in her side, and unless she did something about it she would bleed to death. She had the ability to write novels; Mr Heinemann, the best judge there was, had said that he was waiting impatiently for her first book. She imagined a novel in which the love of one woman for another would be shown as a holy and pure thing. She would speak up for the afflicted. While Una led her about Europe on this holiday, her mind was busy shaping the story. If she appeared distracted and grumpy and odd-looking to Una's friends, it was because the social chatter of people like the Massolas bored her stiff. She was never one to hide her feelings, even for the sake of her little beloved.

On their return to London, John joined the P.E.N. Club, then in its early days under the Presidency of John Galsworthy. Here at the monthly dinners she began to meet well-known writers like I. A. R. Wylie and May Sinclair, and they began to dine with each other outside the Club. On her return from Europe she had thrown herself with her customary fierce concentration into writing the novel. The first attempt when completed was called *After Many Days*. It never saw publication, but it was submitted by the literary agent Audrey Heath to the leading publishers, starting with Heinemann. The declining letters were encouraging. The publishers' readers with whom, through Audrey Heath's introduction, she was able to meet and talk about the manuscript, like the novelist J. D. Beresford who read manuscripts for Collins, professed themselves moved by her story, and Ida Wylie, a very experienced novelist herself, said she was 'most enthusiastic'.

But all the time, even when writing and completing *After Many*

Days she had been at work on another called, at that time, *Octopi* which as *The Unlit Lamp* was to become her first successful book, though not the first she was to publish. By the time *The Unlit Lamp* was ready to submit to a publisher Mr Heinemann had died, and his place had been taken by a very keen, sharp young man named Charles Evans, who was not bound by the promise of his predecessor, and who was to decline *The Unlit Lamp* out of hand when it was submitted to him.

The story line had suggested itself to John when she was on holiday with Una at Lynton in Devon. Into the dining-room of the hotel one evening came – as Una describes it:

> a small wizened old lady and an elderly woman who was quite obviously her maiden daughter. The latter was carrying a shawl and a footwarmer and clutched a bottle of medicine. She fussed for several minutes round the old lady, putting the footwarmer under her feet, the shawl round her shoulders and enquiring if she felt warm enough and not too warm, before she herself attempted to sit down. And John said to me in an undertone: 'Isn't it ghastly to see these unmarried daughters who are just unpaid servants and the old people sucking the very life out of them like octopi!' And then as suddenly: 'I shall write it. I shall write Heinemann's book for him and I shall call it *Octopi*.'

Bullied daughter enslaved to a selfish valetudinarian mother? It did not promise much in the way of a story, but the theme to which she was to relate this glimpse of an unhappy couple did. *The Unlit Lamp* becomes the story of Joan Ogden – and of the struggle between her mother and her woman tutor, Elizabeth Rodney, for her body and her mind.

Joan Ogden is the clever one of the two sisters. She comes under the influence of one of her teachers. Soon it is apparent that what motivates Elizabeth Rodney's interest in Joan is not only to pluck such a bright intellectual brand from the consuming fire of maternal selfishness, but an acute desire to get this girl away and to share a flat with her in London. They take this flat and furnish it together, and a date is set when Joan is to leave home. At literally the last moment the mother makes a sentimental appeal to her not to go, and when Elizabeth comes in the cab to pick her up she tells her that she is staying. A broken-hearted and passionately-phrased parting love-letter from Elizabeth follows after a little, and we are revealed a final glimpse of Joan Ogden, her mother now dead, taking a new position as a sort of domestic nurse to an elderly man whose mental development was arrested when he was a child and who still plays with toys.

It is by the standards of the time a good first novel, conveying with noticeable skill for a beginner subtleties in human relationships that could only have been observed by someone of acute sympathies. For what we see here is an early demonstration of an attitude on the author's part towards sexual relationships between women. *The Unlit Lamp* is in fact an experimental run of the theme of *The Well of Loneliness*.

Ten publishers declined the book before the eleventh took it. Half-way through this suspenseful process, John persuaded herself that she had been too serious. It had taken two years to write *The Unlit Lamp*, and another two to find a publisher for it. It took only five months to write *The Forge*, and it was accepted by the first publisher who saw it. *The Unlit Lamp* had reflected the author's deepest interest. *The Forge* is a quite skilfully-presented social comedy, pointing a moral. It only *pretends* to be serious. A solemn-minded, well-to-do couple, deeply interested in becoming serious artists, plan to devote their lives after marriage to art, she to becoming a painter, he to write novels. They fail, not for want of trying, but because neither of them has any real talent. They are spoilt by their upbringing, and by having had everything given to them that should be won from a struggle with life.

They become bored, fall apart, and separate so that he can finish his novel and she get on with her painting. After a year of separation they are drawn together again, and Hilary Brent, the husband, contrite for all the unhappiness he has caused, confides in his wife the conclusion he has come to, not very profound, that we are all bound by the environment and circumstances which we inherit at our birth and entwine ourselves in as we live our lives.

The Forge, accepted immediately by Arrowsmith, was published three months before *The Unlit Lamp*, which had finally been accepted by Cassell, the eleventh publisher to whom it had been submitted. Newman Flower had recently taken over the proprietorship of Cassells. He was a man of some taste in high-class popular fiction, and he was to succeed in building up the Cassells imprint with a number of very successful names. He shared an interest in spiritualism with Radclyffe Hall, and he employed the same medium, Mrs Osborne Leonard, whom Flower went so far as to consult about his business dealings. But in imparting this information confidentially to a fellow-spiritualist like Radclyffe Hall he added, 'In taking over a huge business like this, one does not want the sceptics to think that it is being run by a freak.'

Once the book was accepted everything prospered happily, and John was very pleased to be settled down with a publisher whom she liked personally, and whose imprint was held in general esteem. *The Unlit Lamp* received excellent notices and was quickly reprinted. Arrowsmith had not done so well with *The Forge*, but their publication of the earlier book gave them an option on her next novel. She quickly satisfied this with *A Saturday Life*, a comedy in the manner of *The Forge*, which Arrowsmith published in the following year, 1925. By then she was already at work on a successor to *The Unlit Lamp*.

Chapter Eight

With the publication of *The Unlit Lamp* in 1924, John began to attract the attention of other writers. Leonard Rees, the Editor of the *Sunday Times*, met her at this period, and found himself amused, interested, and finally deeply attracted by her unusual personality. It was in his home, to which she became a frequent visitor, that she met Ralph Straus, who did the novel reviews for the *Sunday Times*, Edmund Gosse, E. V. Lucas, Augustus John, Clifford Bax and Violet Hunt, and such younger writers as Rebecca West, Edith and Osbert Sitwell, Margaret Irwin and Michael Arlen. Suddenly all the creative writing world of London was open to her. She found that many of these writers had read *The Unlit Lamp*, and had liked it; they took her seriously, and accepted her as one of themselves, as an artist.

In spite of paper rationing, the novel had emerged from the war in a state of vigorous well-being. Borrowers who once for obscure class reasons would have got their books only from Mudies or the Times Book Club, or one of the stores like Harrods or the Army and Navy, were now swallowed up in the broader middle-class public, emancipated by the war and the Education Act from old drudgeries. With leisure now to read, these thronged the thousand-odd branches of Boots The Chemist up and down the country which carried library books as a means of inducing customers to patronize their shops.

This new public was also immensely curious about the authors of the books they read. The gossip columns of the newspapers were quick to catch on to the newsworthiness of authors, especially the author of a new, well-reviewed novel who exhibited in her own appearance or manner some eccentricity that made news. Authors were 'going public' in a sense no Victorian except Dickens had dreamt of.

Una had her hands full, pushing her beloved forward in one direction, shielding her from intrusion in another. She wanted her to be appreciated for her work, and to be liked for her person; at the same time she wanted to shield her from mere vulgar curiosity and profitless visits to unimportant people. She found a helpful ally in Leonard Rees, who was tireless in helping John to meet the right people.

Rees could see what a great help Una was to John. Una had never had any doubt that she herself would be liked. She always had been. It amused Rees to see her in the role of this lioness's *bien aimée*, calmly attempting to persuade the friends who had known her as the Admiral's lady, to accept the friend for whom she had left the Admiral, and to admire qualities which were not immediately apparent to the stranger. The trouble was that John had absolutely no social small-talk, and she had no great intellectual depth which might have been plumbed by some of the intellects she came up against in these circles. It was as though she could pull over herself on these occasions a defensive carapace, from behind which she seemed sometimes to send out little darting attacks against anyone who appeared momentarily startled by her unconventional appearance, her deep voice and her strong features. She had a sharp sense of wit which expressed itself in these circumstances by instantaneous and often graceless comment, uttered in her shy, hardly audible voice; and strangers were apt to appear startled when they found themselves the object of these remarks.

There were some like Leonard Rees and his wife who took this in their stride, and were touched by these little gaucheries which slipped out, as they thought, in unguarded moments, and others, like Alec Waugh, whose generous spirit and overflowing humanity would see interest in everyone and evil in no one. And there were some in these circles who were homosexually inclined, some who had secret 'attachments' and others battling against an attraction with which they were in continuous struggle. They were irritated and distraught, even frightened, when someone like John not only dropped the disguise, but openly claimed to be what they were at such pains to hide. It did not make them like her.

Thirty-seven Holland Road, a pink-brick, Georgian-style house with casement windows opening on to an enclosed brick-walled garden, which they had bought in 1923, was ideal for entertaining. Serious evenings, in which dinner-parties were arranged by Una for their new-found literary friends, started to alternate with those gayer ones, in which Toupie and Honey and Vera and Budge and the others kept the laughter and the gramophone going until the early hours.

It was at one of these serious evenings when, Una's diary notes, Rebecca West and May Sinclair were dining with them, that John told them of an obsequious waiter she had seen that day at a restaurant, busy at his task of keeping the customers at his group of tables satisfied. She said 'I would like to write a novel about the life of a waiter who becomes so sick of food that he allows himself nearly to die of starvation'. The idea caught fire around the table, and they had talked of it until dinner was over. Stimulated by their interest and response, she could not get the idea out of her mind. She lay awake much of the night thinking about it, and began the novel before lunch the next day. She began it with a smile, remembering the lively conversation of the night before. It was finished in six months, and in the terrible tension she by this time shared with the character she had created, as he met his end. In that brief period of time, not only had the story and its title changed, the author had. The novel which, when she started it, she had meant to call *Food*, had become the story of a simple man in search of God: it was called *Adam's Breed*.

The story can be briefly summarized. Gian-Luca, the illegitimate child of a Soho shopkeeper's daughter, who dies giving him birth, is brought up by a strict and unloving grandmother to become a waiter. He marries Maddelena, a devout Christian, but he himself remains outside the church, because no one has taught him that God is love.

Gian-Luca finds the hardest thing to bear in his working life is the sight of people stuffing themselves ceaselessly with food, and he comes so to detest what it is his duty to discuss and recommend that he literally begins to starve himself to death. He becomes ill, and eventually has to give up his work.

In the end he leaves his home and goes out on the high road – to find God, taking with him a suitcase which his wife has packed for him, with changes of shirts and underclothing and socks, and a neatly-packaged little lunch for the first day. The picture of Gian-Luca making his way up Oxford Street from Soho with this homely burden is touching, and is plainly intended to be so.

The final chapters show the material disintegration of an idealist in a harsh practical world. Gian-Luca ends as a tramp in the New Forest as winter comes on and the deer are being hunted. The end is not disillusion, but illusions cleared away. Starving and cold, seeing pain as ever continually inflicted, he finds God – where He is to be found always – at last when he is dying of hunger and exposure. God is in the hearts of each one of us. 'The path of the world was the path of His sorrow, and the sorrow of God was the hope of the world, for to suffer with God was to share in the joy of His ultimate triumph over sorrow.'

Adam's Breed belongs unmistakably to the period in which it was written. One could hardly conceive a book with this theme becoming today the instantaneous success that it was on publication. Newman Flower said that it was the best manuscript he had read in twenty years. One can see now why he thought the title *Food* inappropriate. When the book first appeared in England on March 4 the critics were as enthusiastic as the publisher had been.

The first printing of *Adam's Breed* was 3500 copies, and it was reprinted at the rate of 1500 copies a time seven times during its first year of publication, making a total sale of only 14,000 for one of the most talked-about books of the year. Probably *Passage To India* sold no more in its first year of publication, 1924. But for a third novel by a young woman, it was a good sale, and everybody was anxious to know what she was going to do next.

Personality had a lot to do with literary success at that time. London was more than the capital of England; it *was* England. The great newspapers were there, as were nearly all the writers whose lives in those far-off days fascinated the curious. In the

London scene Radclyffe Hall made a very colourful figure. She was always about – lunching or dining in the best restaurants, or attending First Nights, her striking appearance attracted constant attention, and her picture was often to be found in the papers. Those with longer memories knew who her constant companion was, and the lesbian relationship added to the titillation of gossip. The widely publicized slander case had also added to the interest.

The whole business of publishing is generated by publicity; and those authors who really detest it – like Kipling – cannot help putting up with it and benefiting from it. Everything that Radclyffe Hall did seemed to attract publicity as the lightning-rod does the lightning. If she had been coarse looking and heavily framed she would have looked like the caricature of a man. Instead she had a slim and graceful figure, a masculine-looking one but like that of a man in perfect health at the most vigorous period of his life. If she had had a dissipated unhealthy face, or coarse or repellent features, people would have turned aside, perhaps put off instinctively by what they knew. On the contrary her skin was healthy, her features even and strong. The eyes were especially compelling. It was not a woman's face but it was a very handsome one, and nearly everybody found it attractive. Una was not the only one to succumb to her charm. Their life together had its ups and downs, in which respect it did not differ much from most marriages. John had a temper which frequently flared up, and disappeared as quickly again, leaving not a trace behind. Her remorse was as swift as the temper had been fierce. Their love affair had had its roots in remorse. John felt that by betraying Ladye in the last months of her life she had been responsible for hastening her death. She involved Una in this guilt, and when her temper got out of control she would say that Una had murdered Ladye by seducing her, John. While they worked their way through this tangled psychological forest which obstructed the ultimate fulfilment of their acts of passion, each of them passed through hell. Yet John loved her little companion, and could not bear to see her suffer for long. When she saw that she had hurt her she overwhelmed her with presents and tears of regret, and promises never to do it again. The hurt and the bliss of reconciliation followed each other with such frequency, as we can see from Una's diary, that it perhaps was part of the act of love, a stimulation to passion, the sadistic expression of the abnormality of its character, almost a necessary preliminary to the thunderclap of its fulfilment which left them both exhausted but complete. It was an essential part of the bond that held them together in this passionate, painful, wonderful attachment which was to last all their lives. And Una was blissfully happy. She had exchanged the petted life of an Admiral's wife in a fashionable station for the tempestuous one of being the object of desire of a homosexual lover; and she was satisfied with the exchange. She believed that John was a genius, and she devoted her whole life to making her known and her work admired.

Although John's writing had introduced her to a new social world, and to some extent she had chosen to drop out of the giddy one in which the lesbians kept up their courage and their humour in a society which constantly by side-glances of disapproval reminded them of their ostracism, there were forceful friends with strong personalities among that group who simply would not allow themselves to be dropped, who loved darling Johnny for herself, and who knew quite well that she belonged to them, and would have to return to them in the end. These were women like Natalie Barney in Paris, Romaine Brooks, Toupie Lowther. Dominant personalities themselves, they refused to be forgotten or dispensed with. They came back to have 'blood rows' over trifles, to confide their own private griefs when some lover jilted them, to ask for help to rescue some young woman from illness or a broken love-affair; or simply, just for a laugh for old times' sake, as mates together in a largely hostile world, loving mates who had their own secret jokes and fears, their own private world of joy and pain.

Toupie Lowther gave a fancy dress ball that November. It was quite a different affair from a *thé dansant* at Augustus John's, or a Sunday evening, say, at Leonard Rees's when literary giants met and socialized. There could be dancing and music and drink at all such gatherings. But Toupie's was remembered for something else, for laughter free and unrestrained.

Someone had once cast Toupie's horoscope, and described violence as her outstanding characteristic. She was of an athletic build, large, forceful, energetic, bearing in life a distinct resemblance to Aurora Freemantle in Compton Mackenzie's *Extraordinary Women*, who is described by Mackenzie as so masculine as almost to convey the uncomfortable impression that she really was a man dressed up in women's attire – someone they could laugh at and with. Called Brother, she was constantly teased for her desperate love-affairs which so often ended unhappily. She was quite oblivious of Una's desire to shake her off as John became the object of attention of famous literary people.

And, from time to time, John was glad of that. Too much refinement got on her nerves. The chatter of the literary set sometimes sounded to her like parrots screaming in the jungle. The sadistic *gamin* in her nature longed to shock them with a vulgar word or an obscene anecdote. She was not made to be respectable; she winced like a nervous horse when they tried to drop that harness on her.

But with Brother and Romaine or Natalie, and a score of others, she could relax. She could feel the humour bubbling up in her as from a spring, and the warmth of love and happiness for everyone round her spreading through her veins. She went to Toupie's ball dressed as an Indian Chief. The costume suited her; she revelled in the admiring glances and the firm young bodies she could clasp to her in the dances which did not cease until five o'clock in the morning.

Chapter Nine

John had finished *Adam's Breed* in November, 1925, and the first galleys had arrived just before Christmas which they spent with the Temples at Datchet. Andrea had returned for her Christmas holidays as the first proofs arrived, to find that with last-minute Christmas shopping distracting her elders, theatres and dinner and luncheon parties taking toll of their time, she saw even less of them than usual.

With the housemaid, Dickie, Andrea was despatched to Datchet by train, while John and Una fitted in a sitting with Mrs Leonard on the 23rd, paid their usual visit to place a wreath at the catacomb in Highgate on Christmas Eve, and drove down to Datchet for midnight Mass that evening.

On the last day of the old year they returned to London 'and we intercepted a letter to Andrea and questioned her'. After luncheon they questioned her further. The year ends with this note: 'John and I lay in bed and heard the bells and saw our eleventh new year in together' – while in another room Andrea lay with her guilty secret.

What should have been a joyous time with a new book on the point of coming out was in fact plagued by family troubles, and it is difficult to know whether the Visettis or Una's family were the greatest worry. Andrea's little problem was disposed of handily by a joint attack – 'John and I breakfasted in our room and then talked to Andrea for a long time'. Then she was packed off to her father for a week, and put out of mind until a week later Minna – Una's mother – dined – and 'heard all about Andrea'. The day following Dr Grant came to discuss Andrea. On the 12th Andrea returned from her visit to her father. On the 19th Andrea is given a farewell lecture, and then accompanied by Dickie the maid is taken to Charing Cross to catch her train for school. What her sin was is never revealed. But there is certainly something rather startling in these two lecturing this young sinner.

There was a great Visetti crisis in January. It was precipitated by one of those fantastic financial muddles into which Marie Visetti time after time allowed their affairs to drift. Rows reminiscent of the Kensington days reverberated in the house in Phillimore Gardens which John had provided for them. Under the strain of being called to account Marie collapsed and was carried off to a nursing home. When she recovered she clung like a limpet to the nursing home and refused to be taken home to Alberto. They had to go in the car and physically remove her and restore her to her home. Whereupon Alberto immediately fell ill with a soaring temperature. That subsided, and simultaneously Marie's temper rose. Alberto thereupon fell into a decline, and Marie, full of remorse, wept silently. Alberto recovered, Marie got vile-tempered. The nurse rang up to say that Marie had been so rude to her that she was leaving that minute.

And as if Andrea and the Visettis had not created enough worry, Admiral Troubridge died in Biarritz on 28th January. He had been attending a *thé dansant* and had gone out for a breath of air when he suddenly collapsed and did not recover consciousness. In Una's diary for that date he rates only a marginal note 'Admiral Troubridge died at Biarritz'. The scribble implies immense relief. But they were awoken to what was involved by Una's mother on the telephone at 8.15 next morning, reminding Una that her separation allowance, which was almost the sole source of her income, was certain to be affected by his death, and Minna urged her to get on to the Admiralty right away. Una spent the morning on the phone, and after luncheon went to see the Accountant-General who broke to her the appalling news that her pension would be £225 per year, and Andrea's £24. She went on to her mother's to talk this over. The atmosphere there was anything but pleasant and the air was heavy with charges and recriminations. 'Intolerable' Una called it, and went home to John.

She made up her mind to apply for a supplementary compassionate allowance, and this required much visiting of associations like the Officers Families' Fund and the Ministry of Pensions, and much beating of the breast about the cost of supporting life on a widow's pension, all rather difficult for someone constantly lunching at expensive restaurants and always to be seen at First Nights.

The Memorial Service to Admiral Troubridge took place at Westminster Cathedral on 1st February, and was attended by a very distinguished congregation. The widow was there, accompanied by the daughter, who had two days off from school for the occasion. His death could not have come at a more inconvenient time. *Adam's Breed* was on the point of coming out, caricaturists and journalists were besieging Holland Street, and a second printing before publication had been proudly announced by its publisher. While John should have been attending to all this, she was forced to take the dogs for walks. She was frequently deprived of Una's company. One can easily imagine – one does not have to imagine, it is there to read in the diary – John fuming at this distraction from the business on hand.

Even when the Memorial Service was over, and publication day approached, the Admiral's spirit could not be laid to rest. Una's mother, never one for tact, made a fresh attempt to draw Una away from John. She reminded her daughter that she was now a widow, and free to marry again, and with the financial outlook so bleak, she owed it to her future to leave Holland Street, and set up an establishment of her own.

For this well-meant proposal Minna received a blast from Una. Did she not realize after all this time that she loved John more than she could ever love anyone else? She would never see her mother again unless she gave an instant apology for an unheard-of insult. Of course she told John all. From that beloved breast no secrets were hid.

It was these constant pricks and barbs they had to put up with which not only gave to the passion that united them a sadistic twist, pain being its spur, but built up in them an aversion to those whose lives were tranquil and untroubled by what made theirs rich and tumultuous. Love-making in these circumstances could never become the dull habitual response to appetite or the weak flickering of lust, no more than a feeble groping in the dark. Fantasy played too large a part in it, and the fantasy began before they lay clasped in each other's arms. John had to be the man-lover, Una the feminine body clinging to the male body that has brought her to life. It was too long and artificial a process to be hastily summoned up on the sexual impulse of the moment. It was a fantasy that had to be lived every minute of the day and night, and it was grossly impertinent of Minna to imply that it could be turned off like a light switch.

What struck others as disconcerting and strange in John's appearance and manner was essential to the maintenance of this fantasy. Since Una shared in it, acting out her own more receptive part, and retaining her full attractiveness to men and women, she was not conscious of the effect this relationship had on others. She thought that they did not appreciate John because her John would not allow her virtues to show. And she was fortified in this impression by the pleasure intellectual women like Ellen Glasgow, Ida Wylie, Violet Hunt and May Sinclair showed in John's company.

In March the third and fourth impressions of *Adam's Breed* were advertised in the press, in April the fifth impression, and in May the general strike came to put a stop to everything, including temporarily the sale of books. After a week of inactivity they offered to do their bit by driving patients who needed urgent treatment to and from Charing Cross Hospital. The next day:

> We drove Mrs Nice to Sutton to see her deaf child and enquired for a boy at Peckham with a crushed foot. Lunched Lyons at Sutton and so home through Brixton, Camberwell, Peckham, Tooting, Clapham.

The day after:

> John and I after early breakfast to Mrs Leonard's. (for a sitting). and we lunched at the hotel at Purley. Then to Peckham and fetched the small boy to Charing Cross Hospital to have his foot dressed, and took him back to Peckham. On

way to hospital heard rumours strike was over. Confirmed at Hospital. Got home and heard U.S.A. subscription *Adams Breed* 2350.

The year had ended amidst the vexations already reported, but also with the exciting but confidential news that *Adam's Breed*, together with Sylvia Townsend Warner's *Lolly Willows* and Liam O'Flaherty's *The Informer*, had gone up to the final committee for the Prix Femina. Early in April 1927 *Adam's Breed* was given the prize, and this was capped in December of that year by the award of the James Tait Black prize for the best novel of the year, a 'double' that in the history of the two major prizes had occurred only once before – with E. M. Forster's *Passage To India* two years earlier.

Chapter Ten

This arduous life demanded a holiday, and they went – of all places! – to Bergh Island, Weymouth, the station where Troubridge had faced his court-martial. When they returned to London on 26th June they had been away for nearly a month, and they had talked over a daring step which John was about to take, the Admiral now being out of the way. It was to tell their story in the form of a novel. Una takes up the account.*

It was after the success of *Adam's Breed* that John came to me one day with unusual gravity and asked for my decision on a serious matter: she had long wanted to write a book on sexual inversion, a novel that would be accessible to the general public who did not have access to technical treatises. At one time she had thought of making it a 'period' book, built round an actual personality of the early nineteenth century. But her instinct had told her that in any case she must postpone such a book until her name was made; until her unusual theme would get a hearing as being the work of an established writer.

It was her absolute conviction that such a book could only be written by a sexual invert, who alone could be qualified by personal knowledge and experience to speak on behalf of a misunderstood and misjudged minority.

It was with this conviction that she came to me, telling me that in her view the time was ripe, and although the publication of such a book might mean the shipwreck of her whole career, she was fully prepared to make any sacrifice except – the sacrifice of my peace of mind.

She pointed out that in view of our union and of all the years that we had shared a home, what affected her must also

* *The Life and Death of Radclyffe Hall*, p. 81.

affect me and that I would be included in any condemnation. Therefore she placed the decision in my hands and would write or refrain as I should decide.

I am glad to remember that my reply was made without so much as an instant's hesitation: I told her to write what was in her heart, that so far as any effect on myself was concerned, I was sick to death of ambiguities, and only wished to be known for what I was and to dwell with her in the palace of truth.

Ten days later John began notes for *Stephen*, the title which *The Well of Loneliness* was to bear until the book was nearly completed.

Radclyffe Hall had only the feelings of the hopeless Visettis to consider, and as they were financially entirely dependent on her, and the greatest possible nuisances anyway, and as she was completely secure financially, talk of the shipwreck of her career was overdoing it. She was risking nothing except a year or two of work on a book which in the end she might not be allowed to publish. But for Una it was different. The Troubridge family were prominent and well connected. Her mother and her sister were still very much about, and her sister had just married (for the second time) J. L. Garvin, the Editor of *The Observer*. Una had a child at school. Her cousins were thick upon the ground in London and Ireland. The identification of her as one of the central figures in the novel would only serve to reawaken the old scandal. She had given up everything for the sake of this infatuation, and she was now instantly prepared to give fresh shock to her friends and connections, simply to show this woman how much she loved her.

Of course they had often talked about the rigid attitude of society towards sexual inversion, and Radclyffe Hall did genuinely believe that she was now in a position to help her fellow-sufferers by presenting their plight sympathetically in a novel. But she was wrong in thinking that only an invert could write truthfully about the suffering of inverts. It was to be the attempt to treat the abnormal as normal that was so to shock authority when the book was published. Far from helping her fellow-sufferers, her action was temporarily to stiffen opposition and close the ranks against the oppressed minority whom it had been her aim to help.

She had one of the most important qualities a creative artist needs, the ability to concentrate and see the task through. She started making her first notes for *Stephen* on 20 July, 1926. They spent October in Paris where they took three communicating rooms in the Hôtel du Pont Royal in the Rue du Bac, turning one of these into a writing-room. By the time they returned to London in November she had written the first four chapters of the book, and these were read aloud to Audrey Heath, her literary agent, by Una.

It was not an atmosphere conducive to creative work. But she was by now gripped herself by the romantic parable she was weaving about her own beginnings, and the slow discovery she had made of the psychological trick nature had played on her. She pressed on, in spite of these domestic distractions, writing night after night into the small hours. By the middle of March Audrey Heath had listened to nine chapters. Carl Brandt, the American literary agent who was in London, turned up to lunch, read some of the chapters and went away immensely enthusiastic.

Una fussed about her, trying to prevent her from overworking, and driving her nearly to madness by her intense care. It is the last thing an artist wants when absorbed by his subject. To appease Una more than anything else she took a day off and they went to Maidenhead. They lunched again at Skindles: 'a lovely day, and we wiped out a painful memory' noted Una ecstatically that night.

By mid-May fourteen chapters were done. By the end of July, when they left for a holiday in Brittany, a year after the first notes had been made for the book, twenty-nine chapters had been written. She had reached the half-way point in her story. On her return she wrote on, day after day and night after night until two or three in the morning.

One day in November 1927, when totting up the score, the book for the first time was referred to as *The Well of Loneliness*, not as *Stephen*. The title was another of Una's inspirations. John was nearing the end, she was experiencing the author's excitement at seeing his work emerge in its final shape.

In March 1928 the diary reports 'We had tea with Mr Scaife (of Houghton-Mifflin) at Garland's Hotel, Suffolk Street, and met Havelock Ellis, who has promised to read *The Well of Loneliness* when it is finished.' It was their host, Roger Scaife, who suggested that Havelock Ellis should be asked to write a foreword.

On 5th April, when Andrea was on holiday, Una came home one afternoon to find that John had finished *The Well of Loneliness*.

By 16th April it was typed and bound, and copies were despatched to Newman Flower at Cassells and to Carl Brandt in America. Two afternoons later, car and chauffeur were summoned to drive to the address in Brixton in South London, which Havelock Ellis had given them for the manuscript, where they hoped to leave it instead of having it mailed, only to find their bird had flown. She did not leave the manuscript, but wrote instead. A few days later:

> Dear 'Radclyffe Hall' (Ellis wrote from Little Frieth, Henley-on-Thames) I am so sorry that you came in vain to my den at Brixton. It is my permanent address (and parcels left with the caretaker would be safe) but I am seldom there . . . It had not occurred to me that you would call merely on the chance of finding me in.

Havelock Ellis had quickly spotted that Radclyffe Hall was an invert, and he was more interested in her condition than he was in her novel. 'It would be a great advantage', he replied, 'to have an opportunity of talking more seriously than was possible at Garland's Hotel.'

He thereupon gives explicit directions for finding his remote cottage in Oxfordshire, then adds warningly:

> As you know, I would not be able to see my way to writing any Preface for this novel, but I am deeply interested in the subject, having had many near friends, both men and women, who are, they sometimes say – 'so' and if the book appeals to me I would be glad to express an opinion that might be used.

Chapter Eleven

It is only in these present times that it has become the habit to boast of obscure beginnings and early hardships. Fifty years ago when the author of *The Well of Loneliness* set out to tell her own story, the Victorian romantic idea still dominated the novel, and it was no more than natural for the novelist to claim for the Gordons of Bramley greater prominence than had ever been known by the Radclyffe-Halls, who had descended by way of clergymen, private tutors and doctors. Dr Radclyffe-Hall, John's mid-Victorian grandfather, who himself had spent much time and money in tracing back to a suitable beginning his own family history would, as a doctor interested in psychological study, have agreed unhesitatingly with the decision to tell the story; and, as a friend of Bulwer-Lytton's, and a man with the literary tastes of his time, he would have seen nothing wrong in making Sir Philip Gordon a more elevated figure than 'Rat' Radclyffe-Hall would have appeared, if he had been taken directly from life, and plumped down in the pages of a novel.

The background to *The Well of Loneliness* at least is authentic. Sir Philip Gordon's large estate, not very far from Upton-on-Severn, is in the district where Radclyffe Hall had her hunting box. This was the country over which she had hunted, and about which she had written with such feeling in *Songs of Three Counties*. She knew it as well as if she had been born there, and as love of the land was to play a large part in the story, the childhood chapters are important in bringing us to a sympathetic understanding of Stephen Gordon's warped nature and her strange upbringing.

When, ten years after their marriage, the Lady Anna Gordon is to present her husband with a first child, he so confidently assumes it will be a son who will inherit his title and land, that he chooses

Radclyffe Hall at the time of the slander trial in 1920.

Una Troubridge in 1924, painted by Romaine Brooks.

for the baby before its arrival the name of Stephen, and even makes preliminary plans about Harrow and Oxford. But the child when it arrives is a girl – a narrow-hipped, wide-shouldered little tadpole of a baby. Stubbornly he has the child christened Stephen. He comes to adore the little girl, while his wife as the child grows older has difficulty in hiding her lack of sympathy with her.

We are soon made aware that Stephen is not normal. Her mother's antagonism to her is the first hint. When Stephen has her first childhood 'pashes', they are directed towards women. She falls in love, not with one of the grooms but one of the housemaids, Collins. The silly girl responds instinctively, kisses her, and is unconsciously attracted to the child. Stephen becomes passionately attached to Collins, but one day, glimpsing her in the arms of one of the footmen, a blind rage seizes her, and she throws a broken flowerpot and cuts the man's face open; then runs sobbing to her father bewildered and frightened. These and other incidents are taken straight from the young life of Marguerite Radclyffe Hall, as we know from Una's patient account of it.

John had always been a compulsive novel reader, and it was natural for her to invent the sort of background common to so many of the late Victorian and Edwardian novels she had read as a child and a young woman. Her own absent father whom she did not meet until she was fifteen, and saw again only on his deathbed, whose wealth provided everything by which she and the Visettis lived, was invested with the pitying, understanding love, not to mention the title, which were Sir Philip Gordon's; and her mother, there before her eyes every day, a bad-tempered, unsympathetic, spoilt and silly woman, abandoned by her father and living with the equally silly Alberto Visetti, was elevated to the position of wife to Sir Philip and hard, unsympathetic mother to Stephen Gordon. Sir Philip dies as the result of an accident, and mother and daughter are left alone in a mutually antagonistic state. As Mrs Visetti and Marguerite Radclyffe Hall had been in Kensington when Radclyffe Radclyffe-Hall deserted his wife and new-born child.

Two things happen to Stephen when she becomes a young woman, one before Sir Philip's death, the other after. She has grown into a strikingly beautiful but rather odd-looking girl. The oddness comes from the masculinity of her figure and movements. She attracts at this stage both men and women, but she herself is drawn only to women. She suspects, but is not yet sure, that she is abnormal.

She is proposed to by a young neighbour, Martin Hallam, who has been her constant companion in the outdoor activities that she loves, and the shock, and the sudden feeling of physical repulsion which overcomes her, forces her to examine her nature. Her suspicion that she is homosexual is painfully confirmed when, after her father's death, living alone with her mother at Morton, she falls in love with a young married woman in the neighbourhood, Angela Crosby. This young girl, burdened with a boring husband, does not rebuff her; nor does she yield to her: she leads her on. For Angela it is only an anodyne against boredom; for Stephen it is a passion of deep intensity. Already, this early in the story, Radclyffe Hall is reminding us of her high purpose in writing this book:

> She (Stephen) loved deeply, far more deeply than many a one who could fearlessly proclaim herself a lover. Since this is a hard and sad truth for the telling; those whom nature has sacrificed to her ends – her mysterious ends that often lie hidden – are sometimes endowed with a vast will to loving, with an endless capacity for suffering also, which must go hand in hand with their love.

Stephen leaves home when her mother learns of the intrigue from the husband who has accidentally discovered it. Before she leaves, Stephen finds from some marginal scribbles in a few books at the back of the shelves in her father's library – Krafft-Ebing and others – that her father must have known of her impediment all the time. The outburst of despair this knowledge draws from Stephen, as she sits alone in the library, sets the text for the story that follows.

You knew! All the time you knew this thing, but because of your pity you wouldn't tell me. Oh, father – and there are so many of us – thousands of miserable, unwanted people, who have no right to love, no right to compassion because they are maimed, hideously maimed and ugly – God is cruel; He let us get flawed in the making.

Miss Puddleton, who is Stephen's governess, elects to leave the house with her. It is conceivable that old Mrs Diehl, John's grandmother who, at many points in *The Well* is so obviously reflected in the figure of Puddle, was aware of her grand-daughter's sexual inversion, and was as sympathetic and understanding of it as Puddle is shown to be. Perhaps Stephen's cry to Puddle: 'Why have I been afflicted with a body that must never be indulged, that must always be repressed until it grows much stronger than my spirit because of this unnatural repression?' was answered by old Mrs Diehl with words something like those with which Puddle comforts the agonized Stephen: 'Where you go, I go, Stephen. All that you're suffering at this moment I've suffered. It was when I was very young like you – but I still remember.'

It is quite possible that John's departure from the Visetti household was precipitated by some scandal in which she had become involved. We know from Una's account that she fell in love in turn with several of Visetti's pupils who were lodging in the house. Una gives one a name, Agnes Nichols, one of Visetti's brightest pupils whose flawless soprano voice was to make for her a successful career as a concert artiste. Una tells us that John worshipped this voice and the body that contained it, and followed her to the Continent and to cities all over England for some years in the initial stages of her career. John was 18 at the time, Agnes Nichols 25. John had just come into the first portion of her money. We know that she had no sooner settled her grandmother in the house on Campden Hill than she went on her travels.

On the advice of a male homosexual acquaintance, Jonathan

Brockett, who is aware by empathy of the distress that she is suffering because she will not openly admit to her homosexual temperament, Stephen leaves England and goes to live in Paris. There Brockett introduces her to homosexual society, and there she buys a house and settles down to write.

In 1914 the war comes. Stephen joins the Breakspear Unit – a Unit of Englishwomen attached to the French Army Ambulance Corps, and here she meets Mary Hamilton. When armistice comes she returns to the house in Paris, taking Mary Hamilton with her. For some weeks Stephen makes no physical advances to Mary. A sense of honour stops her, even though the girl makes no secret of her desire for it; and the strain on both of them is intense. Although the language in which this protracted restraint is presented is novelettish, the sense of strain is vividly conveyed, and the reader sees some of the handicaps of perversion. No doubt this more or less accurately reflects John's wooing of Una while Ladye was still alive. Una had been 'unhappy and depressed' when she met Radclyffe Hall, who was not free either to seduce this unhappy young wife at this particular time. But in those walks at Watergate Bay in September 1915, Una, as we know from her book, must have heard the words, or something like them, that are echoed in Stephen Gordon's speech to Mary.

> I am one of those whom God marked on the forehead. Like Cain, I am marked and blemished. If you come to me the world will abhor you, will persecute you, will call you unclean. Our love may be faithful even unto death and beyond, yet the world will call it unclean.

In *The Well of Loneliness* it is Mary Hamilton who finds the strain in the end intolerable. She turns on Stephen one night to announce that she is going home to England – to get away from an association that is leading nowhere. Whereupon Stephen breaks down . . . 'she spoke roughly; the words when they came were cruel. She spared neither the girl who must listen to them nor herself who must force herself to stand there and "listen", "Have you understood? Do you realize now what it's going to mean if you give yourself to me? . . . It's too much to ask. I had to tell you – forgive me, Mary." '

To which Mary replies, in words that reflect almost exactly Una's answer to her question about relating their story:

> What do I care for all you've told me? What do I care for the world's opinion. What do I care for anything but you, and you just as you are, I love you . . . Can't you understand that all that I am belongs to you, Stephen?

But *The Well of Loneliness* is not just a cry of pain from the deprived abnormal, asking only to be understood; it tells the truth of what abnormal love is like, the dry aftertaste of passionate love when it cannot create, when it is sterile.

> For now they were in the grip of Creation, of Creation's terrific urge to create; the urge that will sometimes sweep blindly forward alike into fruitful and sterile channels. The well nigh intolerable life force would grip them, making them a part of its own existence; so that they who might never create a new life, were yet one at such moments with the fountain of living . . . Oh, great and incomprehensible unreason!

This fictional love-affair is to end in tragedy; its sterility willed it so. There is a subtle but basic difference here between the male-woman lover and the female-woman loved one; and Radclyffe Hall the true invert acknowledges this:

> There comes a time in all passionate attachments when life, real life, must be faced again with its varied and endless obligations, when the lover knows in his innermost heart that the halcyon days are over. He may well regret this prosaic intrusion . . . (yet) will bend his neck to the yoke of existence. To every devoted and ardent woman there comes this moment of poignant regretting . . . Not yet, not yet – just a little longer; until Nature, abhorring her idleness, forces on her the labour of procreation.
>
> But in such relationships as Mary's and Stephen's, Nature must pay for experimenting. She may even have to pay very

dearly for it; it all depends on the sexual mixture. A drop too little of the male in the lover (note Radclyffe Hall identifies the male lover with herself, the loved one with Una) and mighty indeed will be the wastage. And yet there are cases – and Stephen's was one – in which the male will emerge triumphant; in which passion combined with real devotion will become a spur rather than a deterrent; in which love and endeavour will fight side by side in a desperate struggle to find some solution.

What she is getting at here is her own need to work. They settle down, she to her writing, Mary to overseeing the running of the house. Soon Stephen becomes so immersed in her book that she neglects Mary; an echo this, perhaps, of Una's loneliness and John's conscience about it. Nearly all Una's old friends could not bear Radclyffe Hall. Una had a gift for friendship, and suddenly everything was lost. The loss had come in two stages. The Admiral's failure had cut off many of their old naval friends, but Una's taking up with the notorious Radclyffe Hall had separated many more. Not a single friend of her early days, except possibly an artist or two remained. By the time *The Well of Loneliness* came to be written, she had as friends, judging by the absence of reference to any others in the diary, only the ladies in the Society for Psychical Research, and the homosexual and cheerful crowd who in London at this time kept themselves to themselves.

When John decided to write a novel with sexual inversion as the theme, she could draw only on her own experience. Autobiography, even when disguised as fiction, always involves others. But she had the consent of the chief figure in her story, Una; and there was no one else she need fear. Her father could be translated into Sir Philip Gordon; Grandma Diehl into Miss Puddleton. All that she needed was the *mise-en-scène*, and Paris offered everything that she wanted. In the Hôtel du Pont Royal in the rue du Bac they found exactly what they were looking for – three rooms, one of which could be used as a writing-room. Close by the hotel, on the river bank, with blessed convenience was the *Vert Galant*, where one ate well, something these two always insisted on.

If their London friends had vanished, their Paris friendships had grown since their first shy visit to the city in 1921. The key to this had been Natalie Barney, and it was fitting that in 1928 she should appear in *The Well* as Valerie Seymour, hardly changed from what she was in life. This handsome American woman, who had come to Paris as a young and wealthy girl in the closing years of the 19th century, had become over the years an intellectual force there. Her beautiful house on the rue Jacob had become the literary salon of Paris where such figures as Marcel Proust, Colette, d'Annunzio, Paul Valery, Paul Morand, André Gide and Rémy de Gourmont might be seen on Friday afternoons, when Natalie Barney was 'at Home'.

Born in Dayton, Ohio, Natalie had something of the huge frame and blondness one is ready to associate with pioneers. She was an expert horsewoman, and rode astride in the Bois de Boulogne every day. It was Rèmy de Gourmont who, seeing her for the first time in the Bois in her riding habit, mounted on her horse, named her *l'Amazone*, a name quickly taken up by everyone in Paris when he immortalized her in his *Lettres à l'Amazone*.

In 1924 Romaine Brooks, the artist, who was Natalie Barney's lover, had come to London with Natalie, where Romaine had some commissions to execute. Romaine was a dark striking-looking woman, at this time just fifty, with a very curious and twisted family background. Her mother, who was a widow, was immensely wealthy, and was devoted to a son who lived on the edge of madness, and who needed constant supervision and attention. Mrs Brooks had tried to make Romaine his nurse, and for years as a young girl, she had been forced into contact with her mad brother, as they travelled about Europe from resort to fashionable resort, looking for medical help which Mrs Brooks never ceased to believe could restore her son to sanity.

When she was 21, Romaine had broken away, had forced her mother to give her an allowance, and had gone to Rome to study art. She had had an illegitimate child who died, and she married a man who turned out to be a homosexual. She threw him out. Her experiences and her temperament had shaped her into a most unusual young woman, passionate but completely homosexual.

When she became the Amazon's lover, she found peace and inspiration for her work, just as Radclyffe Hall had found it in her first lasting affair with Mabel Batten. Romaine's devotion to Natalie Barney was as complete as John's had been to Mrs Batten.

Nevertheless, fancies stray. Among other portraits she painted in London on this visit in 1924 was Una's. The sittings, a dozen of them, took place in late May. They are noted carefully in the margins of the diary, not in the main body of it. Una says nothing of what she and Romaine talked about. Nor did she confide anything to John. But that the talk became intimate and meaningful can be guessed from subsequent correspondence.

On the 9th June John was taken to see the finished portrait. As it had not been commissioned, and as Romaine was by this time too busy an artist to waste time on unproductive work, she must have expected John to buy it. But no offer was forthcoming, and no opinion was recorded in the diary.

In the following summer of 1925, Baroness Emile d'Erlanger arranged an Exhibition of Romaine's paintings at L'Alpine Club Gallery in London, and once again Natalie Barney and Romaine descended on the city. For the opening of the exhibition, a whole troop of their distinguished friends came over from Paris, and on the Baroness's insistence, wealthy and aristocratic London attended the opening, and admired and bought the paintings. John and Una were drawn into an unending round of social engagements, and their friendship with Natalie and Romaine ripened. The cloud occasioned by the contretemps appeared to have blown away. So that when in the summer of 1926 they decided to visit Paris, and settle down there to start the great novel, they were amongst friends and in surroundings that stimulated them, and lent fire and zeal to the writing.

Even so, the visit got off to a bad start. The diary records on the first day, 'Tea at Natalie's

> who was charming, and made me read *The Forge* aloud. Romaine came in and made a hideous scene, abusing *The Forge*, John and Natalie like a fishwife.

But notably not Una. But these sudden explosions of temperament were the business and colour of life. Hard feelings never lasted, and soon all was rapture between them again. Tempests which had seemed likely to blow their attachments to destruction, died down as quickly as they had sprung up. In *The Well of Loneliness*, the writing of which occupied every day during this visit, it was the Amazon whose spirit bore them all up. In this passage, she is disguised as Valerie Seymour.

> For Valerie, placid and self-assured, created an atmosphere of courage. Everyone felt very normal and brave when they gathered together at Valerie Seymour's. There she was, this charming and cultivated woman, a kind of light-house in a storm-swept ocean. The waves had lashed round her feet in vain; winds had howled; clouds had spewed forth their hail and their lightning; torrents had deluged but not destroyed her. The storms, gathering force, broke and drifted away, leaving behind them the shipwrecked, the drowning. But when they looked up, the poor spluttering victims, why what should they see but Valerie Seymour! Then a few would strike out boldly for the shore, at the sight of this indestructible creature.

Many afternoons and evenings were spent in the rue Jacob. They were dazzled by these candlelit suppers, evening concerts, and afternoons devoted to readings of poetry and prose. After the sombre years of psychical research, followed by the relief of chattering fun with 'les girls' at Chip Chase, or at the Ham Bone or Orange Tree Clubs in London, the atmosphere in the rue Jacob was as pure and elevated as the music of a flute after the discordance of ragtime. Here in Paris, amongst these friends, was the ideal ambience to write the book about Stephen – nameless at this stage – which was to become *The Well of Loneliness*.

But John knew that her own homosexual experiences had not all been on this elevated level. On this same visit, seeking copy, they also experimented with homosexual night-life in Paris, and the fruits of this research appear in the visit to Alec's Bar, 'the meeting-place of the most miserable of all those who comprise this miserable army', where they were addressed as '*Ma Soeur*', and were compelled to reply in the same way, or with 'Mon Frère'.

The end of *The Well of Loneliness* is contrived. It had to be, for in real life the story was not yet ended. So far *The Well* had been a fictionalized but recognizable account of the author's upbringing and experiences. She had intended from the beginning that this should be a *moral* book. Its announced intention was not to show the pleasures of homosexual love, but the painful sacrifices those who could not help but turn to it had to endure.

In the book the young man who had proposed to Stephen, Martin Hallam, from whom she had turned away horrified and disgusted, comes back to find her, having been faithful in memory to her all these years. But he falls in love instead with Mary, and in spite of herself Mary responds. It is when Stephen sees the depth of this love that she sacrifices herself for Mary's happiness. She allows Mary to believe that she has been having an affair with Valerie Seymour. Mary escapes, broken-hearted, to Martin's arms – Stephen is left alone at the end of the book with a soliloquy that states in dramatic terms the fate and destiny of the forsaken ones in this perverse love:

'they possessed her. Her barren womb became fruitful – it acted with its fearful and sterile burden' ... And then there was only one voice, her own:
'Acknowledge us, Oh God, before the whole world. Give us also the right to our existence.'

This novel is transparently an account of their life together. It is a plea for understanding and sympathy for those oppressed with the stigma of homosexuality. Such an open discussion of a forbidden subject at this time was bound to stir up a storm. The war had liberated a lot of old repressions, and the novels of the mid-twenties were definitely more outspoken and less reticent than those in the decade leading up to the war, when H. G. Wells had shocked with *Ann Veronica*, and even more with *The New Machiavelli*. But he had not dealt with deviant sex. D. H. Lawrence had loosened the bond, and the police and the magistrates' courts had been very active with *The White Peacock* and *The Rainbow*. James Joyce was published only in France, and that master of the topical, Frank Harris, scenting the curiosity about sex, had issued in 1922, his *My Life and Loves*, but he too had taken the precaution of having it published in France, not in England. But meanwhile the translation of Freud's *Die Traumdeutung*, which had been published just before the war, had made people interested in the vagaries of the sexual temperament, and the time was ripe for a book like *The Well of Loneliness*. Only established authority was not ready to allow it.

Chapter Twelve

She had finished *The Well of Loneliness* in an exalted mood. No one had seen it, or heard extracts from it, except Audrey Heath and Carl Brandt. Audrey had swooned over the reading of successive chapters and Carl Brandt had reported to Audrey that it was 'great'. She was encouraged by Havelock Ellis's willingness to read the manuscript. She felt none of the misgivings and doubts that had attacked her when she had finished her other books. *The Well of Loneliness* was the story of her life, and in telling of her own battle she had seen herself as champion of her oppressed sisters and brothers. She did not think of the book in terms of its possible commercial success. In fact she thought it might be a disappointment to her publisher, and in order that her good friend Newman Flower of Cassells, who had been the first to recognize her talent, should know what he was in for with this successor to *Adam's Breed*, for which he had been waiting impatiently, even to the point of offering her a contract before reading it, she wrote a letter before the manuscript could reach him through Audrey Heath telling him that, having attained literary success, she had now put her pen at the service of some of the most persecuted and misunderstood people in the world. She went on:

> In a word, I have written a long and very serious novel entirely upon the subject of sexual inversion. So far as I know, nothing of the kind has ever been attempted before in fiction. Hitherto the subject has either been treated as pornography, or introduced as an episode as in *Dusty Answer*, or veiled as in *A Regiment of Women*. I have treated it as a fact in nature – a simple, though at present tragic, fact. I have written the life of a woman who is a born invert, and have done so with what I believe to be sincerity and truth; and while I have refused to camouflage in any way, I think I have avoided all unnecessary coarseness.

She goes on to say that there is a possibility, no more, of a foreword by Havelock Ellis. Then she entreats him:

> I need not say how sorry I should be to sever my connection with Cassells, but unless you feel, upon reading the book, that you are prepared to go all out on it and to stand behind it to the last ditch, then for both our sakes, as also for the sakes of those for whom I have written, please don't take it. (16 April 1928).

She ends by saying that 'although my book may not be worthy of so vast and so immensely important a subject, I feel very strongly that the subject is more than worthy of my book', a sentence which illustrates as much as anything she said in this letter her elevated and excited state of mind at the prospect of battle ahead. She was in a militant mood, and Una's daily diary entries are hushed in tone, and her handwriting shaky with the immense strain of their shared confidences.

Alas, Newman Flower could return only a low-spirited answer to her challenge. Protesting that 'as a piece of literary work this is one of the finest books that has gone through my hands', he said quite simply that he could not publish it. 'It would, I feel sure, do a lot of harm to our other books here.' And for once the publisher's excuse to authors who have some claim on them, that 'for a book of this type Cassells is not quite the right house', had some justification. Cassells purveyed chiefly circulating library fiction, and the views of the Head Librarians of Borough and Commercial Lending Libraries loomed heavily over this trade. But, writing to Audrey Heath, her agent, he added: 'I cannot tell you how distressed I am that she should be passing from us. I have had great pride in her work, as you know, but naturally Miss Radclyffe Hall writes what she feels she wishes to write, and one cannot blame her. She is a great artist, and I take off my hat to her.'

It had taken Newman Flower less than a week to make up his mind. Heinemann, who were the next to see it, took only half that time. Charles Evans's letter to Audrey Heath was spirited and lively, but equally unrewarding:

'Personally,' he wrote, 'neither Bayard [his partner] or myself find anything to object to in the way in which the subject is treated, but we do feel (and this is the fundamental reason for our decision not to publish) that the book will be regarded as propaganda, and that inevitably the publishers of it will have to meet not only severe criticism but a chorus of fanatical abuse which, although unjustifiable, may nevertheless do them considerable damage. That consequence we are not prepared to face, and so we must decline the book, but I wish you would assure Miss Radclyffe Hall of our sincere regret that our courage is not as great as hers, and tell her how profoundly the book has moved us both.' (April 27 1928).

Martin Secker was the next to decline it. He did so on the reasonable (though as it turned out mistaken) grounds that he did not think the book a commercial proposition, but said that reading the manuscript had impressed him with Radclyffe Hall's gifts, and when this book was out of the way he would be very happy to make a contract for her future work. He did not reveal that he had in the press a witty novel by Compton Mackenzie satirizing lesbianism, and that among its flamboyant characters was one who might well be taken for Radclyffe Hall.

The book was next shown to Jonathan Cape, and at last it went to the right quarter. Jonathan Cape and his partner, Wren Howard, who was about seven years Jonathan's junior, had started up their firm in 1921, and by a combination of experience and taste, and with the aid of the valuable connection Jonathan had made with an equally young American, Don Brace of Harcourt Brace, they had built it up in a few years into a substantial young business. Unlike Heinemann or Cassells they did not rely altogether on the commercial libraries, but sold directly to the public through book shops. By good fortune, but also because they were guided by Edward Garnett, the best editor in London, they had captured from America Sinclair Lewis and Ernest Hemingway, both of them at the beginning of their profitable careers.

Jonathan Cape was a self-made man whose whole working life had been spent with books. He had a natural sense of discrimination, and a very sharp instinct for turning a penny. For some years before the war he had been the chief traveller for Duckworths, the publishers, and had returned there as manager after serving in the ranks in the army during the first war. It was in this way that he met his future partner, a young ex-officer who had been at Cambridge before the war, and was now learning the book business with the Medici Press, who were Fine Art publishers and had a successful bookshop just off Bond Street. Howard was a good-looking, shy, conventional young man from Hampstead, with a concealed artistic nature which expressed itself in a fine italic handwriting, a love of fine type faces and of beautiful books, papers and bindings. He was the epitome of hard commonsense, but allied with this was an almost sensual love of books as objects of art. His admirable taste was to give Cape books a distinctive, elegant appearance which did much to attract authors to the list. It was Jonathan who, exuding charm and confidence – he had the good fortune to look not unlike the ambassador on the boxes of de Reszke cigarettes – captured the authors and captivated the agents with his adroit and profitable, but unpredictable moves, which quickly became legend in the trade. Typical of these was the early stroke of reprinting Sir Charles Doughty's admired classic *Arabia Deserta* – available up to this time only in three volumes at eighteen guineas the set – in one volume handsomely produced at nine guineas. He succeeded not only in selling the first printing of five thousand copies out of hand, but – admitted to later by Lawrence of Arabia – in attracting to his list the fabulously rewarding *Seven Pillars of Wisdom*.

By 1928 Cape was beginning to be very much admired as a discriminating publisher, with a real talent for putting his books over. While Charles Evans shied away from propaganda, Jonathan Cape saw that in dealing with a new wide public and a popular press whose combined circulations ran into the millions, it was an essential weapon in the modern publisher's armoury. Propaganda had got a bad name in the war. It was taken to mean stuffing unasked-for opinions, usually lies, down unwilling throats. But the real essence of propaganda was the same as the essence of publishing; to make more widely known. Nobody would be so foolish as to think that in publishing *The Well of Loneliness* the firm of Jonathan Cape was advocating more liberty for sexual inverts. In publishing the book he was simply saying that there was a case to be put. It was here put in an impeccable way by an artist who confessed that she herself was marked with this brand.

It was a book made for the Cape list, and both parties to the agreement, celebrating over lunch at the Berkeley, were prepared to go forward heart and soul together, as the author had asked her old friend Newman Flower to do. Of course Jonathan would not have been unmindful of the fact that he was taking on to his list the winner of last year's Prix Femina,* a poet of some distinction, and the admired author of several ready-published novels. He was paying a larger than usual advance, £500, compared with the advance of £100 paid by Cassells for *Adam's Breed*. But it was a calculated gamble and exercising his charm, Jonathan took the author into his confidence, pointing out that he was taking a financial risk – he was astute enough to say nothing about the legal risk which would have made her suspicious of his sincerity – and that this justified him in adopting unusual measures to mitigate the risk. His proposal was to do a limited edition of 1250 copies at 25s, three times the usual price of a novel of this length. If the book 'caught on' – by which he meant but did not say, without attracting the attention of the police, he would do a much larger general edition.

Radclyffe Hall was not so pleased with the idea of a limited edition. She wanted the doctrine in the book shouted from the housetops. A comparatively expensive limited edition suggested to her mind under-the-counter sales to the prurient and curious, and being quite impervious to Jonathan's masculine charm she looked at him coldly while he unfolded this strategy. But Jonathan was so businesslike, so confident, so genuinely admiring of the book, that she could not stand out against his wide experience and proven skill. At the celebratory lunch she agreed to this proposal.

Within a few days, Havelock Ellis's foreword which he termed

---

* The award of the James Tait Black prize to *Adam's Breed* had not at this stage been announced.

Beresford Egan's cartoon
for the lampoon 'The Sink of Solitude' (see page 186)

Radclyffe Hall and Una Troubridge
in Edy Craig's Garden at Smallhythe in 1931.

a 'commentary', turned up. It was brief but succinct with just the message she wanted. 'It possesses', he wrote, 'a notable psychological and sociological significance.'

Now, conscious that this strategy did not fit well with the picture of the reformist publisher issuing soberly and carefully a novel which in Havelock Ellis's words 'presents in a completely faithful and uncompromising form, one particular aspect of sexual life as it exists amongst us today,' Jonathan changed his plan. Nothing if not adroit, he decided to print 1500 copies of an unlimited edition, and to reduce the price to 15s; then to hold standing type to await the verdict of the public, not to mention the reception by public authority, before venturing further.

Michael Howard, the historian of the firm, tells us that the book was produced in a large format in sombre black binding, with a plain wrapper. Review copies were sent out only to the serious daily papers and periodicals, not to the popular papers likely to blow the story up into a sensational news-feature. Jonathan sent out to a selected list of influential people some carefully studied letters with complimentary copies. Michael Howard quotes an extract from the one sent to Hugh Walpole, the Chairman of the Book Society selectors, in which you can almost hear Jonathan tiptoeing so as not to alarm:

> I don't want to strike an attitude – portrait of a publisher doing something daring and heroic – but I realize that the publication of *The Well of Loneliness* may be called into question unless it is soberly and carefully published.

Publication day was fixed for 27 July, 1928. It was now mid-June.

Meanwhile in America the book was going through as difficult a birth. Doubleday, who had an option arising from the publication of *Adam's Breed*, declined it, as Harper, who were the next to see it, also did. Roger Scaife of Houghton Mifflin, at whose tea-party John had had the good fortune to meet Havelock Ellis, had since his return to America sent John a copy of Amy Lowell's *Collected Poems*, and had kept up a flow of friendly letters with anxious enquiries as to how everything was going with the book.

He now had his desire to read it gratified, but could only write back regretfully that the Boston Watch and Ward Society would mean death to the book if a Boston publisher took it on.

And suddenly Blanche Knopf appeared in London. This sparkling, highly intelligent wife and partner of Alfred Knopf was accustomed never to let a year pass without descending on Europe, and herding on to the Knopf list any intellectual or trend-setting author demonstrating his talent at that moment. As a result of this close attention to the European scene, the Knopf list had become over the decade or so it had been in existence a highly individualized one that clearly bore the stamp of the personal taste of the Knopfs.

But although intellectual agreement between them was wonderfully close, the partners were each of them dominating personalities who held their opinions with great force, yielding to each other when necessary, not in submissive silence. Few publishing relationships have been so fruitful, and so much envied and discussed. For out of the sometimes vituperative arguments generally conducted by cable and letter had come on to the Knopf list the kind of books that came to be recognized in Europe and America as Knopf books and no other. They were this in appearance as well as content, Alfred having strong views of a rather Gothic nature on type-faces and typographical layouts, and the same passion for startling colours in binding cloths as he displayed in the shirts and ties he wore.

But it was the contents of the books that set them apart from all other publishers' books. There was a substratum of sound twentieth-century Americana, personified in the work of Mencken. For its time it was advanced, representing liberal ideas in a granitically conservative, capitalist society. The mark of the list was undoubtedly European-intellectual, liberal again, searching, poetic in character; a reaching out from nineteenth-century fixed, complacent bourgeois virtues to the ineluctable promise of the twentieth century. So marked was this experimentalism that it was even possible to think that the Knopfs preferred the outré and the unusual to the commonplace, so that if the Nobel award for literature was given to some novelist in Calabria or a

Greek pastoralist poet, his work would be sure to be found already translated on the Knopf list. They had their share of commercial successes too – Thomas Mann and André Gide, for instance – but these were almost certain to carry some meaningful message or to be contemporary literature in classical forms. What they shied away from without doubt was anything to do with the vexed and troublesome question of sex.

Petite Blanche, totally feminine in manner but with a mind of steel, met Radclyffe Hall at a reception given by Heinemann at their Windmill Press, and Blanche, never one to miss a chance, asked who was doing *The Well of Loneliness* in America. When she heard that the issue was not yet settled, she asked if she might have an option for two weeks, and back in London that night John and Una delivered to her at the Carlton Hotel a copy of the manuscript.

At once the Knopf acquisitive-defensive pattern came into play. Blanche read it, and had it read (although she had promised Radclyffe Hall she would not let it out of her hands), and cabled and wrote extensively to New York. The book was a dangerous one, and it dealt with sex all right, but it was obviously an important one. It came out clearly with a definite attitude towards a subject that had long been avoided or dealt with only in fanciful or allegorical terms: homosexuality in women. It satisfied the Knopfian desire to be in the van. On the other hand it might be banned, and strong as the Knopfs were for intellectual adventure, they had equally strong instincts about profit and loss. In the end it was a tug-of-war. Blanche wanted the book, and Alfred was putting up obstacles.

By the 12th June when the two-week option expired, the Knopfs offered a contract. But it contained a clause by which the author was to be held solely responsible, financially and legally, for any difficulties, delays and expenses arising in connection with the publication of her book.

This was not standing heart and soul behind the book, which was the condition demanded by the author from any publisher who took it on, and the author bristled. Mrs Knopf explained that all their English authors had signed contracts with this particular clause in it. The author growled and sent the contract back signed, but with this clause struck from it, and so that the Knopf lawyers might have a chance to think again she agreed to the option being extended until 22nd June. But she was firm. She wrote to Carl Brandt on 21 June instructing him, if Knopf did not accept the contract as she had returned it, to offer the book next to Harcourt Brace. May Lamberton Becker, the literary editor of the *Herald Tribune*, who was in England and was privy to all that was going on, was a great friend of Ellen Harcourt, and was prepared to cable her the moment the Knopf option expired to be on the lookout for a very important book.

On 23rd June the Knopfs yielded, as one can assume all along they had meant to do. They were merely arriving by the accustomed process at their own agreement to go ahead. Within a fortnight they were setting the book up, and Blanche Knopf was writing from a sanatorium in Baden-Baden whither these tiresome events and the culmination of an arduous annual visit had sent her: 'I am so happy about everything, and so glad we are doing you'; and Alfred, writing to the author for the first time, glowed with as much sincerity and earnestness as the curate did to his bishop about the state of his breakfast egg:

> I have now finished it (*The Well of Loneliness*) and feel very happy indeed we are to publish it. It strikes me as a very fine book indeed and the first half of it is simply superb. I have very great hopes for its success, and will assure you, in any case, of a very good-looking volume. (June 19/1928).

Ten days after this letter was written, the book was published in London. Such reviews as there were immediately after publication discussed the book seriously. It was praised for being an honest attempt to present a difficult problem, but one marred perhaps by the author's insistence on the reader's sympathy for the invert as a great tragic figure marked with the brand of Cain. But nobody expressed alarm that this doctrine should be thus openly propagated. The reviews dealt strictly with the book's literary merits, and ignored its message in judging it as a novel.

Until Mr James Douglas, the Editor of the *Sunday Express*

turned to it in the August dog-days, three weeks after publication, as the theme for his weekly article which, too often, condemned in outraged tones and explicit detail vices, mainly sexual, which at first mention were declared to be unspeakable, and were then discussed at some length. Female homosexuality was the ideal subject for his column. In a style which uncomfortably reminds one of the late Vice-President Agnew's, he thundered:

> I am well aware that sexual inversion and perversion are horrors which exist among us today. They flaunt themselves in public places with increasing effrontery and more insolently provocative bravado. The decadent apostles of the most hideous and loathsome vices no longer conceal their degeneracy and their degradation . . . They do not shun publicity. On the contrary, they seek it, and they take a delight in their flamboyant notoriety. The consequence is that this pestilence is devastating young souls.

He ended with a demand that the publishers should admit having made a grave mistake, and withdraw the book at once. If they failed to do so, he there and then appealed to the Home Secretary to set the law in motion by instructing the Director of Public Prosecutions to consider whether the book was fit for circulation. He ended his sermon with a warning to 'Our novelists and our men of letters . . . to keep their house in order', warning them that literature had not yet recovered from the harm done to it by the Oscar Wilde scandal.

This article appeared on Sunday 19 August. On Friday the 17th James Douglas had sent Jonathan Cape a proof of his article attacking the book, and the next morning, Saturday, the *Daily Express* ran banner announcements and put up posters on bookstalls heralding the article, and urging everyone to buy the Sunday edition. The result was the predictable one, that public curiosity was aroused, messengers were sent post-haste from the bookshops to Cape's Trade Counter, and the remainder of the first printing was sold out that morning. Already in the previous week, seeing the demand growing for the book, Cape had put in an order to his printer for a second impression of 3000 copies. And now on this Saturday morning he took an apparently impulsive, but I think carefully calculated step to put him in the clear with the law, and at the same time keep public interest in the book going. He wrote the Home Secretary, drawing his attention to James Douglas's article, sending him a copy of the book and a selection of the serious reviews, and inviting his opinion of it. If the Home Secretary considered that he had erred, he announced himself ready to withdraw the book. But he neglected to tell the author, who was in London only a telephone-call away, what he was doing.

On Sunday Una noted: 'John and I breakfasted in bed. Attack against book in *Sunday Express*'.

Early on Monday morning it was of course necessary for Jonathan to tell John of the letter he had written to the Home Secretary, and not unnaturally she was greatly upset. A heated interview took place at Jonathan's office. He propounded the subtlety of his action and the good results which might flow from it. He urged her to wait and see what reply the Home Secretary made, and meanwhile he pointed out the beneficial results of this publicity which had quite exhausted the first printing.

By the first post on Tuesday morning the Home Secretary's reply was received, signed by the great man, Sir William Joynson-Hicks, himself, not by an anonymous civil servant. It was unequivocal. Jix, as he was known to everybody, said he had read the book himself and was in no doubt that it was obscene. Unless the book were immediately withdrawn, proceedings would be started for its suppression. In view of the offer he had made to the Home Secretary, Jonathan had no other recourse. A telegram was sent to the printers to stop all work on the reprint, and Jonathan addressed a letter to *The Times*:

> We have today received a request from the Home Secretary, asking us to discontinue publication of Miss Radclyffe Hall's *The Well of Loneliness*. We have already expressed our willingness to fall in with the wishes of the Home Office in this matter, and we have therefore stopped publication.
>
> I have the honour to be
> Your obedient servant
> *Jonathan Cape.*

Such prompt obedience, such abject humility before a public servant's threat was not a bit like Jonathan Cape, but his method of obeying was entirely characteristic. In writing to the printer to confirm his telegram of 22nd August, he said:

> Please make moulds of the type as quickly as possible, and deliver them here. The type should be kept standing after moulding until further notice.

Instructions that sat rather oddly with his breast-beating letter to *The Times*, and with his humble undertaking to the Home Secretary. It was this contradiction between his professed intention and his action, unearthed by a sharp-nosed detective-inspector enquiring at the printers, and reporting his findings mono-syllabically in the witness box, which was to weigh heavily against the book when it came to trial.

The deviousness with which Jonathan met each obstacle, and even seemed to derive advantage from it, is fascinating. A number of leading publishers, as we have seen, were not prepared to venture on this book at all. If they had, and it had been attacked in the press in this open way, most publishers would have quietly with-drawn it, on the grounds of expediency in regard to the harm it might do to the work of other authors on their list; or would have persisted, and waited for the Director of Public Prosecutions to open the action. Or, if they believed sufficiently in the literary quality of the work, might have put up a spirited defence and derived some credit from the resulting collision with authority.

But Jonathan did not select one of these alternatives; his response was a judicious mingling of them all. He got credit from authority by undertaking to withdraw the book from sale; he then flew moulds of the type to Paris, sub-leased the rights to an English-language publisher there, and proceeded through this firm, the Pegasus Press, to solicit orders from English booksellers.

Enter on the scene Mr John Holroyd-Reece, proprietor of the Pegasus Press in Paris. A man of taste and discrimination, he had completely revolutionized the whole conception of paperback publishing in the decades between the wars. Born of a German father Johann Riesz, who was a well-known socialist leader, and a Scottish mother, this remarkable youth had begun school in Dresden, but was later sent to a preparatory school in England, and then to one of its great public schools, Repton, for his entry to which he anglicized his name to Reece. Somewhere along the way he was to come under the patronage of a rich man, Percy Ingham, who was to back the various enterprises into which he leaped after the First War, when with the true dash and bravado to be expected of one who had made the headlines as a co-respondent while still at boarding school, he had become military governor of Zahle and Moalaka at the young age, even for a warrior, of 21.

His adventures after the war were equally dramatic. He married Dorothy Holroyd, whose name he took over and hyphenated to his own. He became the proprietor of a girls' school in the North of England which had been owned by one of Percy Ingham's sisters. Later on he was to gain control of a girls' school near Florence. He found his way into publishing when Victor Gollancz, whom he had known at Repton and socially afterwards in London, joined Ernest Benn, the English publishers. Under Gollancz's vigorous direction, until he started his own firm in 1929, Ernest Benn were very active, and Holroyd-Reece was appointed their Continental representative.

Here Reece soon saw that the old-fashioned Tauchnitz 'Collection of British Authors,' first issued in 1841 by the Baron Tauchnitz, and aimed at the leisurely, well-to-do travellers of Victorian times, needed more than their discreet typography and mournful outward appearance livened up. All sorts of undertakings and restrictions and limitations had been imposed on the Baron by the dictatorial Publishers' Council of mid-Victorian times, for English publishers were very jealous of competing editions in what they lordly regarded as their market. Holroyd-Reece saw that times had changed, and so had the quality of the English-speaking visitors.

He had founded the Pegasus Press in Paris in 1927, and as its business was the publishing of continental editions, he kept an eye on Tauchnitz, while working out plans for launching, with the financial support of Percy Ingham, a new, up-dated, dashing series of continental paperbacks.

And then in 1928, a great piece of luck came his way, when Wren Howard of Jonathan Cape flew to Paris with moulds of the type of the suppressed *The Well of Loneliness*, with the intention of licensing the new firm of Pegasus Press to produce a cloth-bound edition on the Continent.

It happened that Holroyd-Reece knew Radclyffe Hall. By chance he had spent the last two Christmases in her company, as the Holroyd-Reeces had old friends in Datchet where John and Una were accustomed to spend Christmas with the Temples. Christmas calls had been exchanged. Holroyd-Reece had learnt the nature of the book Radclyffe Hall was working on, and had made sympathetic and approbatory noises with a view to getting the continental rights later on.

The proposal that Pegasus Press should issue an edition in Paris went a long way towards mollifying John's anti-Cape feeling. Jonathan Cape supplied Reece with a list of unfulfilled English orders, and an overseas mailing list. Unfortunately Holroyd-Reece was a greedy man, and the orders from English booksellers being bigger than he had hoped for, he appointed a bookseller in London to act as his agent and distributor, and one shipment to this man, Leopold Hill, consisting of 250 copies, came under the notice of Customs Officers, who impounded the books as porno-graphic. After a few days the Customs, no doubt in consultation with the Metropolitan Police, released the shipment. The police allowed a few days to elapse, and then obtained search warrants under the 1861 Obscene Publications Act, and seizing copies of *The Well of Loneliness* at Leopold Hill's and at another leading bookseller's on Charing Cross Road, they applied to the magis-trate for summonses against Leopold Hill and Jonathan Cape, who had come forward to claim ownership of the copies at the other booksellers, to show cause why these books should not be destroyed.

Jonathan and Holroyd-Reece had no recourse but to defend the book in the Magistrate's Court; if they had not, Radclyffe Hall, all her war-paint on by this time, would have whipped them into it. There was little to lose and everything to gain by the action. If the case was lost, the book could continue to sell on the Continent. If it was won, and it might well be won, the English market would be open to the Pegasus Press edition in which Jonathan now had a financial interest. Meanwhile the publicity was enough to gladden any publisher's heart, and it was having an immensely stimulating effect on the sales in Paris. Holroyd-Reece reported from there that orders were pouring in by letter and cable from all over the world. Sir William Joynson-Hicks became the target for indignant press reports. He was accused by the *Daily Herald*, not in possession of all the facts, of having imposed a secret censorship on the book, whereas all this maligned gentleman had done was to answer the publisher's request whether he thought the book indictable. 'Jix Judges A Book – *Well of Loneliness* Banned At His Request' said the *Daily Herald* in banner headlines across the front page, while the *Daily Express*, coming to the support of its Sunday editor, reminded the Home Secretary of his duty, and while at the same time virtuously proclaiming its traditional opposition to any interference with the rights of self-expression, declared:

> But every now and then there is an affront to decency and morals so flagrant and infamous that it deserves the notice and action of the State. Such an affront is contained in this book.

Shaw and Wells, never to be left out of any public debate at this time, had their opinions solicited, and in the words of the *Daily Herald*, added the weight of their authority to the protest against the attack on the freedom of the Press by the Home Secretary and the Customs authorities. Mr Shaw was quoted as saying 'If this sort of thing is to happen and no protest be made against it, no books will be published at all in England'. Mr Wells denounced the seizure of the books and said that he doubted very much whether the action was legal. 'I hope the owner of the seized copies will take early action.' While in Paris Holroyd-Reece declared himself an English subject with two votes in the City of London, and he challenged the Public Prosecutor to take action against him in England. He also pointed out that his firm was registered under French law , and he would request the French authorities to give him the customary commercial protection.

The book was being kept well in the forefront of everyone's attention, and Jonathan, who had other plans afoot, must have been rubbing his hands with satisfaction, even though a warrant had been served demanding his appearance at Bow Street on 14th November.

Chapter Thirteen

When *The Well of Loneliness* was published in 1928, the definition of obscenity in English law had been pronounced seventy years before by Lord Justic Cockburn: 'I think the test of obscenity is this, whether the tendency of the matter charged as obscenity is to deprave and corrupt those whose minds are open to such immoral influences, and into whose hands a publication of this sort might fall.'

In the state of society of England in 1857, there was little difficulty in passing through Parliament the Obscene Publications Act, based on this dictum. Thereafter the test was simply to be this: would the book, if it fell into the hands of someone weak-minded, or not yet arrived at a maturity of judgement, tend by suggestion to impel them towards vice? If it did, there was an end of it. The author could not speak in his own defence, or call witnesses such as his fellow-authors to attest to his good character and the high level of his art. A corrupting thing must be rooted out.

But as society as a whole became more sophisticated, and the level of education broadened, a feeling of resentment grew against this excessive interference of the State in matters in which the individual likes to think he is his own best judge. There came a division between the law, and what people generally thought of the law. *The Well* fell into this in-between period.

In 1928, when the Home Secretary was asked by the publisher to say whether *The Well of Loneliness* was obscene, he had no alternative, basing his opinion on the law as it stood then, to saying that it was, and if the book were not withdrawn he would instruct the Director of Public Prosecutions to proceed against it. To that extent one must sympathize with the notorious Sir William Joynson-Hicks, who subsequently defended himself on this point in an able article in *The Nineteenth Century and After*.

Not only prosecuted under the definition of that out-of-date Act, but procedurally prevented from making a proper defence, because the author was not allowed to defend her high purpose in writing it; the Magistrate could refuse to hear evidence from her fellow-authors as to her standing in the profession of letters; and distinguished public men and women could not be called to give evidence of the book's value as literature or science.

But change was in the wind, although it was to take another thirty years before Parliament passed an act to amend the Act of 1857. At least there were grounds for hope in the changing temper of the times that the Magistrate might agree to allow evidence as to the importance of the book, and that is why so many eminent authors and scientists were assembled in the court room that day.

That great men who profess broad views are not always willing to stand up for them in public becomes painfully clear as one turns over the letters from those invited by the defence, who were reluctant or hesitant for one reason or another to come forward and speak on behalf of the book. Sometimes the excuse is that the book lacked literary merit, the honest view of Professor Gilbert Murray who said he profoundly disliked police prosecutions of literature but thought one would succeed in this case. Sometimes it is all too plain that female homosexuality was particularly abhorrent to many. Sometimes it is a cowardly evasion such as John Galsworthy's: 'I am not prepared to go into the witness box on behalf of Miss Radclyffe Hall's *The Well of Loneliness*. I am too busy a man, and I am not sure that the freedom of letters is in question.' As President of P.E.N. of which Radclyffe Hall was a member, this was an extraordinary remark, for P.E.N.'s charter is based on the freedom to write and speak one's opinion.

Much more admirable because it was honest, was the reply from Hermon Ould, the General Secretary of P.E.N., a homosexual himself, who was 'sorry he could not make a stand', because to do so would imply that he was speaking for the whole membership of P.E.N.

Another homosexually-inclined author of considerable prominence on the contemporary scene, Hugh Walpole, wrote to

Cape that he would have admired his courage if Cape had stuck to his guns instead of submitting himself to the Home Secretary's judgement, and then abandoning the book. 'I dislike intensely all the publicity given to abnormality, which ought, I think, to be let lie on both sides.'

Altogether these letters provide a revealing view of the state of mind of society towards this subject at this particular time. From bishops and generals, from too many writers, comes the answer, although often muffled up in excuses, that the less said about this subject the better.

But those who did support it were eminent, fearless and vocal. It was declared 'a masterpiece' by Sir Michael Sadler, the Master of University College, Oxford, and the father of Michael Sadleir, the author and publisher, who, perhaps to protect his own reputation from the reverberations frequently caused by the emphatic utterance of his father's opinion, introduced a differentiating 'i' into the family name. 'To suppress it', he went on:

> would, I think, be contrary to the public interest. It is poignant, vivid, deeply felt. It is in the same category as Rousseau's *Confessions*. The book is a psychological study rather than an essay in fiction.

Arnold Bennett, always ready to spring to the defence of authors, and never behindhand in offering instruction on any subject, told the lawyers how the case should be conducted:

> The Prosecuting Counsel will without doubt ask questions and demand an answer, 'Yes' or 'No'. It should be left to the most impressive witnesses either to insist on answering such questions in their own way, or to ask the permission of the Court to explain ... [Bennet thereupon gives a specific instance.] If the Prosecuting Counsel asks: 'Do you think this book is a proper one to put in the hands of young persons?', the witness should absolutely refuse to say Yes or No. He should add, 'and I say the same for the bible and Shakespeare.'

But Arnold Bennett in this case was offering gratuitous advice.

He was against a book 'which had been banned, whether officially or unofficially, no matter how foolishly or stupidly, by properly established authority' being smuggled into the country. And as this was what the case was about, he was of little help to the Defence.

Dr Karen Stephen, the famous psychiatrist, got to the heart of the whole matter by saying that while she did not feel that the psychology of the book was wholly true, 'it is a seriously written piece of literature, and ought not to shock the ordinary novel-reading public. The fact that it deals with inversion in a serious spirit does not seem to me reason for suppressing it.'

But she thought, and rightly, 'my attitude to questions of sexuality whether moral or perverse would be fundamentally different from the Magistrate's, and the support of a Freudian would probably be harmful rather than helpful.'

In the United States the test under Lord Justice Cockburn's ruling had been applied, but with the greater adaptability of American courts to changing conditions and the greater freedom of magistrates to inject common sense as opposed to a rigid adherence to the letter of the law, the test had gradually undergone a change, and it was accepted that it was no part of the duty of courts to exercise a censorship over literary productions, on the admired American grounds that to confer upon any individual such a power would be to invite abuse and threaten freedom of speech. The chances of the survival of *The Well of Loneliness* in the United States was therefore rather better than in England. But in some degree the risk was also greater, for the book could there be haled into court by a common informer, and in New York there was a Society for the Suppression of Vice, and its Secretary, a Mr John S. Sumner, had been very active in recent years in taking to court not only dangerous new novels like James Branch Cabell's *Jurgen*, but accepted classics like Theophile Gautier's *Mademoiselle de Maupin*. At the time of the trial in England an American publisher had not yet been found for the book, but Mr Sumner, reading in the New York press an account of the trial in England, must already have been sniffing his prey.

It did not take him long to pounce when the book was issued.

It was before the Chief Magistrate of London, Sir Chartres Biron, that Jonathan Cape and Mr Leopold Hill were arraigned. Neither offender appeared in person, Jonathan Cape at the time of the trial, in fact, being on the high seas speeding to America. The defendants were represented by Counsel. The solicitors acting for Jonathan Cape and the Pegasus Press in Paris, Rubinstein, Nash & Co., had briefed Mr Norman Birkett, one of the most distinguished Counsel then at the Bar, and J. B. Melville, K.C. a younger but brilliant man who was to play the star part in the proceedings. The partner of the solicitors in charge of the case was Harold Rubinstein, whose literary interests and enthusiasms I have already mentioned. He had busied himself in collecting more than forty eminent literary men and women ready to bear witness to the high literary quality of the work and its artistic intention, if the magistrate would admit them, and among these, arrayed along the benches at the trial, were such figures as E. M. Forster, Desmond McCarthy, Hugh Walpole, Leonard and Virginia Woolf, Rose Macaulay, A. P. Herbert, V. Sackville-West, Laurence Housman, Storm Jameson and Julian Huxley.

A disappointment had been Havelock Ellis's failure to come forward as a witness.

'I hope you will not misunderstand me if I say at once that I should *not* be willing to be a witness. I *never* have been in the witness box. There are two good reasons against it. The first is that I do not possess the personal qualities that make a good witness, and would probably make a bad impression, and certainly not a good impression. The second is that being the author of a book on this very subject that has been judicially condemned, I am "tarred with the same brush". The less said about me the better for you.' (20 October, 1928.)

What he could have attested to, if the magistrate had admitted his evidence, is what he had acknowledged in the short prefatory paragraph he had written for the book where he testified that it

possesses a notable psychological and sociological significance. So far as I know it is the first English novel which presents in a completely faithful and uncompromising form one particular aspect of sexual life as it exists among us today.

But as the magistrate was intent on stamping out any such revelations, it is doubtful if Havelock Ellis's intervention would have been of any value. All it signifies for the reader of another generation is the courage which Radclyffe Hall showed in writing *The Well of Loneliness*. More than thirty years had passed since Havelock Ellis had published the first volume of his immensely important *Studies in the Psychology of Sex*. Volume I was entitled *Sexual Inversion*, and dealt scientifically with the very subject which Radclyffe Hall was now presenting in a novel. In 1898 George Bedborough, the Editor of *The Adult* who also sold books, was arrested and brought to trial for selling *Sexual Inversion*, and in the event Havelock Ellis did nothing. In the end George Bedborough was bound over, and an undertaking was given by the author Havelock Ellis that he would never again publish his sex books in Britain. As Arthur Calder-Marshall writes in *Lewd, Blasphemous and Obscene** where this affair is very clearly set out, 'It was the consistent cowardice of Havelock Ellis at every stage after he had finished his bold book that turned a blow for sexual freedom into one against it.' In the considerable batch of letters between Havelock Ellis and Radclyffe Hall which came into my possession after Una's death, this discreet evasiveness, detectable in his account in his autobiography *My Life*, of his very peculiar relationship with his wife, Edith Lees, is plain. He was not the stuff of which soldiers are made, a scholar with a brain but not much of a spine. Radclyffe Hall, for all her flamboyant behaviour, shines beside him.

At the trial Radclyffe Hall sat at the solicitors' table wearing a leather coat with an astrakhan collar, and the black Spanish hat made familiar in many photographs of her. A reporter from the *Daily Herald*, who gives a breathless but lively report of the proceedings, noted that... 'her hair is closely cropped. Her features are refined and well-chiselled, the expression in the eyes being one of mingled pain and sadness'. This was not her cus-

* Hutchinson, London, 1972.

tomary expression; the eyes could, and even did on this occasion, frequently flash with temper, and she is best remembered by her friends as, in Una's words 'a great laugher'. Resignation was certainly not her forté but everybody was conscious of being an actor in this drama from the Chief Magistrate – 'white-haired, clean-shaven, tight-lipped', in the same reporter's phrase – who used a quill pen and had beside him a copy of *The Well of Loneliness*, to Sir Archibald Bodkin, Director of Public Prosecutions, who was present in person to sit beside the Counsel, Mr Fulton, who had been briefed by the Crown to lead the prosecution.

It is not difficult to imagine the feelings of Radclyffe Hall as this drama unfolded. When she began the book she knew that there were certain risks in writing it. She could not disguise the fact that it would be her own story. She did not mind that; she had always frankly admitted her inversion. Disguising it seemed an admission of shame which she refused to make. She wanted now to explain and defend what unthinking people were too ready to condemn. At first she had no thought of the book as being a crusade on behalf of all inverts. It was only as the story developed, and she introduced characters drawn from the lesbian world she knew in Paris and London and exposed their private tragedies, that she persuaded herself that she was speaking on behalf of all the afflicted. She had finished the book in that conviction, and this had compelled her to write to Newman Flower as she had done, and later to abandon Mrs Knopf when her agent could easily have forced the Knopfs to carry out their part of the agreement.

Everything that had happened since with Jonathan Cape, James Douglas, Sir William Joynson-Hicks, the police, and now in this court-room scene, deepened in her the impression that she was defending the helpless and the weak against the oppressions of authority. It was a grief to her that the law as it stood meant that she was to play no part in the proceedings. She sat there, eyeing the magistrate belligerently, and continually interrupted and contradicted him until he had to threaten to have her evicted from the court.

Sir Chartres Biron tried hard to be magisterial and just, but it was plain that the subject of homosexuality was not congenial to him. He listened without comment to Mr Norman Birkett's contention that the relationship between the two main characters the book portrayed was one of normal friendship. It was a weak beginning, for there was too much evidence to the contrary in the book which lay on the Bench before the magistrate, and which it was plain, from his comments throughout the trial, he had closely read. After the luncheon interval in the course of which Mr Norman Birkett was violently and loudly attacked by the author for this misrepresentation of her well-known views, he retracted this submission, and after that there was really no case, as the magistrate emphasized in his summing-up.

It was Mr Melville, taking over in the afternoon, eloquent, young and forceful, who put forward the view that this book discussed a social question that nobody could deny existed . . .

> So we are agreed, I think, in this Court that the theme itself is not to be proscribed: The question is the treatment of the theme . . . It is impossible to say that this is a book which should be banned as an indecent publication. The moral of the book, is it not this? These people who are born with this misfortune cannot expect charity and understanding. To those at large it says there should be toleration and understanding for those who are God's creatures. I submit to you Sir, that this book is written in a reverent spirit; that it is not written in a manner calculated to excite libidinous thoughts, but is an attempt to deal with a social question that exists. From its literary side there can be no dispute. It would be presumptuous for me to add a word to the tributes which have been paid to it from all sides. I do beg of you to say that this is not a case in which you, Sir, acting judicially, feel yourself compelled to say it is an indecent publication, because I know that you will act upon the principles which you in your judicial office must always act, and that is, that if you feel this case is even doubtful, it will not be resolved upon the side of the suppression of a work which is a thoughtful work, which has been said on all sides to be a fine literary work.

But the magistrate was not to be swayed by these familiar

arguments, or impressed by the gallery of distinguished onlookers, all obviously sympathetic to the defence. He had with difficulty kept his temper at several stages in the proceedings. That he had read the book closely but with bias in his mind was apparent from his judgement. He instanced Stephen's infatuation for Angela, the young married woman she first has a passion for. It is made plain in the book that this infatuation was not consummated in an unnatural way. There is nothing more than fondling and kissing. But to Sir Chartres Biron, here is the seduction by a pervert of a married woman:

> who, of course, I admit at once, is not described as a woman of any particular morality, but that was not present to the mind of Stephen when she seduced her and persuaded her reluctantly to indulge in these horrible practices.

We begin to see that even judicial minds may be open to immoral influences if the magistrate in the case has allowed his imagination to be inflamed to a degree that pictured a depravity that cannot be found in the story.

It must have been very early on apparent to those who were listening in court which way the judgement was going to go. 'Horrible practices' was the phrase reiterated continuously to describe the relationship between the women; and it was particularly abhorrent to the magistrate's mind that this depraved sexual experience should be represented as being elevating to the spirit.

> 'I have to be satisfied', he began his judgement, 'before I can order this book to be seized and destroyed (if I come to that conclusion) that at common law it is an obscene libel.'

He proceeded to satisfy himself in a very direct manner. First he commented on the fact that the two men responsible for the resurrection of the book after its professed withdrawal, Jonathan Cape and Leopold Hill, had neither of them been called into the witness box by the defence, and had therefore not been called upon to explain why Cape, having voluntarily withdrawn the book from publication after discussion with the Home Secretary, had arranged to have it produced in Paris and imported through Hill and sold in England surreptitiously.

Next he went on to consider the point ably put forward by Mr Melville, that nowhere in the work was there any detailed description of these offences, which anyway were not illegal between women. But, the magistrate pointed out, the reader's imagination must be at work between what was actually described and what the author hinted at. Homosexual relationships, whether between men or between women, 'involve acts of the most horrible, unnatural and disgusting obscenity. Therefore if I find in this book that those practices are defended or in any way held out to admiration, no reasonable person could say that the book . . . is not an obscene publication.'

Finally, it was the attitude of the author towards her subject that the magistrate found obscene. If the story had been presented as a moral lesson, if the victims – he would say the subjects – of these congenital deformities had been presented as struggling against their inborn handicaps, endeavouring to resist the tendencies which they prompted, then the book might have been said to have a moral purpose. But, on the contrary, they were shown as entirely satisfied with their state of degradation, and this book asked only that they be accorded their place in society.

> The whole note of this book is a passionate and almost hysterical plea for the toleration and recognition of these people who, in the view presented in this book, are people who ought to be tolerated and recognized, and their practices tolerated and recognized, in decent society . . . Not merely that, but there is a much more serious matter, the actual physical acts of the women indulging in unnatural vices are described in the most alluring terms; their result is described as giving these women extraordinary rest, contentment and pleasure; and not only that, but it is actually put forward that it improves their mental balance and capacity.

Sir Chartres Biron came swiftly to his conclusion.

> I have no hesitation in saying that this is an obscene libel, that it would tend to corrupt those into whose hands it might fall, and that the publication of this book is an offence against decency, an obscene libel, and I shall order it to be destroyed.

So away from the court went the Spanish hat with the striking face beneath it, pressed in by a crowd of admirers, not only from among the ranks of literary witnesses but from the general public too. The case had attracted wide attention, but pending an appeal, *The Well of Loneliness* could not come into England, and the only hope now was the American edition, which had also been suffering pre-natal troubles of a critical kind.

On Friday 14th December, the appeal was heard before Sir Robert Wallace and eleven magistrates sitting at the Quarter Sessions. It followed much the same course as the hearing at the Magistrate's Court. Mr Melville was as eloquent on behalf of his clients as he had been at the previous hearing. Sir Thomas Inskip, the Attorney-General, said nothing new. Inspector John Protheroe who had organized the seizure of the books, and who claimed himself to have read it, was as monosyllabic as before, and Mr Tanner, the printer, was no more revealing in his acknowledgement of the curious instructions he had had from the publisher charged with this offence.

The question remained as before: 'will this book corrupt?' The Attorney-General had no doubt. He confessed himself shocked by the temerity of the thing:

> It is a missionary work, appealing for recognition of the status of people who engage in these practices, and there is not a word to suggest that people who do this are a pest to society and to their own sex.

All Mr Melville's eloquence again went for nothing, for the Chairman of the Court, issuing judgement, was briefer, more incisive and condemnatory than the Attorney-General had been in his opening. He agreed that there were plenty of people who would neither be depraved nor corrupted by reading a book like this, but it was those whose minds, as Chief Justice Cockburn had said, are open to such immoral influences and into whose hands a publication of this sort might fall, who have to be considered.

> The character of this book cannot be quite fairly gathered from the reading of isolated passages. They give an indication

as to the general tendency of the book, but the book must be taken as a whole. I might just say in a sentence what the view of the Court is: that this book is a very subtle book; it is a book which is insinuating in the way in which it is propounded, and probably much the more dangerous because of that fact. But in the view of this Court it is a most dangerous and corrupting book, a book the general tendency of which would be to corrupt the minds of the general body of those who read it, a book which if it does not commend unnatural practices certainly condones them, and suggests that those who are guilty of them should not receive the consequences in this world which they deserve to suffer. The view of this Court, put in a word, is that this is a disgusting book when properly read – a disgusting book – that it is an obscene book and a book prejudicial to the morals of the community. In our view the Order made by the Magistrate was a perfectly correct one and the Appeal will be dismissed with costs.

Some time before this the alarm bells had rung in America. Blanche Knopf who had written from the sanatorium to say 'so happy we are doing you', and had subsequently sent a card from the *Aquitania* promising the author 'Full Steam Ahead', found on her arrival in New York in mid-September that the outlook was far from hopeful. As part of his publicity campaign for the book Knopf had produced a 4-page leaflet quoting *in extenso* Havelock Ellis's commentary, and had sent this out as a supplement to their Fall Catalogue. This had reached the press at the very time when the events following James Douglas's condemnation of the book and the Home Secretary's action had come on the wires. With the Knopfs' claims on behalf of the book, supported by Havelock Ellis's praise for it, coupled with the press reports from England telling of the Home Secretary's personal intervention in the matter, the drama was fully set out, and the news stories had only to conclude by saying that they awaited with much interest the publication of the book by Knopf for some premonitory tremors to be felt in the publishing office in New York.

Within a week of her return to New York, Blanche Knopf was

writing to convey to the author a very different prospect than the decision to go 'Full Steam Ahead'.

> While orders are coming in for the book they are not coming in any great quantities from the better type of booksellers, but rather from dealers who expect a sensational demand for the book from people who expect something very salacious. I am convinced that, handle the book as we might, we could never avoid selling it as a dirty book, which is the last thing you or any of us want to see happen in connection with it.

The odour of legal advice is very marked in the next paragraph:

> Our decision not to publish it will, I am sure, come as a very great shock to you, but you must view the situation from our point of view. You are an English author, and you secured a reputable English publisher for this book. The English publisher, on request of a public authority, withdrew the book from circulation, and in this withdrawal you acquiesced. You made no attempt to compel him to carry out the terms of his agreement and thus bring the matter to the attention of the Courts, the only bodies competent to render a legally binding decision. We are thus faced with the hopeless prospect of attempting to defend a book which has not been defended in its author's own country.

Mrs Knopf then proceeds to lay the blame for their difficulty on Cape's early publication date. If simultaneous publication had been effected this difficulty would not have arisen. It is hard to see what difference this would have made. If her earlier argument for abandoning the book was a valid one – that it could only be sold as pornography – simultaneous publication would not have avoided this. James Douglas would still have raised his strident voice; Sir William Joynson-Hicks would still have been Home Secretary; Jonathan Cape's impulsive move would not have been checked by any consideration for the Knopfs.

Finally Mrs Knopf advises Radclyffe Hall to keep the book entirely out of the American market, 'if you can persuade yourself of the wisdom of this course.' She then proposes cancelling the agreement insofar as it relates to *The Well of Loneliness*, 'but preserving it for the next two books you may write. We should,' she concluded 'be prepared to pocket the substantial loss of the printers' bills that have been incurred.'

Mrs Knopf whatever her other qualities – and they were many – was plainly no psychologist, and she had read *The Well of Loneliness* in vain if she had not recognized that this was not a book written for profit or fame, but was a passionately-expressed *apologia pro vita sua*, and could not be set aside, no matter what the prohibition. Nor could she possibly have understood what sort of a woman Radclyffe Hall was, a very direct character who detested doing business with women and, angry at this rebuff, had no intention of doing any more business with Knopf. Her agent in New York, the astute Carl Brandt, saw the weakness of the Knopfs' position, and recognized the palpable bluff in Blanche's letter. Mrs Knopf had not consulted him before writing to Radclyffe Hall, but had sent him a copy of the letter. He immediately insisted on Knopf carrying out their agreement to publish, and he cabled Audrey Heath that he had done so. Whereupon he got this cable for his pains:

> In view disgraceful termination contract John absolutely refuses any compromise with Knopf Stop Has already received alternative offers and has signed contract with Cape who guarantees full copyright protection.*

At first sight it is odd that the man whose impetuous action in writing to the Home Secretary had brought about this drama should in the end have been the one who brought about a solution. Jonathan Cape and Radclyffe Hall were alike in many ways. Jonathan was a powerful persuader; broad wisdom seemed to flow from him, and the impression that it was genuine, disinterested wisdom was fortified by the dignity of his bearing, the handsome if rather bilious-complexioned face, the mellifluous voice. John's frightening temper had sprung into flame when she learnt that without consulting her, he had sent a copy of the book

* Under the existing copyright law in America temporary copyright protection was accorded to a book manufactured outside the United States provided that an American edition was published within six months of the date of the *ad interim* registration which had to be within two months of original publication. To obtain full copyright protection therefore, an American edition of *The Well of Loneliness* had to be published before January 27, 1929.

to the Home Secretary, offering to withdraw it from publication if the minister thought his motives in publishing it were wrong. And for the unseemly haste and the public gestures of regret with which he had withdrawn it, she had felt that she could never forgive him. There had seemed to her something surreptitious in the arrangement to issue the book through the Pegasus Press in Paris, and her direct nature abhorred the idea that he should be doing this with her book while at the same time he was dissociating himself from it in his letter to *The Times*.

By this time *The Well of Loneliness* had become with her a personally conducted crusade waged on behalf of all inverts; an attempt to bring into the light of day a subject which had been whispered about and dealt with furtively in the shadows. To be, by association, involved in actions which were similar in hypocrisy and duplicity to the conduct her book condemned, was utterly revolting to her proud disposition, and she stormed and made things difficult for those around her.

But Jonathan rode the storm. He had obtained her permission to manufacture *The Well of Loneliness* in France, and already the Pegasus edition was displayed in every English bookshop in Paris. When the Knopf deal fell through he was at hand to tell her of his plans for starting up a business of his own in America. He came up with the proposal to issue all her books in the United States in a collected edition. As *The Well of Loneliness*, to preserve copyright, needed to be published before the end of the year, he proposed that he should take over from her the American rights with power to sublease the publishing rights to a suitable American publisher who could accomplish this, since he could not do it himself in time. But he would retain the right to include it in the collected edition his American branch would issue in due course.

Again she agreed, reluctantly and stormily, as there was no other course, and her respect for Cape's acumen and skill, even though some of his actions appeared to compromise her high purpose, began to overcome her doubts. By the time the Bow Street trial was on, Jonathan was on the high seas, and Howard was left to hold the breach. The Bow Street magistrate's judgement was given on 16 November. Three days later Howard had an interview with her, and this letter follows:

Dear Howard,

I am afraid that it was a pretty unpleasant interview for all three of us, but somehow I do think it was a good thing to put forth all grievances and thrash them out frankly, even at the risk of some hard speaking, and that it has cleared the air for a return to our former happy relations. I have really felt sore about the whole thing, and these things are better out than in, especially at such a time of strain for us all . . .

Quite soon all our troubles should be over, we have now only one more fence to cross. Melville seems to think that we had quite a good chance, but in any case after the Appeal we can all look the public fearlessly in the face, and no-one can say that we have left off before we had to.

Yours sincerely,
Radclyffe Hall.

No doubt it was agreed at this meeting that Jonathan Cape should appeal, and that Radclyffe Hall should bear a proportion of the cost. A week later Jonathan cabled from New York that he could arrange publication of *The Well of Loneliness* with Covici Friede, the book to appear by mid-December, thus protecting the copyright. Donald Friede had offered an advance of ten thousand dollars against a fifteen per cent royalty – very good terms indeed. Jonathan had back a cable from Audrey Heath: 'HALL ACCEPTS FRIEDE OFFER BUT WISHES IF POSSIBLE HAVE HALF ADVANCE ON SIGNATURE OF AGREEMENT.' This provision was because her experiences with Knopf had shaken her confidence in American publishers. But this confidence was rapidly to be restored as *The Well of Loneliness* set out on its triumphant course in America.

Chapter Fourteen

They were less dismayed than one might expect from the dismissal of the appeal. There were compensations. Good news was flowing in fast from other quarters, Reece reporting an increasing demand for the Pegasus edition in Paris, and Jonathan Cape sending a reassuring cable from New York about the sales of the Covici Friede edition which was published two days after the appeal was dismissed by the English courts.

There is no doubt, too, that they were beginning to find pleasure in the publicity and excitement engendered by all this. A state of siege existed at 37 Holland Street, flattering to its occupants, mounted by reporters from European and American papers begging for interviews and photographs. There is something satisfying to an author of a suppressed book in being able to answer back to authority in this way, and John, her aggressive instincts on behalf of sexual inversion now thoroughly aroused said, as well as some expected, some incautious things which made headlines and news stories for the popular press. This, alas, had the effect of putting off some of her more useful allies, who disliked appearing to be championing lesbianism, when what they wanted to defend was liberty of expression.

Christmas was approaching. The holiday was to be spent at Rye, a town with which they were to be closely associated for the remainder of their time in England. In September they had first seen in Rye a cottage up for sale called Journey's End, which belonged to a Mrs Harvey. They were as much taken with the town and the ancient Mermaid Hotel, as with the cottage which had its full share of inconveniences. They came and went weekend after weekend, looking it over and comparing it with other alternatives, and on 21st October they finally took it.

There had been little chance to do much about getting it ready for occupation during the daily excitements connected with the preparation for the Bow Street hearing, and the subsequent trials in November and December, especially as they had to dispose of 37 Holland Street and take a *pied-à-terre* flat in London at the same time. But all was accomplished, and on 20th December, Andrea accompanying them, they set off by car for Rye and the Christmas holiday.

There were the by now customary temperamental outbursts. These two were so devoted to each other that they resented anyone who was not ready instantly to see in the little exasperations of daily existence, the same degree of intentional malevolence which they saw in them. On Christmas Day, after the exchange of presents, Andrea and two other guests, Patience Ross of the Heath agency and a friend of hers, went out for a walk together on Camber Sands, and came in nearly half-an-hour late for Christmas dinner. The ensuing silence could have been cut with a knife. Later John and Una went for a walk together, and Una as usual restored peace. It was these sudden little gusts of fierce and quite unpredictable temper which were shaking loose so many of their old friends.

Part of the reason for disposing of Holland Street, and keeping a flat in London and a cottage in Rye, was to get rid of domestic responsibility in England. They had determined to go abroad for a long stay, with the idea in mind of settling there if they could find a suitable place. Andrea was now eighteen, and would soon be off their hands, not that she had ever been allowed to be a burden. She was to sit a scholarship examination for Oxford. When she did, to everybody's surprise, except her teachers', she was awarded it.

While England had suppressed *The Well of Loneliness*, Gallimard, the leading French publisher, had undertaken a French translation, to the annoyance of all women French writers it was said, who for years had been trying to break down the barriers which kept them off this mainly male list. The Pegasus Press edition had already been reprinted three times, and a fourth impression was in the press. Longing secretly for approval and to be lionized, and feeling the interest in the book in England begin

173

to die away as other matters came to occupy the headlines, John and Una departed for Paris in February 1929.

What a place to be if you were famous (or notorious), and rich in the splendid spring of 1929. Radclyffe Hall was both, and they were soon meeting not only the fashionable ladies who preferred sapphic love, but famous American writers like Louis Bromfield, Stephen Vincent Benet and his wife, and Ezra Pound. It was perhaps odd that none of these friendships was sustained. There would follow from the first encounter several meetings, and ecstatic admiration of each other's work. Then something would supervene. The spell would be broken. Nothing for instance could exceed their liking for Stephen Vincent Benet personally, and their admiration for his work. Lying on their bed in their Paris hotel, Una read *John Brown's Body* aloud to John for eight hours without stopping. Benet showed them the original manuscript. They met for lunch and dinner – a beautiful friendship seemed to be forming. Then – what was it? The flamboyant appearance of this man-woman and her lover, the outrageous things she could say in public places about perversion? Something – it may have been only the New England character crying 'enough'; suddenly it would be all over.

It was the ladies in Paris who really took them to their hearts. In the beautiful house in the rue Jacob, they met Ezra Pound and Maurice Rostand. Natalie Barney was not a bit dismayed by the recognizable portrait of her in *The Well of Loneliness*, or for that matter in Compton Mackenzie's *Extraordinary Women*. She was to live on in Paris until she was 95, without losing her taste for the amusement she still then managed to extract from life. Then there was Toupie Lowther, whose home was in London but who made frequent appearances in Paris, and the attractive Duchesse de Clermont-Tonnèrre, whom they saw much of on this visit. Dolly Wilde, Oscar's attractive niece, was living in Paris, and both John and Una lost their hearts to her. 'Wilde himself lives again here in Paris', wrote Una ecstatically to Audrey Heath, 'in the person of a niece so like him in fact that it is uncanny – and like him, of course, also in nature, but I think – as far as a superficial estimate can judge – the better man.' (14:3:29.)

Luncheon parties, dinner parties, excursions were arranged. Our British visitors were being feted. Displays of *The Well of Loneliness* were massed in every bookshop window, accompanied by blown-up photographs of John, and the book and its author were attracting an immense amount of interest.

The icy winter of 1929 had not yet relaxed its grip, and even the tops of the palms in Monte Carlo were turning brown with the frost, and snow lay briefly along the Croisette in Cannes. In Paris the Seine was solidly frozen, and John and Una shivered in their hotel. They were eating rich food, getting no exercise at all, deprived of their proper allowance of sleep by late parties, and the excitement of meeting new people, constantly being stared at and whispered about. It was all very bad for two middle-aged ladies, with fragile digestions, unreliable blood pressures, who were subject to exciting bursts of news from abroad. A cable from Jonathan a fortnight after they had reached Paris told them that the sales of *The Well of Loneliness* in New York were touching 40,000. Then, at the end of February, came a letter to say that Mr John S. Sumner, Secretary of the New York Society for the Suppression of Vice, had informed the authorities that *The Well* was an 'obscene, lewd, lascivious, indecent and disgusting book', and had demanded that it should be suppressed and the authorities, after examining it, had sustained Mr Sumner's objection. The publishers had entered an appeal. These gestures of authority's disapproval merely fanned the flames of public interest in the book. Jonathan, who was making an extended visit to New York while establishing his new company, Cape and Harrison Smith, could report that 'it was going strong all over the U.S.', and soon Donald Friede, the American publisher of it, arriving in Paris, could tell them that the sales already exceeded 50,000 copies.

Meanwhile Mr Morris Ernst, a partner in the firm of Greenbaum, Wolff and Ernst, and a noted champion of the freedom of the press, had thrown himself heart and soul into the defence, and had prepared a memorandum for the court's enlightenment, tracing the history of the law relating to obscenity both in England and the United States, comparing *The Well of Loneliness* with works ranging from *The Satyricon* of Petronius Arbiter to Theophile Gautier's *Mademoiselle de Maupin*, both of which had been the subject of recent court actions and had been vindicated. He reminded the court that a strenuous letter of protest against the suppression of the novel in England had been signed by, among others, Storm Jameson, Sheila Kaye-Smith, Lawrence Binyon, Ashley Dukes, John Drinkwater, T. S. Eliot, E. M. Forster, Julian Huxley, Rose Macaulay, Lytton Strachey and Virginia Woolf. And he listed the names of seventy-five distinguished men of letters in the United States who had signified that they were ready to protest against any attempt to suppress *The Well of Loneliness* in the United States. The memorandum reminded the Judges that this was a criminal prosecution. Moreover it was a prosecution based on the publication of a book. 'The Penal Statute is in derogation of our Federal and State Constitutions guaranteeing the freedom of the press. Hence it should be administered by our courts with the greatest reluctance.' The information which had led to the bringing of this case, said Mr Ernst firmly, should be dismissed, and the defendants acquitted.

It was a noteworthy and exhaustive piece of pleading, and it achieved its purpose. On 19 April, 1929 the Court of Special Service in New York handed down its judgement. It was admirably brief. The defendants were charged with violation of section 1141 of the Penal Law by offering for sale a book known as *The Well of Loneliness* which book, it was alleged, is obscene, lewd, lascivious, filthy and indecent. The book in question, the Judges noted, deals with a delicate social problem and could not be said to be in violation of the law, unless written in a manner that was obscene, lewd, lascivious, etc. and thus tending to deprave and corrupt minds open to immoral influences. 'After a careful reading of the entire book we conclude that the book in question is not in violation of the law and each of the defendants is acquitted.'

No rhetorical fireworks, no talk as in the English Court of this being 'a most dangerous and corrupting book . . . a book which if it does not commend unnatural practices certainly condones them and suggests that those who are guilty of them should not receive the consequences in this world which they deserve to suffer'. Just the simple statement that 'This is a criminal prosecution, and as judges of the facts and the law we are not called upon, nor is it within our province, to pass an opinion as to the merits and demerits thereof, but only as to whether same is in violation of the law'. *The Well of Loneliness* was free to be restored to circulation in the United States.

It is not difficult to imagine the excitement when this news was received in Paris. First a cable to Donald Friede from John: 'Please express to my American brothers and sisters of the pen, and indeed to all who have rallied on behalf of *The Well of Loneliness*, my heartfelt thanks and deep gratitude'. Next a letter to Audrey Heath: 'Will you write to all the nations of the earth ... (telling them of this Court's decision) – 'I feel this American decision should greatly help in our translations'. 'Hip! Hip!' she exclaimed in another less didactic letter to Audrey. 'The news is splendid, and if this goes on we all look like making money, as Una always said we would. I am simply delighted, as you can imagine, and feel ten years younger ...'

There was much to occupy their attention in Paris. Willette Kershaw, the actress, wanted to dramatize *The Well of Loneliness* and put it on in Paris, and agreeable discussions about this occupied their attention. Una was conducting the enormous correspondence about *The Well* with Audrey Heath and the American publishers. The letters all had to be written by hand, because she detested the typewriter.

They had met Colette at Natalie Barney's on their previous visits when *Chéri* had been the talk of Paris. At that time Una had had no thought of anyone but darling Johnny, and had subdued her own cleverness and sharpness in order not to appear to be drawing attention from her loved one. In the spring of 1929, John's fame was beyond doubt, and Colette had just published *La Naissance du Jour*, and was being overwhelmed by a fresh wave of veneration. Una conceived the idea of translating Colette's books, and introducing her to the English public, and she set about the task by beginning with *Chéri*. It was her persistence in getting Secker and Warburg finally to publish that book that introduced Colette to the large and appreciative English public which proved to be waiting for her. Meanwhile they were seeing Colette, who was charming, unpunctual, forgetful, every other day or so, and Una was hard at work on the translation of *Chéri*.

What with lunches at the *Cheval Pie* and the *Vert Galant*, and walks in the Bois with the two dogs they had bought, and parties every day, and cables and correspondence so extensive that a secretary finally had to come to the hotel; what with being stared at and whispered about, and having the pleasure of being greeted as important personages every time they went into Smith's and Bretanos; what with the heady excitement of Paris in April and May, with the horse-chestnuts in bloom, and 'Paris looking wonderful' as Una continually remarks in her journal, they were having the time of their lives.

There was even a smile to be spared for those who sought to take commercial advantage of the notoriety of *The Well of Loneliness*. The Milne Literary Agency wrote to ask, as the book was banned in England, if they might make one hundred type-script copies which, such was the demand for it, could be sold for £10 apiece. John said 'No' to this. And also 'No' to a Miss Grace Little of Los Angeles, who wished to use her name in a Radclyffe Hall Club to bring together 'in a congenial group a number of women interested in living their own lives without the so-called necessity of male companionship'.

But every now and then the sudden gloom that descends on the psychopathic mind would darken everything, and they would feel suicidal. At such a time, John wrote 'Darling Robin' (Audrey Heath):

> I don't seem able to get on with things at all, and am growing to simply dread being *me*, and being known by so many people. I want to be Annie Jones of Putney who lives in a villa with Father and Mother and plays in the local lawn tennis tournaments! Or better still, a retired ironmonger with a fat bank account, a wife and four children – I want to read the Lessons on Sunday feeling placid because all sinners are

damned, and because unlike Lot, I have never been tempted to rape my elderly daughters.*

Last night we went with a man we know to a bar frequented by male inverts. It was really quite seemly, not at all like 'Alec's'† (by the way 'Alec' has blown out his brains!) but somehow the whole thing was deeply depressing. Everyone was trying to be light-hearted while looking deeply unhappy. The songs varied between the sloppy sentimental – lost virtue, lost love, lost hope, lost youth, and the grossly obscene accompanied by gestures – that part was exactly like my description.

There was an amazing youth called Charpini who sang in an enormous soprano voice. He is now the rage with both men and women, a very marked type himself, half a woman. He seemed quite a nice creature. We were introduced to him. Before taking up his present career he sold writing paper etc at the Louvre, but being unable to cope with such trifles, got into an awful muddle, I am told, and nearly wrecked the entire department. What does it all mean, and what are we to do to help such people? He is very good-looking at the present moment, but that will not last, and then drugs or drink or both and a slippery toboggan down hill and to whatever will be Alec's in a couple of years – It is not always gay in Paris! (March 19, 1929).

Then the maddening Danes in their edition translated as 'They shot the fox', the sentence 'they killed not so very far from Worcester'. 'Oh no, I have no words' John wails to Darling Audrey, instructing her to write to the publisher at once, and have this and other imbecile and ignorant errors rectified. For another and similar misdemeanour, her Dutch publisher can go STRAIGHT TO HELL! – her own capital letters and exclamation mark.

But the most grievous blow of all was a Macy advertisement in the New York *World* linking Compton Mackenzie's *Extraordinary Women* with *The Well of Loneliness*.

* Lot can hardly be said to have raped his daughters. The charge could lie the other way. See Genesis 19: 30-38.
† *The Well of Loneliness*, pp. 393-396.

Radclyffe Hall has written an Extraordinary Book. She herself is an EXTRAORDINARY WOMAN, and one who figures largely in a brilliant satiric fictional divertissement by Compton Mackenzie entitled EXTRAORDINARY WOMEN, published by the Vanguard Press.

On 4 April she wrote to Audrey Heath thanking her for having acted so promptly in the matter of this advertisement, two cuttings of which had been sent to her by outraged friends. Audrey had persuaded the American publishers not to repeat the advertisement under penalty of being sued for slander.

> Yet now I must say a bitter thing. Do you know what would happen in an English court of law were I to be tempted to attack Mackenzie? The case would be given against me at once, because I would not deny being an invert. It would therefore follow that nothing could be too bad to write or to say about me; indeed I do not doubt that Mackenzie would be praised for having been so chaste and so temperate. The result would be that his book would sell thousands, and with every copy a fresh blow would be struck for the persecution of inversion. This I will tell you here and now – in the Autumn I am coming back to England, prior to settling in on my French translation (if the Gallimard contract really goes through), but here and now I renounce my country for ever, nor will I ever lift a hand to help England in the future. Nothing that has gone before has hurt me like the publication of *Extraordinary Women* in an ordinary edition.* In it I see only a personal insult, for the Government that allows such a book to go free is doing so with a considered intention, and this being so I am done with England. I shake its dust from my spiritual feet . . .

This is John in one of her black rages when anything can be said and that often expressed incoherently. It was mere chance that *Extraordinary Women* and *The Well of Loneliness* should have been published simultaneously. They both deal with the same subject, lesbianism, but one does it wittily and with considerable literary skill,

---

* She meant that her book had been suppressed while Mackenzie's had got away with it, first as a limited edition, then in a general unlimited edition.

and the other with fanatical fierceness and a notable lack of humour.

Extraordinary Women, which is dedicated to Norman Douglas, depicts a group of lesbians holidaying on the Island of Sirene (Capri) which John and Una had visited in 1923. It was where Romaine Brooks had her villa, and where Natalie Barney and the Duchesse de Clermont-Tonnèrre and others came to stay. There is an unmistakable likeness in one of the chief characters, Hermina de Randan, to Radclyffe Hall. It may have been accidental, but it may also have been a desire to tease, and how could such a witty young novelist resist a character like Radclyffe Hall, the very caricature of the predatory lesbian with 'her finely-cut profile, the slight hardness of which was accentuated by her dark complexion and sharp arrogant eyes'. The likeness is further made clear in 'hobbies like spiritualism and gardening and collecting old furniture . . . sometimes provided more than idle diversion, as when the drums and tambourines of Eudozia, the Greek medium, had to be rescued from the aspersions of male investigators, or Mrs Rubjohn's ectoplasm defended against attempted man-handling by the Society for Psychical Research'.

Madame de Randan has a great friend, Anastasia Sabrecoff, who bears a distinct likeness to Una – 'stepping out dauntlessly towards an old age of penury'.

Radclyffe Hall's and Una's likenesses are not the only ones it is possible to identify in this delicate yet biting little comedy, and there must have been considerable fuss and squawking among this group at being observed and then held up to fun. But only John seems to have got wildly upset by it. At the time of her stay in Capri, she would not have minded, but not forgotten was the humiliation of being exposed to some ridicule in the court over her psychical investigations, and now that she had become a literary figure, she was taking herself with immense seriousness. Inversion is not a joke, it is tragedy in *The Well of Loneliness*.

While Andrea was sitting her examination for the scholarship, Una's royalty account from her translations reached her, and in the luxurious holiday mood of Paris she bought John a set of sapphire and diamond cuff-links. She received between £60 and £80 for a translation, and had managed to extract a small royalty from each of the publishers of the five books she had by now translated. Her income from all this was of course modest. But she was prepared to lay it all as tribute at the feet of her beloved.

When one of Una's frequent colds assailed her, John nursed her, never leaving her side day and night, except once when Una's temperature had come down, to go out to the shops. She came back with her arms full of long-stemmed roses, with madeleines, brioches and oranges, to tempt her darling to eat again.

By early May, with the contract for the dramatic production of *The Well of Loneliness* signed, and Gallimard's translation starting to come in in proof, they wanted to get away from Paris to the Riviera where the sun could help to put the colour back into Una's cheeks. They settled down at the Golf Hotel at Beauvallon, near St Raphael. There they stayed for two months, bathing every day and getting very sunburnt.

Natalie Barney's house, Mas Natalie, was in the hills above the town, and Romaine Brooks had rented a villa. Colette's house was at St Tropez, only a short drive away. There were continual exchanges of visits with them and others of the sisterhood who were taking their holidays on the Riviera. Bathing parties, with cocktails and dinner, and dancing afterwards at one or other of the villas, were the usual thing. The laughter in the warm night air is perfectly caught in *Extraordinary Women*. Gilbert Frankau and his wife were also nearby neighbours, and they dined with them and were entertained by them in return.*

Una was in ecstasies. She wrote to Robin:

> It's marvellous to see John turning dark brown and smoothing out! But it frets us to think *you've* had a specially exhausting and harassing time while we were wallowing. Of course I never saw any of all this till John brought me – tho' it's an old familiar story to her. But to me all new and wonderful. I spend most of my time stark naked clutching a bottle of coconut oil, so as to cultivate a rich copper hue *all over* – no mixed grill for me! John is working at the *World*.†

* 'Gilbert Frankau's isn't a villa, it's a palace!' says the diary.
† This was a novel which she finally abandoned after several attempts at rewriting it.

Miss Kershaw, who was dramatizing *The Well of Loneliness* and putting it on in Paris, was proving troublesome. The nature of her naughtiness is not easy to identify from the letters and the indignant diary entries, but it is probable that she objected to a constantly interfering author, especially one who took herself and her theme so solemnly. Cuts were necessary to compress this long novel into a three-act play, but each cut was a knife in the side of the sensitive author, and finally John tried to cancel the contract. Miss Kershaw took strong objection to this, and lawyers were called in. Mr Goddard came all the way to Boulogne at a weekend to discuss this with his client, who drove down from Paris. In the midst of all this Marie Visetti had to have an operation – on, of all days, Friday 13 September – but little time could be spared for her, with Miss Kershaw on the point of producing a mangled version of the work on the Paris stage. They managed to delay the production by issuing a writ, and in October they were recalled to London by Goddard for discussion with counsel, Sir Patrick Hastings.*

By this time, October 1929, John had abandoned the unfinished *World* and had begun a new book which at this stage and for some time after, she was to call *The Carpenter's Son*. When it appeared three years later, it bore the title *The Master of the House*. It was her last major work, and much pain, even physical pain, went into the writing of it.

* Miss Kershaw subsequently revised her scenario to meet the author's objections, but Radclyffe Hall refused to consider it until new contracts were exchanged. This was August of the following year, 1930. Whereupon Miss Kershaw, who seems to have had a temper as fiery as John's, defied the injunction and went ahead and produced *The Well of Loneliness* in Paris. It had only a short run at the beginning of September, but this was enough to stimulate the sales of the Pegasus edition, and to give Holroyd Reece the idea of issuing *The Well of Loneliness* in the *Albatross*, a paperback series which he had now started. John rejected this suggestion on the grounds that Tauchnitz had an option on the paperback rights, and that anyway these rights belonged to Jonathan Cape.

Chapter Fifteen

A strong vein of common sense had always marked Radclyffe Hall's business dealings. She might say outrageous things in defence of abnormality; she might dress flamboyantly, and altogether seem to behave in an exaggerated way. But when it came down to business she was the true daughter of her father, who had left more money than he inherited without doing a stroke of work all his life, and the true grand-daughter of Dr Radclyffe-Hall, who began as medical practitioner and ended up the rich owner of a health spa, and of a great deal of England's green acreage surrounding it. You have to be an egoist to care about acquiring and retaining wealth. Together with a firm confidence in your own judgement, you have to care enough about principles of financial conduct not to have them trifled with. John was a clear-thinking egoist who was extravagant but long-sighted. Her letters to her agents, her publishers and lawyers, are models of incisiveness. And they are completely dictatorial. Nothing offends her more than devious conduct in business, and just as Jonathan Cape was very much in the dog-house for his letter to the Home Secretary, so 'darling Robin', her English agent, for whom she had felt a fleeting passion, and Carl Brandt, her American agent, are frequently rapped over the knuckles for putting expediency or profit before principle.

It is easy enough to make a figure of fun of her. Those broad-brimmed Spanish hats and suits cut like a man's, the firm, the almost devout devotion to sexual abnormality; the immense seriousness with which she proclaimed her own case, and defended others who found happiness and release only in abnormal practices, can so easily be caricatured. As she had grown older she had lost a little of her youthful lithesomeness, her eyes had become more hooded, her nose had sharpened, and her likeness to an eagle had become more marked. She was still a striking-looking woman, but what had been wild, secretive and exotic in her youth when she had been shy and withdrawn, and had spent as much time in the hunting-field as in the drawing-room, seemed a little clamorous when she was given maximum exposure in the press of the world as the central figure in an autobiography wearing the light disguise of fiction, and dealing with homosexuality among women.

What defeated the caricaturists was her earnestness. You can't make a laughing-stock out of vice; it only becomes funny when respectable people are caught up in its whirlwind. So, while the parodists were quickly away on the job, and *The Sink of Solitude* – a mock-heroic poem, author anonymous but plainly someone with the wit of A. P. Herbert or Jack Squire – appeared on the heels of *The Well of Loneliness*, it scoffed at James Douglas and Jonathan Cape and Joynson-Hicks much more than it did at Radclyffe Hall:

> The Isles of Greece where burning Sappho sang,
> We analyse in terms of Freud and Jung;
> Though Sappho burned with a peculiar flame,
> God understands her, we must do the same;
> And of such eccentricities say,
> ''Tis true, 'tis pity: she was made that way'.

But for the canting hypocrisy of James Douglas, the editor of the *Sunday Express*:

> While decadents the moral issues shirk,
> He girds his loins (if any) for the right,
> Exclaiming – 'Onward-Christians-to-the-fight'.

And for Jix and Cape,

> *Two* men in Sodom can avert God's spleen,
> *Two* men can keep the British Empire clean:
> *Two* men by filthy books are never flecked.
> Two *good* men – never mind their intellect!
> So JOYNSON-HICKS to JONATHAN sent a letter,
> And CAPE withdrew – he ought to have known better.

For such as these the poem has only merciless scorn.

What cut at her deepest feelings in this parody was the full-page Beresford Egan cartoon which illustrated it. This drawing shows Radclyffe Hall with feet and hands nailed to a cross, knees bent in agony in the same position as Christ is shown in the historical scene of the crucifixion. Pressed against her thighs is a naked girl, and on the cross-bar perches Cupid cocking a snook at the anguished victim, while in the lower corner stands Sir William Joynson-Hicks, wiping his hands and wearing the satisfied look of one who has just dispensed justice where it was long overdue.

Parodists are always in danger of going too far, but the over-wrought closing pages of *The Well* offered a temptation too difficult to resist. Stephen gives up her Mary, allowing her to go the way of normal love; and abandoned, calls on her God in lines in which she cries out for pity and understanding for her kind, as Christ in his agony on the cross had cried, 'My God, my God, why hast thou forsaken me?'

How fundamental to John was her religion? She was a convert to the Catholic faith. She made her confessions regularly, and attended Mass once or twice a week, and she was generous financially more than once to local churches where she worshipped, which found themselves in financial difficulties. But one cannot get over the impression that she was restless and chafing against the discipline which her adopted religion demanded of her if she wished to remain within its fold. She submitted, but not without frequent rebellions. She talked a great deal about the necessity for the Catholic church to alter its ruling over both divorce and birth control, although by their very nature these questions were purely hypothetical in her case.

There seem to have been no religious influences in her early life. The Visettis never mention religion, and her father had been a Free-Thinker. She grew up a lonely child; the image persists of a thin pale girl lost in the large garden on Addison Road, falling in love with her step-father's pupils. But a solitary, rich young girl, who despised her mother as her father had done, and who looked forward to the day when she would be independent, and could get away. The life hereafter for her must have signified the one she would know when she could break away from home.

Probably she gave no thought to religion until she became Mabel Batten's lover. By then she knew that she was a congenital invert. But in 1908 or 1909, if the fashionable Mrs Batten's confessor was the agent through whom she was converted, her homosexual nature would not have been admitted, and there would have been no need to refer to it subsequently – although one wonders how she dealt with sins like infidelity.

To have become a Catholic as Una did at the age of nineteen, without excessive emotional involvement, exchanging the established Church of England for the more disciplined, but not too harshly disciplined Roman faith, was one thing. To have reached out to it as a means of salvation from an inner turbulence of spirit was another. Of the two, John was the more devout, but the less assured. But one cannot escape the conclusion that she got more satisfaction out of her communings with the hereafter through the mediumship of Mrs Osborne Leonard than through the fabric and the formalism of the Catholic Church.

But the events following the publication of *The Well of Loneliness* deepened her faith, and Beresford Egan's cartoon was the spear which pierced the side of this crucified figure. From this time on, although she was yet to have her last infidelity, her mind was turning towards God, her craft of writing was to be dedicated to His service.

In the South of France that summer of 1929, when they were regaining their composure and health, Radclyffe Hall was ostensibly working on *The World*, the novel which she was shortly to abandon. The theme that gradually crept into her mind during that holiday, although she was not to start writing it down for several months, was suggested by the rocky, primitive background of the little coastal villages of Provence, and by the simple folk who inhabited them. She was in a mood in which rustic innocence and lack of sophistication made a particular appeal. The ignominious rejection of her book by authority seemed to her proof that compassion had gone out of the world. She began to think of a character in a setting such as this who might possess that ancient virtue, and whose life and death might reawaken the world to what it had lost.

She became haunted by this theme, seeing in her imagination a boy of our own times, the son of a carpenter as Jesus was, who as he grew up in the carpenter's shop would have memories and impulses that he did not understand, that linked him with the carpenter's son of Nazareth.

She could not get this character out of her mind, and one day, as their car made its way through Fréjus, a little village near St Tropez, she called the chauffeur to stop. 'Look', she said to Una excitedly, pointing to a low stone archway, beneath which there was a carpenter's bench and a carpenter at work, 'there is my story. That's where Christophe Bénédit was born'.

For she had already so named him, and she had talked over her plan with Una. The very name of the family, the Bénédits, suggests the close analogy she wanted to draw with the Holy Family. Christophe is to be the boy who grows up into the modern suffering figure. His father is the carpenter Jousé, his mother Marie, his young friend and cousin Jan, who is to be the modern John the Baptist. Her story as she designed it was to begin in Provence and end in Palestine during the First World War when Christophe and Jan, taking part in the campaign to liberate the Holy Land from the Turks, are sent out on night patrol, and Christophe meets his end, retreading Christ's way to Calvary.

There is nothing intrinsically wrong imaginatively, and nothing scientifically unacceptable, in assuming that a simple peasant's son in Provence might be on a plane in time with a spirit who had lived terrestrially two thousand years earlier in a similar family and in similar circumstances. We now accept that time is relative, and although our views on what happens when the body and the soul part company at death differ widely, at least the Christian view is that the soul lives on. Perhaps the most widely accepted, because it is the gentlest view, is that the human being, in Dr Arnold Toynbee's striking phrase, is ephemeral in himself, a wave that rises and falls, a bubble that forms and bursts on the surface of that immortal sea which brought us hither, and of which our souls have had glimpses in 'a season of fine weather'. That sense of the continuity of the soul would justify the conception of a powerful psyche continuing to vibrate, and someone now living might be tuned in on those vibrations. He who had been the carpenter's son in Nazareth two thousand years before might strike responsive chords in the carpenter's son in Provence. On that assumption the story of *The Master of the House* is based.

The trouble with such a theme is literary acceptance, not intellectual approval of a possible scientific phenomenon. Modernizing Christ's life diminishes the glory and the brightness that myth has attached to it. H. G. Wells attempted something nearly similar in *The Undying Fire* in 1919, in which the story of Job and his trials is transposed into modern post-war terms.

But Job is a very earthy human being. His arguments with Divine Justice are those of an embattled man asking only for a fair deal. Wells seems to get exactly right the sporting attitude of God and Satan on which the whole appeal of the story is based, and this is also beautifully brought out in the translation of the New English Bible. As members of the court of heaven are assembling for a regular meeting God asks Satan where he has been. 'Ranging the earth', says Satan, 'from end to end'. The Lord then asks him if in the course of his travels he has run across his servant Job, and boasts a little of the devotion and piety this man displays towards him. He has reason to be grateful, says Satan sourly, you have been more than generous to him. But just you try taking away some of what you have given him, and then how he will curse and revile you. 'So be it', replied God, rising to the challenge. 'Try it, and we shall see'. The testing of poor Job, painful in the extreme, is the result of this encounter between these two rivals.

This wonderful story reaches back to a time when God had hardly withdrawn His hand from the task of first creation, and when individual attention could be given to complainants like Job. Anthropomorphism was natural to such a time, and in the hands of an experienced novelist like Wells, the fundamental unchanging nature of man but the revolutionary conditions of the world he has constructed for himself, offer some fine ironies when the Job legend is retold of a modern man.

But Christ was not an earthy human being. He is the Son of God, coequal with the Judge. Also he is a modern figure, living in Roman-occupied Palestine, a society much closer to ours than to the tribal one in which Job plays his part. In that more crowded world, there could no longer be a convincing dialogue between God and a man; the action had to be expressed in action, Jesus shown cleansing the Temple, feeding the multitude, healing the sick and raising the dead, being tried before a crowded court, crucified before an excited city on holiday. Only in the stable at the time of His birth was He with His father and mother, and only in the Garden where He suffered the final Passion while His followers slept, was He alone and ignored. The bible affords us only the barest glimpse of His childhood.

Radclyffe Hall catches the simplicity and innocence of her Christophe, but these are the marks of any lonely child's life. There is an attempt to lighten the solemnity with the introduction of a mischievous younger brother to Christophe, and a drunken old fisherman, and a designing widow looking for a husband, all of whom play important parts in the plot. But their presence and their actions do not make up for the excessive weight that must be given to Christophe's holiness if the link with another carpenter's Son is to be made credible, and if the end of the story, repeating the pattern of Christ's sacrifice, is to be accepted as showing what compassion can do to help in a world dedicated to self-destruction.

Though they had vowed never to set foot there again, they had to return to England to deal with the troublesome matter of the writ against Willette Kershaw, and found themselves caught and held by the peculiar attractions of England for the English-born. After all, it was home to both of them, and the ancient town of Rye never ceased, in all the troubled years that lay ahead, to exert a fascination over them. The idea of living abroad faded, and it was now that they took the little house in Watchbell Street, opposite the Catholic Church, and here all summer long John worked at *The Carpenter's Son*, while Una, arrayed in a boiler suit with her hair in a scarf, worked with the builders at The Black Boy, the name they had given to the house.

Or did, when she was not ill. Or when John was not ill or in pain. Una's illnesses were frequent and were aggravated and extended by her 'nerves'. John's illnesses were only occasionally physical in origin. More often they were psychosomatic, as in the case of the stigmata, which suddenly assailed her, and which was to require X-ray treatment before it cleared up.

There can be little doubt that this experience came from the hysterical concentration she was now giving, and had been giving ever since the previous October, to the writing of *The Carpenter's Son* and that it was, if such a term exists, hypochondriacal stigmatism. She lived herself into the part of Christophe Bénédit so deeply that, at a further rebound, the vibrations in space of Christ's psyche, picked up unknowingly by the innocent Christophe, fell on her, who was Christophe's creator. There comes a point in the story where Christophe is lured to an assignation by a girl he admires, who is amused and excited by the prospect of seducing him. But when by some dumb instinct rather than from desire he puts out his arms to take her, the stabbing pains in his muscles force him to put them down again.

Something of the same pain afflicted John. She complained to Una of a growing discomfort in the palm of her right hand. Then her left hand was equally affected, and the pain increased in intensity to such a point that she was unable to sleep. A red stain appeared in the centre of both palms which gradually extended as far as the wrist, as though some liquid had been poured into the palm and had overflowed. The doctor recommended X-rays, but this produced such unbearable agony that she had to stop. Gradually the pain desisted, and the stain disappeared.

So the year passed away. A change had come over them. Once their house had been crowded with friends, and the talk had gone on late at night. There had always been the bustle of excitement and planning in the air.

One by one these friends had dropped away. It was not that

they disapproved of the association between John and Una. Many of them, the majority in fact, were homosexuals or artists leading vagabond lives, or simply jolly forty-year-old girls, left-overs from the war, liberated but not free in a class-striated society like England's, where morals were often what your own kind approved of, or did not openly disapprove of. One begins to see why they seem to belong to an earlier age. In 1930 the post-war idiosyncracies, and the amusement and interest provided by outrageous behaviour, were being given the cold stare, not the indulgent smile they had once provoked in the relief from the tension of war. Of course John's uncertain temper had something to do with it too. She had alienated many people, and Una, once the most gregarious and charming of girls, closed in on herself with her beloved and too often they were by themselves night after night, weekend after weekend, in this charming home they were making out of The Black Boy. Only 'darling Robin' came to stay, but then everybody was in bed by eleven, not up talking or dancing until three or four a.m. as in the old days. Robin came to take instructions, or to listen to chapters of the work in progress, not to laugh the night away as once they all did.

The friends were local ones. Three delightful women living together in an equally delightful cottage and garden at Small Hythe a few miles away – Edy Craig, Christopher St John and Tony Atwood, who gave John a piece of the true cross, which John imaginatively and immediately transformed into a symbol which Christophe has, which, when he has chucked away his rifle and bayonet, he clutches to his breast as he walks towards the enemy trenches. Francis Yeats-Brown had a house in Rye and was a frequent visitor. And Sheila Kaye-Smith, the Sussex novelist as she was called, highly successful at that time, who had married an Anglican priest, Penrose Fry, who had since become converted to Catholicism; 'The small fry', they were called affectionately. Until they in turn offended, and the house was empty of visitors.

But this was still a year or two ahead. A few days after Christmas in 1930 Noel Coward and Lord Amherst drove over from the house where Coward lived with his mother at Goudhurst, and

Una notes in her diary that night – 'howls of laughter', and 'Noel *adored* The Black Boy.'

During all this time they were having frequent sittings with Mrs Leonard, who had now retired to a villa near Margate. John had long retired from the Society for Psychical Research, and there was no longer the excuse as far as Catholic authority was concerned that they were 'investigating' with the object of adding to knowledge. No record is kept of what they did at these séances, but they had to be paid for, and they had to motor ninety miles or so to attend an hour's sitting.

But the one thing these sittings did not bring was quiet nerves and health, and whatever the consequence of the dialogue with the discarnate, it did not include charity towards one's neighbours. One cannot help seeing that as they lost close friends and became lonely, they were drawn more towards one another, but by uncontrollable spasms, not by the steady flow of deep physical and mental love which had driven each of them to give up so much for the other. John worked more and more alone, not taking Una into her confidence. Una was more often in bed than up and about, and one cannot help feeling that this is a dumb plea to her partner for sympathy and love. While John was writing *The Master of the House* she slept separately, was chaste, dedicated to the purity of her subject, except when some inner fury with herself about her work – the kind that all artists know – drove her to a sexual frenzy of which the invalid was the grateful recipient.

But it seems as though whenever they turned from looking lovingly, despairingly, or angrily at one another, they turned gleams of uncharitableness on any victim close to hand. A parlour-maid, caught being sick in the early morning, is condemned without a hearing, and not only instantly dismissed but packed off to her family so that her morals may be attended to. Andrea has been in disgrace for nearly a year, and is not being spoken to, invited down, or her existence noticed at this period, during which, on 5 November, 1931, she came of age, an anniversary which merits only a marginal note in Una's diary. Christmas comes in 1931, and with it the proofs of *The Master of the House*, which Jonathan Cape has accepted. Christmas comes, and they put up holly and mistletoe in the hall and study, and the three boys, as they are called, at Small Hythe come over to join them for midnight Mass, and for Christmas dinner come also 'the small fry'. But, Una notes, 'my John was so tired she had to give in after dinner and go to bed'. The New Year, for the first time, is not seen in together. The whole day was spent in marking proofs, and the year ends without Una's record of how many of these new years she has seen in with her beloved. An air of tension and mounting crisis looms through the record.

The Master of the House was published on 29 February, 1932. Its aim was high, and so was the author's reputation at this point, so that instantaneous reviews in the important Sunday papers hailed it as another striking book from the pen of the author of *Adam's Breed* and *The Well of Loneliness*. But to the weeklies which had had time to digest it, and which often reflect the coming mood which casts its shadow before, chiefly because their reviews are written by younger men, it was pretentious and inflated and dull, and this verdict ate into the heart of this very sensitive author who, for the two years that she had been writing it, had lived so intensely and emotively in the atmosphere of her story, that when she approached the description of his martyrdom she had experienced the excruciating pain of the stigmata. They had brought her intense suffering, but joy had lifted her spirit at this sign that she was sharing Christ's agony. She was emerging triumphant and exhausted when these reviews and the flagging sales of the book after publication struck her like a blow.

One sees, looking at it from this distance, that the book in fact fails through over-earnestness, a mood antipathic to the time in the early thirties when it was published. We were then entering the second decade following the First War. The half-hearted attempt to set things back to where they had been in 1914 had soon been followed by the period of 'drink-and-forget', and the late twenties in Europe had witnessed a carnival which only spent itself as the harsh economic effects of over-spending had ended in the World Depression. One recaptures the mood of these years so easily by running one's eye over the best-selling novels of those years, which like milestones mark the mood of the time, passing from *If Winter Comes* to *Point Counter Point*, from that to *The Fountain*, and from that to Orwell's *The Road to Wigan Pier*. From solemn rededication to ironic reflection, and from that to an earnest search to find a key to the puzzling existence; and from that to a book about working class conditions which plainly pointed to the road back to war, the solution having evaded us.

It was soon apparent that the publishers were fighting off that boredom which always settles on them when a book doesn't 'catch on' – the only cure for which is to get on with another author and book. Howard, telephoned to by Una for a report on how things were doing, was tactless enough to be rather depressing about the outlook, and this was not the sort of thing these ladies took lying down. He was soon recalled to a sense of duty by Miss Heath, on the instructions of her author, and a little later he made amends by sending a telegram to say that the 10,000 mark had been passed. But this was poor comfort for an author who had now passed the 100,000 mark with *The Well of Loneliness* in the USA, and gloomy was the outlook.

To add to their anxieties at this moment they learned from their American agent that the firm of Cape and Harrison Smith in the United States was going bankrupt, while the American edition of *The Master of the House* was still in the press. They tried to make contact with Jonathan to confirm this, but he had gone to ground. This was on Friday. On Saturday morning they drove to London and bearded him at his office. Jonathan admitted that Cape-Ballou, as the firm had become, was going into liquidation the following Tuesday, and he thereupon signed a release of the American rights of *The Master of the House*. Nevertheless it was a sad blow, coming at a time when the book was not doing particularly well in England.

It was a year for retrenchment. Instead of going to France for the summer they decided to go to Bath where they would be more in touch with developments affecting publication in America. Ever since February, when the book was published, Una had been ill. It had started with 'flu and a high temperature, which John caught devotedly nursing her. They shared the great bed together, but John recovered and Una did not. When they went to Bath in June, Una was still ill and very sorry for herself, but she noted in her diary that 'my beloved is tired and anxious', and she determined to make an effort to get better so that John's holiday should not be spoilt.

But her condition continued to deteriorate, and at last a specialist was called in from London. His examination was soon over, and his advice was abrupt and urgent. An immediate hysterectomy was necessary. She was rushed to the nursing home at 27 Welbeck Street, was operated on the following day, and for a week or more was close to death. During all this time John did not leave her side, except late at night to walk down to the hotel at the end of the street and snatch a few hours sleep.

When Una had recovered sufficiently to be moved she was driven to Brighton, and there at the Royal Crescent Hotel they stayed for two months, the devoted John pushing Una up and down the mile of front from Black Rock to Roedean every day, and only at intervals turning to her desk, where she wrote the short stories that were to make up *Miss Ogilvy Finds Herself*.

On Christmas Day, when they returned to The Black Boy, Andrea reappeared after a long absence, and on New Year's Day they all drove to London. There were no celebrations. They spent a quiet and peaceful afternoon and evening in the hotel, lying in bed and listening to the New Year coming in – 'only clocks and hooters and yells – no bells ringing'. Nineteen thirty-two had been a sad and trying year, and still the clouds had not cleared away. Something ominous seemed to hang over the future.

Chapter Sixteen

Of Andrea, they had seen little in this year. She had appeared suddenly one day in December 1931, her first visit to them since Easter. A letter which came ahead of that visit hinted of ominous news. The diary is mute on details, but by now one can read between the lines:

> John and I received Andrea at 11.30 in the library. She went at 3.30, leaving us appalled. We talked all the rest of the day and evening.

However, while not asked for Christmas, she was invited to come and spend a day at Rye before returning to Oxford. As usual she blotted her copybook. She missed her train and did not arrive until after luncheon. By which time she was in disgrace, John was not visible, and Una records of the visit only that

> I lectured her all afternoon and she returned to London after tea.

Once again, a sense of duty prevailed, and she was invited to come down for Easter week, during her Easter vacation. She arrived, as arranged, on the Tuesday afternoon. But Una had taken a chill in the morning and had retired to bed, and John was at her book, and not to be disturbed. Una kept to her bed on John's instructions the following day, and on the third day they all drove up to London, dropping Andrea off on the way. All that Andrea had had was some lonely walks on the marsh, and the week's visit was curtailed to one of two days in which there was no communication at all.

During that summer of 1932 Andrea came down from Oxford, and joined a repertory acting company. They did not see her, even though Una had been dangerously ill. It is possible that Andrea was not even told of her mother's operation. Then on Christmas Day, she called on them. She must have apologized or asked for their help, because in a moment their whole attitude changed, and on this occasion it is recorded, 'We talked over her problems, poor child'.

Their relationship with her was curious but easily understandable. Una had been devoted to 'Cubby' when she was a baby, but from the time she fell under John's spell her attitude to everyone close to her – her mother and sister, particularly, but her friends too – had undergone a fundamental change. John completely dominated her, and she became from the beginning a slave to her moods. John had no feeling at all for children, and although she was indulgent to Andrea at first, this lasted only as long as she was wooing Una. Thereafter the child was plainly a trouble to her, and there can be no doubt that the frequent periods of disgrace she was made to endure were at John's instigation. At the beginning when Cubby was sent to her boarding school at Harpenden, Una went to the Speech Days and other parental occasions, but she soon gave this up. These absences, if only for a day, distressed and disturbed her darling.

They seem never to have visited her at Oxford during her three years there. They appeared quite happy to get along without any contact with her at all. If she made the approach, and was submissive, and above all if she appealed to them for sympathy and help, then the fountains of generosity started to flow, and they smothered her with attention. But it is plain that this spirited girl frequently rebelled against the domination of John, and as she grew older could not stomach moral lectures from this pair, and at last flung out of the house where she had never been made welcome.

But once she had admitted her fault, as on this occasion, and John had accepted what must have been an apology, they were all over her. She came to lunch with them several times and they went to have tea with her in her lodgings.

Suddenly they felt that they must have a flat in London; they had been too much away from theatres, absent too long from their friends. They took a *pied-à-terre* at 17 Talbot House, and John accepted an invitation to go to speak to the English Club at Oxford. Over five hundred crowded the Taylorian Hall, and there was a reception after at the Randolph to meet her. She also lectured at University College in London to an enthusiastic audience.

But after a brief flurry of engagements and theatrical first nights, the loneliness returned. They found that they were having most of their meals in restaurants, and their friends no longer responded to their advances, or at least their responses were unflatteringly delayed. Then they both began to suffer from boils, and spent much of their time nursing these and feeling sorry for themselves. Back at Rye for a weekend they walked in the streets of the old town at night, just for the sake of the companionableness offered by the few hurrying figures who, unlike the people in the crowded London streets, threw a greeting or a friendly smile in their direction.

Returning to London they were even glad to see Andrea, who was playing in something at Wimbledon which they drove out to see. They bought her a fur coat at Harrods, and all was well between them again until she fell in love with a most suitable young man, Toby Warren, and Andrea, encouraged by recent kindnesses, brought him along for inspection. He was very youthful, only 23 to Andrea's 22, and very much in love with Andrea. He was plainly anxious to make a good impression on Andrea's mother, and on this formidable lady with whom the mother lived. And he succeeded, politeness and submission winning the day.

All went well until a luncheon was arranged at which Lady Warren came to meet Lady Troubridge; and this time all did *not* go well. John was in one of her moods, and Lady Warren's grand manners exacerbated it. John said some outrageous things, clearly designed to shock. Andrea was near to tears, and Una white and tense, and Lady Warren grew very dim and distant, until the party was over and Andrea escaped with the Warrens.

Andrea did not communicate with them after this scene, and more than a month passed without their being consulted in any way, or knowing what was afoot about the marriage, until their curiosity got the better of them, and they invited her to lunch.

She came, and spoke her mind. Voices were raised, and from this girl burst at long last her resentment of all she had been made to suffer during all the years she had lived with them. She was in tears when she left, 'very insolent' according to Una, but so choked with sobs and anguish that the insolence could not have been very articulate. But whatever had remained unintelligible she put in a still more insolent letter ten days later, saying she was to be married in a fortnight's time, and would not see them again.

In the next few days came a formal invitation to the wedding on the fifteenth of November 1933, at St Mary's Church, Cadogan Street. The invitation had Una's name written across it, with John's pointedly excluded. Of course Una did not attend. John would not have permitted it. It is also true to say that Una would not have dreamt of going without John. Her submission now was complete. But her anguish was not. There was much still to bear in the years that remained to them.

Chapter Seventeen

There keeps coming into my mind the story told me when I was a boy of the inspiration behind a piece of music which for a season I played unceasingly on the gramophone – the *Valse Triste*. The tale told me was that this piece by Tchaikovsky described the dance in which Death invites a dying woman to share with him as she leaves life on his arm. The slowing tempo of the music at the end as they leave this world used thereafter to induce in me a feeling of inconsolable sadness. As I have been writing the last few chapters about these two lives, that image and the sadness have both come back to me. The dance of love begun at Watergate Bay in Cornwall twenty years before had then the lively and beguiling lilt of courtship. The passion may have been unnatural, but it had the innocence and freshness of any beginning of love, when soul speaks to soul.

Both the tempo and the volume had increased to *vivace* and *fortissimo* with those lively and happy times when in post-war London and Brighton and Paris they had danced the nights away, and had laughed and played with the sisterhood. Then had come the great limelit hour of *The Well of Loneliness*, and authorship which had been a part-time occupation and indulgence became after this a mission, while the physical excesses from which they could recover quickly enough when young, now induced extended hangovers from emotional storms which left them battered and sore and sick physically. The friends dropped away, and the search for something – the search the egoist never ceases to make to prove that he is right – intensified. They were coming now near the breaking point, and the tempo of the waltz – which had ensured fatality the moment the invitation to it was accepted – started to slow down. From 1934 onwards there could be only one end to this passionate partnership.

They had been busy in the closing months of 1933 buying and renovating The Forecastle in Rye, the fourth place of residence they had established in as many years in that ancient town. They had gone first to the little Tudor cottage called Journey's End, where they had found installed as housekeeper that immortal character, Mrs Bourne, something of whose likeness can be traced in *The Sixth Beatitude*, John's last novel, which reflects the love they had come to have for this most individual of towns, with its arrogant motto, 'God save England and the Towne of Rye'. When the lease on Journey's End ran out they had set up at The Mermaid, the town's celebrated hostelry. The rooms were beautiful, and the fireplaces were ornamental and plentiful. But the draughts created by the winds roaring up the English Channel which came whistling through cracks and nooks and crannies in the historic frame of the ancient building were too much for such delicate bodies.

So they had bought the house at 8 Watchbell Street. It was a plain little house, and it was surrounded entirely by shops, but it was exactly opposite the Catholic church. From the sitting-room, when the church door was open, they could look right up the nave, and see the statue of the Sacred Heart softly illuminated by the votive candles burning before it.

This was in 1930, when John was writing *The Master of the House*. While she wrote, Una's strong antiquarian instincts came into play. Una discovered that in the 14th century the house had been part of the monastery of Friars Heremite of St Augustine. While John was lost in concentration over her book, she pulled the little place apart, tearing away Victorian additions, and getting back as nearly as possible to the original form in the 14th century. When it was finished, they named it The Black Boy, and John gave it as a present to Una. It was here that Mabel Bourne came permanently into their service, to remain with them until the end of their lives.

But they did not enjoy Watchbell Street for long. In Hucksteps, where Journey's End stood, a small house became available at a very cheap price. They sold The Black Boy and bought The Forecastle, which was to be their last home in England. This exchange took place in the winter of 1933. Again John gave the new house to Una as a present. The work of renovating, redecorating and furnishing it took them months of delightful anguish, and when it was all ready it looked so pretty and inviting that they were ready to settle down and never leave it again.

But Una felt that, before they did, they should have a holiday abroad. Knowing Una by the nineteenth volume of her diary, one can see that she was beginning to be aware that her constant illnesses must be trying to a companion deeply immersed in a book. Things had not been going well for John as an author. After the profound disappointment over the reception of *The Master of the House*, she had had to suffer the comparative lack of attention paid to *Miss Ogilvy Finds Herself* which was published by Heinemann, and Harcourt Brace in America, just before they moved into their new home. There is no one so difficult to live with as an author suffering the pangs of being unjustly neglected.

During all this trying time, Una had been almost continuously ill. She had never been strong, but there is a difference between a charming invalid in negligee with a headache, a cold, or an upset tummy, who can be wooed back to health with presents of peaches and grapes and eau-de-Cologne, with caresses and passionate concern; and a beloved in a crisis involving surgery and the possibility of permanent disablement, or even death.

Una's hysterectomy had coincided with their return to England after the giddy excitements of Paris and the South of France, in the afterglow of the publication of *The Well of Loneliness*. John had thrown everything aside at that moment in her deep concern for Una, who, as she recovered, one senses took the advantage a spoilt child would have done of this attention, and played it out as long as she could. Rarely a day passes in which there is not a note in her diary for 1933 of headaches or simply 'not feeling well'. Obscure ailments are 'John to Mass. I not well cd not go. Afternoon we had tea Cassons and dined Ivy'. The next day 'Neither of us well'. The day after 'I stayed in all afternoon with painter's colic', while John takes the dog Mitsie for a walk, and ten dozen carnations arrive, telegraphed from a Prague fan. The next evening they go to 'When Ladies Meet', a first night at the Lyric. 'Quite a good show, everyone there.' Then, 'We came home and undressed, but were hungry and dressed again, and to the Arts (Club) for sandwiches.'

This must have been a distracting time for John, and one marvels at the patience of someone who in her relations with others was so quick and impatient. Her devotion and loyalty to Una were very deep, and nothing but the sensual demands of her passionate nature could have made her break them. Una, so intelligent and sensitive herself, should have remembered what happened when Ladye ailed too long. She was sharp enough to note what she calls 'the hunting vein' in John's eye, but, too sure that their love could never break, she suspected only passing flirtations, and for those she had long trained herself to be tolerant.

But when Una suggested that they should go back to Bagnols-sur-Mer for a holiday before John settled down to her Rye novel, John did not want to go abroad. Later in their remorseful search for how it all began, John was to tell Una that she felt instinctively that she should not leave England. A sense that something awful was going to happen would not vanish. She kept these feelings to herself, and all Una was to remember, recording it later, was 'how earnestly she opposed me, and how I overcame her protests in my anxiety for her health'.

But it was Una who succumbed with enteritis, as soon as they arrived at Bagnols, and instead of being able to take the waters and the baths John found herself, as she had done the summer before in Bath, nursing the chronic invalid which Una seemed unhappily to have become. Undoubtedly the suffering was genuine, but it was also a pitiful cry for attention from an abstracted gaze. John was always impatient with weakness when it was a disguised appeal for sympathy. She had shown this same impatience with Mabel Batten when Una had appeared on the scene nineteen years before, when she had found it so difficult to steal away in pursuit of her new love. The new lover had not yet appeared, but she was trembling with the sense of some impending experience, and in no mood to share the sombre shaded darkness of a sick-room. Outside the waves of the Atlantic came rolling, bright with life and vigour upon the shore. She longed to be out there, and she instantly and gladly complied with Una's suggestion that they should send for a nurse from the American Hospital in Paris, so that John might be released to enjoy the sun and air. The next day Evguenia Souline arrived.

The first impression she made was of a stolid, plain-looking young woman whose English when it emerged from what seemed to be an immense shyness, was incomprehensibly accented. 'Oh, a foreigner,' groaned John. This did not help the first awkward moments. Evguenia had a very pale skin, and the slanting eyes of an Asiatic. She turned out to be a well-trained and competent nurse, and she soon made Una comfortable. They learnt that she was Russian, the daughter of a Cossack general killed in the Civil war.

She seemed rather frightened of the two ladies, and she had good reason for her fears, for Radclyffe Hall with whom she shared a table in the dining-room, and with whom she sat down-stairs when the invalid had been settled for the night, began to make rather alarming remarks to her. Remarks of an intimate and surprising nature that at first shocked her, and then held her suspended as though she were being mesmerized.

'I think you are beautiful,' said a low and thrilling voice behind her on the second morning after her arrival, when she was buying some necessary supplies at the chemist's. Evguenia clung to her impassivity as to a shield, but she knew quite well whose voice it was, Miss Radclyffe Hall's. When they sat on at table after dinner, while the music played among the palm trees in the drawing-room, and the sea lay like a pool of spilled silver outside, and the rich food and splendid wine dulled fears, the conversation kept coming back to love, and Miss Hall, who urged her to call her Johnnie, laughed aloud at Evguenia's attempts to pronounce the unfamiliar name. John found Souline a beautiful name, and adopted it instead of Evguenia. When they walked along the beach in the moonlight before turning in, their hips touched. A night or two after her arrival, when they had been for such a stroll and had re-entered the hotel, Miss Hall followed her to her room.

After a few strained minutes she kissed her. And suddenly the kiss became savage. Souline's lips were bruised, the strong arms crushed her; she cried out. Then she said to Miss Hall, 'This is the only way I know how to kiss.' It was meant to be a reproof. Or was it? She could hardly at thirty have been so unaware of what she was doing. Rereading a letter of John's to Souline which recalls this scene, we know what happened. Evguenia put her strong young arms around John's body and pressed her fresh lips, firmly and virtuously closed, against John's, little guessing what powers of excitation they had in that form for the burning figure before her. What had until then been no more than a mild flirtation turned in that moment into a passionate desire for freshness, innocence, the pure undefiled body of unblemished youth. This is not an interpretation contrived by the biographer; it is there for anyone to see who reads the six hundred letters of every degree of passion and disillusion that were to pour from John in the next nine years.

But John was nothing if not honest, and as soon as Una was up again, and Evguenia had returned to the hospital, she told Una frankly of what had happened – something that Una had already begun to guess, as Ladye had done in Una's case twenty years earlier. She did not hide from her the intensity of the experience. John told Una that she meant to see Evguenia again when they were in Paris on their way to Sirmione on Lake Garda, where Micky Jacobs had taken a house for them for September.

The shock of this revelation to Una must have been considerable. She was such a romantic herself. I am sure it never occurred to her that their union might be broken by a younger woman drawing John away from her. At first she acted on the assumption that, if she bore it courageously and did not make too much fuss, the danger would depart with Evguenia. But the meeting was already being arranged.

My dear,

We expect to leave here for Paris on the 24th. Only in Paris for a short time on my way to Italy, and *please* may I come and see you at 2.45 on the afternoon of the 26th, if you will. Don't ask anyone to meet me. You know by now that I am shy of people, also there are things I want to say to you – not frightening things. I don't know why I should have a feeling that you are scared of me, but so it is, and I don't want you to be scared. We leave for Italy on the 30th. Yours.

John.

The answer must have been immediate, for there is an added touch of teasing intimacy in the next note:

Your darling stiff little note came yesterday. I wish that I could write French as well as you write English. Only in one place did your English go wrong. In my country one would not – in the circumstances – have begun 'My dear Miss Hall'.

But the meeting when it occurred was inconclusive; nothing happened. John wrote the next day:

My dearest,

A torment of tenderness, of yearning over you, of longing to take you into my arms, and comfort you innocently and most gently, as I would comfort a little child, whispering to you all sorts of foolish words of love that have nothing to do with the body . . . I agonised to take your virginity and bind you to me with the chains of the flesh; because I have so vast a need that my wretched body has become my torment. But through it all my spirit cries out to you, Souline, and it tells you that love is never a sin, that the flesh may be weak, but the spirit is strong. Yesterday it was my spirit that saved you. Must I always save you? God help me, I ought not to write like this for our time is not yet. But I love you, I love you.

So nothing had happened but this outflowing of tenderness. The girl had put up a fight, but not so strenuously that she put off her pursuer. What is so strange in this relationship is that it is the seducer who seems direct in her passion; the hunted one is the devious one, twisting and dodging, in half-hearted attempts at escape, fascinated by what repels her, playing it out like a game. They had arranged to meet again when John would be passing through Paris on the way back to London. John adds a line or two to this letter to Souline: 'Lady Troubridge has been very wonderful. She sends you her love, and asks me to tell you that she will write you from Sirmione.'

But when she does write again, her first letter from Sirmione, it is to say this:

> My beloved,
>   I do not know how I have the strength to write what must be written. I cannot see you in Paris on my way back to England. I thought Una would consent, for she knows how it is with me, with us, and she knows too something that I have not told you, that I am ill with misery. Then I found that she means to keep us apart. I do not blame her. She and I have been together eighteen years. When all the world seemed to be against me at the time of the persecution of *The Well of Loneliness*, Una stood shoulder to shoulder with me, fighting every inch of the terrific battle. She will not end that right, but will insist on it with all the strength that lies – as she well knows – in her physical weakness. She has reminded me that I have always stood for fidelity in the case of inverted unions. I have tried to help my own kind by setting an example. Thousands have turned to me for help, and have found it, judging by their letters. I have a debt of honour to pay.

But in the end Una relented. She agreed first that they might correspond, and then that John might see Souline on their way back through Paris. But she extracted a promise. She asked for John's word of honour not to be unfaithful to her in the fullest and ultimate meaning of the word. John had no choice but to agree, although she must have known by this time that she would have to withdraw that promise.

She had always been a forthright and generous character, and this new absorbing passion drew from her a boundless effort to keep nothing hidden, and a burning desire to shower her beloved with gifts. Souline was poor; she was rich. She sent her the ridiculously extravagant sum of £100 for stamps, to cover the expense she was putting Souline to in answering her letters at 1F.50 a time.

Souline's reactions are baffling to the biographer. She was a young woman of thirty who had lived in Paris since she was seventeen. She seems to have had no men friends, although perhaps her plainness would account for that. But she had a number of very curious attachments to older women, who were wealthy and could order her presence in whatever part of the world they were at the shortest possible notice. The reader might suspect that these relationships were homosexual. But then why does she play the innocent to Radclyffe Hall, who was not only rich but famous, and was beautiful as well. Souline seems to play John as an angler would a fish, first letting the line out, and then reeling in rapidly. When Una's objections have been withdrawn, she writes to say that she thinks after all they had better not see one another in Paris. John answers that they must see each other to discuss future plans. John offers pathetically to sit the other side of the room and not touch her.

> Una knows that you have refused to see me and she offered
> to write and ask you to do so, but this I will not allow her to
> do. My love for you has nothing to do with my devotion to
> Una.

Then suddenly Souline goes to the other extreme. She confesses her love for John, and writes to say that she finds sweetness in obeying her. And she asks the age-old questions, 'Why did you fall in love with me? What will you do to me?' she goes on in the same letter. 'You mustn't hurt me.'

> Be at peace, my beloved coward, [writes John]. Darling,
> listen, I am John, your John, the John you say you love. What
> do you think I would want to do to you? What horrors do
> you think I have in mind? . . . Only, my darling, I am not
> such a freak that the thought of the love of my body ought
> to scare you . . .

Souline then raises the objection that it is 'emotionally wrong'. And John replies:

> Not *emotionally wrong* for your John. I have never felt an
> impulse towards a man in all my life, because I am a con-
> genital invert. For me, to sleep with a man would be wrong
> because it would be an outrage against nature. We do exist –

where's your medical knowledge? – and believe me, you must not think us 'perverted'. Have you ever heard of bi-sexuality? You may be that. You are not a morbid unnatural character who has fallen deeply in love with a devil. There is nothing morbid about your love; it is perfectly in accordance with nature. I think we can hold our heads high, my Souline.

Fortunately the visit to Sirmione provided a breathing-space and fortunately also a notable distraction that engaged their attention. Just outside Sirmione at Gardione was Il Vittoriale, the palatial villa of Gabriel d'Annunzio, and there in residence was the great poet-lover himself. He was now 71 and lived in strict seclusion, seeing no one. His romantic triumphs both as a lover and an adventurer lay well behind him; he would not even receive his old comrades in arms. But he had been a member of the circle centering around the Amazon in Paris when he had been in love with Eleonora Duse. They had heard from Romaine Brooks about him, and in 1934 his heroic exploits as an airman in the war, and his attempt after it to preserve for Italy the Dalmatian Port of Fiume, were still alive in everyone's memory. This is where Una shone in comparison with the just-as-well-born Evguenia; she had social assurance; the drawing-room was her field of battle, where she made her conquests, and she was deter-mined to bring John and d'Annunzio together.

She began by sending an inscribed copy of the Italian translation of *The Well of Loneliness*, *Il Pozza della Solitudine*, to d'Annunzio, accompanied by a note signed by John, to ask whether she might be permitted, accompanied by her friend Lady Troubridge, to pay her respects to the great Italian writer.

Ten days of silence followed the delivery of John's note. Then came a message delivered by telephone that on the following day she could expect a car which would bring a letter from Il Com-mandante.

The car bearing an elderly lady came the next day. With her she brought a huge bouquet of carnations, and a large bowl full of golden muscat grapes, sprinkled with the petals of yellow roses, which were presented to Radclyffe Hall with the greetings of Il Commandante. Next was presented to her a bulky envelope which when opened proved a positive cornucopia. From it poured bracelets for both ladies of rubies, sapphires and platinum fashioned by Mastre Paragon Coppella, the resident goldsmith of the Vittoriale. This was not all. The elderly lady also brought copies of the Commandante's own books inscribed to John. It seemed that the ten days had been spent by the Commandante in reading *Il Pozza della Solitudine*, and this lavish response to her inscribed copy was his reaction to so moving an experience. Then the elderly lady conveyed the message. The Commandante was sure that Lady Troubridge would understand his desire to talk to a fellow-artist alone – '*a tre occhi*', as Una translates his allusion to the fact that he had only the sight of one eye.

Una records in her book* how this visit and the queer friend-ship struck up between John and d'Annunzio occupied the whole of the time they were at Sirmione. Twice subsequently, at his invitation, they returned for visits, but the curious mental affliction from which he was suffering, which prevented him from seeing anyone, even his oldest friends and comrades, dropped a barrier between them at the last moment. But this encounter might have been sent by a kind fate to take the shock of the revela-tion about Evguenia which otherwise these two would have picked over hour by hour until one or both of them were driven to madness.

We see this meeting through John's eyes, for she describes it in one of the daily letters she was by now sending to Souline. No doubt she was deeply impressed by the attention shown to her by the great poet-lover, but her mind was on other things. She could not hasten their return to Paris. Apart from Una's obduracy, Romaine Brooks was coming to stay. 'Once she was fond of me,' confides John, 'but I wasn't of her.' Confident that the girl loved her, and now desired the experience of loving as eagerly as she did herself, she issued instructions, which jarred the fragile grip she had succeeded in establishing on Souline. They were due to arrive in Paris on Sunday evening, September 30. On the next day, Monday:

* *The Life and Death of Radclyffe Hall*, pp. 118-124.

I am coming to take you out to lunch at 12.15. Afterwards we shall go back to your rooms. Please keep the evening free also. I shall be a week in Paris, perhaps even ten days, and during my stay I want you to keep your evenings free. In fact, don't make any engagements for afternoons either. I will pay more money over to you in order that you may have a nest-egg.

Souline's response to these commands was to say that one of her friends, a Mrs Baker, wanted her to sail with her to America on October 3rd, and therefore they wouldn't be able to meet in Paris after all. A telegram was delivered to Souline

I arrive Paris September 22 for ten days. Will you definitely promise to remain Paris during that time, keeping yourself free. Telegraph reply as I am compelled to fix our plans.

'I don't know why it is that you are in such a position,' a furious follow-up letter said, 'that you cannot refuse this woman anything – that whatever she demands of you you have to grant her, even if in so doing you hurt yourself, and me you hurt very dreadfully indeed. But this of course you will have to explain when we meet.'

I must remind you [the letter went on] that you have fallen in love with Radclyffe Hall, not Mary Jones or anyone like her, and Radclyffe Hall has a standard to uphold. Help me with my work, not make me lower that standard.

My beloved, you have some dreadful faults. You wobble, moreover you get all your values wrong. Are you going to give me those ten days in Paris, or are you not? Please say so at once.

You are spoiling my work. I can't write a line because of your tie with this damned woman.

Do try to pull yourself together, darling. Honestly, I'll go mad if you don't.

Before there was time for a reply to the telegram or this letter, she telegraphed that she had taken tickets and would arrive on September 22nd. Her jealousy had plainly been aroused by Mrs Baker. 'This much is clear. I am up against a woman who has only to whistle, and you follow.'

She goes on, as though this obedience to Mrs Baker's commands did not go with the innocence Souline had shown at their first encounter:

> This is the only way I know how to kiss, you said to me in Bagnols, do you remember? And your darling lips were so firm and protective, so chaste and so competent to protect, so unwilling to give, so unwilling to respond. Why? You kissed me like a sister or a child. Bless you, my little white Russian torment.

The remaining days before their departure are taken up with letters, setting Souline's fears at rest.

> Please stop thinking this sort of thing, 'Will John find me a bore because I know nothing? Suppose after all I am really cold – how awful. Suppose I feel nothing at all – what would John do then? Very probably hate me. What ought I to feel, what ought I to do, what is it that John expects me to do?
>
> My dear, and very scared little child – there is such a thing as primitive instinct when we love, and in any case there is John.

But Souline is still afraid. John reassures her:

> Dearest, I shall not do you any hurt. I shall only make you very happy, I hope. If only you knew – it's all so simple. There is nothing to fear, nothing to dread, except inasmuch as all intense feeling is rather a terrifying thing I suppose. But believe me, life isn't complete without it, it's not enough to know of this thing in theory. I marvel at your innocence, I am humble before it, I kneel down and kiss the feet of your innocence. Don't you know that I will be what you'd have me? Gentle, if you would fear me otherwise. Little body of mine, little body that wants me. Am I likely to hurt you, or treat you roughly?

Souline's fears mount the closer they come to the meeting, and when John and Una arrive at the Pont Royal Hotel on Sunday evening, a letter is waiting for John to which she sends a reply by hand.

I am not going to force you to do anything that you don't want to do. Sweetheart, I'm John, not a drunken sailor. Damn it all, I don't want it – or if I do want it I'd rather kill myself than live with a frightened and unwilling woman. And remember you are free. There is no obligation on your part towards me. Perhaps you would rather we met as friends? Stop being scared because by being scared you insult me. Your friend, John.

Then there is silence. What happened? Was it all rapture? A year later John is writing to Souline again, remembering that first day together, when they had lunched and had gone back to Souline's rooms. Because she is such a natural writer the scene as she recreates it is vivid and full of truth and feeling.

I thought of your terror, even though you were greatly loved, and I thought of that evening when you sat at supper all crumpled up and in despair, and when I fed you as though you were a child, and I thought of the moment when I had to leave you alone for the night . . . And I thought of how virginal and innocent you were, how ignorant of physical passion –, you, the most passionate of all women . . . Step by step, very gently, I led you towards fulfilment. I found you a virgin and I made you a lover. And this has made you doubly mine, a most blessed responsibility I have taken – a most sweet and dear burden I shall bear to the end and beyond . . .

In this she was unconsciously accepting the trials that by then she must have guessed were ahead. But for the moment the rapture was intense. Silence closes over those ten days, broken doubtless – but there is no record of this for the diary has now been closed forever – by Una's injured manner, and marked by the shower of valedictory telegrams sent from Boulogne, Folkestone and then on their arrival in London. Souline was to come to London for ten days in November. That prospect alone sustained them both in the desolation of parting:

Nothing is real here after those ten days in Paris, when I held you in my arms and taught you to love, when your heart beat close against my heart, and your mouth was on mine, and our arms were around each other straining our

214

bodies closer and more close, until there was an agony in our loving. When we lay there together, hour after hour, and did not notice the passing of time because you and I had got beyond time. I am a stranger in my own country. Nothing is real, this city isn't real, the life I have come back to isn't real any more, my friends aren't real, my career isn't real. Nothing is real but those ten days in Paris.

Souline, so evasive and fearful before the event, becomes like all lovers, intoxicated with the bliss she has shared. She asks if she has made John happy. John's reply is, 'I found you a child; I have made you a woman.'

And now I want to tell you this, beloved. I am utterly humbled by the goodness of you, by the innocence and chastity of you that I found when I came to take you. I am utterly humbled by your passion, your passion for me that was born of love, and there is our love's fulfilment and glory.

But on one point John is firm: Una is not to be displaced. She tries to persuade her young lover to accept Una, as she has succeeded in persuading Una to accept the fact of Souline. This must have been a bitter pill for Una to swallow. To be displaced by a younger rival was anguish enough; to find that the essential place she had made for herself in John's life as an organizer, arrangement-maker, encourager and critic of her work, was all to vanish in a moment at the whim of a spoilt and foolish girl, was cruel indeed. You have to be born and bred in that race of women which Una so majestically typified to her dying day, in spite of the startling irregularity of her life, to be able to carry on in these circumstances. Grimly at first, then sympathetically as she became involved in their joint lives, carry on she did. It is only just that in the end she should be the one to triumph. But the triumph was as ashes when she saw what it had done to John.

Souline had only a 'Nansen', a letter of identity not a passport, allowing her to reside in France. But she could not get a visa to travel outside the country in which she had established residence, without encountering an immense amount of red tape. John wanted to help her become a naturalized French citizen, which would have removed this disadvantage, and legal firms in London and Paris were jointly charged to proceed with this. But it took a great deal of time, endless references and researches, and meanwhile there was burning Sappho on the British shores ardent for the ten days together in London which had been planned.

Una, 'a perfect brick' as John commented in a letter to Souline, thereupon came to the rescue. Being 'her ladyship', she had entré to important officials, and could short-cut the endless waits in Consulates. Una demonstrated the power of her connections by involving no less a person than the Secretary of State for the Home Office in Souline's case. But if Una was a perfect brick, Souline proved a perfect ass, as she was to do again and again in the trying years ahead, by disappearing without notice to Zurich with a Russian princess, whom she had nursed through her maternity. If it was difficult for a stateless person living in France to become a French citizen without procrastination and endless investigation, it was even more difficult if the stateless person was making application from outside the country. John raged and swore, but kept her sharp temper under control. She suspected the worst in the relationship with the Russian princess, but was reassured when a letter came from Zurich in which she detected 'a little cry of love', Souline asking for reassurance that John still loved her. But the next letter from Zurich was chatter about the Princess; it was 'like a blow at my heart', she wrote. 'How is it possible for you to change so quickly?'

> I must be all to you or nothing [she insisted]. Rather than not be sure of your love, I would tear you completely out of my heart. I would turn to my work, and pray Almighty God you had not killed my inspiration.

But the next day two letters arrive in Rye from Zurich:

> And now the sun is shining over the marsh again. Oh, my love, so terribly apt at wounding – so thoughtless, so much a creature of moods, so terrifyingly a creature of impulses.

This in a few lines sums up Souline. She was not to change in the years that were left. It was revealed that drink had been a problem with her, and John returns again and again to this theme, mildly rebuking her at first because drink is fattening. But Souline seems to delight in recounting her excesses, with perhaps the implication that John has led her astray, and that she drinks to forget.

Finally Una succeeds in obtaining a visa for Souline to visit England for three weeks. A 'perfect brick'; John writing to Souline of all that they owe to Una for the happiness of the meeting just ahead, repeats that phrase.

> She has accepted the situation, and really she has, I think, all but stopped fretting. She is ever so much happier now that she has made up her wise and clever mind to accept the inevitable.

Knowing Souline's muddle-headedness – this terrifying creature of impulses, burning with impatience for the moment when they can be together again, John commands her: 'You will make no effort of any kind to alter any dates that have been arranged by the Home Office for you.' The instructions are repeated and repeated, until at the end of a long letter –

> Darling, I am wild with excitement – aren't you? And if it's possible, I love you more today than yesterday. I keep on loving you more and more. Where will it end? They will write on my grave –
> 'Radclyffe Hall who died of love for Souline'

This meeting at the London flat, sealed off from the world with her loved one while Una remained at The Forecastle in Rye, excited raptures that were to stir the memory with longing when once again they were parted. The phrases in her letters seem to be flung on the paper just as they burst from her. They reflect the abject state of this passion, the longing to protect the loved one; at the same time the throbbing violence that results from the frustrations nature imposes. The longing for a child is there. 'Had I been a man I would have given you a child. I much long for an impudent Chink-faced brat.'

> Press close to me, and be shielded against the hardships of life ... be gracious and merciful because you have the power ... I am thinking of how cold your room must be this

Christmas – the first Christmas of our love, and we not together, the greatest pain the thought of you alone. My little cold and wet dog, I love you with my spirit and mind, all ways . . . I long to wait on you like a servant. I have never in my life felt so terrific an urge as you have roused up in me. I think that if you said to me now that you would not have me any more as a lover I might want to kill you.

She is concerned about Souline's health, and she makes her a regular allowance so that she will not have to work so hard, can buy herself warm clothes and get away from Paris for a holiday. Souline has the Russian temperament; she is derisive about matters which are of great concern to Anglo-Saxon ladies, accustomed to managing their own affairs. Money means nothing to her; she drifts from one financial crisis to another, and this exasperates her lover who, while she slips five-pound or hundred franc notes into letters, keeps urging Souline to check her extravagance.

Souline makes no pretence of being interested in John's books. When the three of them try a summer living together this disregard of genius shocks Una to the core. Wordy battles break out and Souline becomes violent in her abuse. Una knows that it is death to criticize Souline to John, but what can be effected by sniffs, heavenward glances, dignified exits from the room, was done. Life must have been hell for them all. But it was Souline who was forced to retreat. She could not break the bond between these two women. Once it had been fire between them, as it was now between her and John. The fire had died, but John continually makes clear to Souline that she will not abandon Una, and therefore will never force Souline to live with them. She tried to make the difference clear when Souline departed:

> I feel a deep gratitude towards her, a deep respect, and a very deep affection – also an enormously strong sense of duty, all this for reasons I have told you.
>
> My love for you is more like *First Love*. I honour and adore you for the innocence I found in you when I first came to you, and I honour and adore you now for the passion that equals in its completion your erstwhile innocence.

1935 and 1936 passed in this fashion, with frequent visits to Paris, and summer spent in the South of France. By now Souline is becoming a bit of a trial. She resolutely refuses to live with Una, and when she does come to join them in their hotel at Beauvallon or Grasse, her temperament makes life difficult for them all. John's love for her is unwavering, but now she frequently rebukes her for acts of unkindness, for showing lack of generosity or manners, omissions which she once would have smiled over indulgently.

The book which John had started in the autumn of 1934, just after she had fallen in love with Souline, and which she told Souline she had inspired, finally had to be abandoned. She describes it as a psychological study of a man who avoids all pain until in the end he is made to face it. She is now (1935) at work on *The Sixth Beatitude*. 'It is coming through very fast, just as *Adam's Breed* did,' she exults to Souline. Gripped by it, she sometimes wrote all night, and after a few hours sleep would join her secretary and work all day with her, rewriting and correcting. Unable even to spare a moment to write to her beloved, she agreed unthinkingly to Una's suggestion that Una should write and tell Souline the splendid news of the way the book was coming, and of John's temporary total immersion in it. This unleashed a storm. John received a sharp letter in reply telling her not to abuse Una's kindness. John capitulated:

> Next time she wants to write to you I'll stop her. The result will be that she will feel left out and offended. Never mind. I love-love-love Souline. I do know what you mean. It's your natural good breeding and delicacy of feeling. She genuinely likes you, Souline.

It was an intense relationship that brought her fierce joy, but was never without its stab of pain. Can it have been worth it? These hundreds of passionate letters prove that it was. But the emotional strain was immense, and it began to affect John physically. A breakdown was looming before her at the beginning of 1937.

Souline had been particularly trying in the summer of 1936.

She was hopelessly extravagant, and was continually toying with wild ideas for cashing the capital in the form of War Loan which John had settled on her, to start businesses for which she had no aptitude or training.

Souline's own health, always precarious, seemed progressively to fail as her restlessness increased. Her lungs were X-rayed, and she was found to have a tubercular infection, not serious enough to put her to bed, but effectively preventing her from carrying on with nursing. John at this time was engaged in the long process of obtaining for Souline British naturalization papers, a first step in which was to exchange her French 'Nansen' for an English 'Nansen'. War seemed unavoidable in Europe, and this was the only way in which they could avoid possible separation. Souline was unwilling, knowing that England meant Una. She used the excuse that the English climate would be bad for a convalescent from tuberculosis. But John baited the hook well: 'Here in my own country I can do so much for you. Moreover one day you will inherit English money. England is the right place to be your home. You have had War Loan bought for you, and I have made ample provision for you after my death.'

But even this would not persuade this obstinate girl, and once again John capitulated, persuading Una that they should shut up The Forecastle, and find a home in France or Italy.

Una agreed – she had no alternative, and no means of her own, except her small pension, to keep up an establishment without John's help. But one must give her the credit of supposing that this was the last factor in determining her agreement. What she still hoped was that this attraction would wear off, and she had good grounds for thinking that it might, in spite of the extreme attraction of this young woman. Evguenia was spoilt, headstrong, had a temper as quick and lively as John's, alternated between moods of wild optimism and abysmal despair, and although it was expected of her, she had not succeeded in reading one of John's books. She made no secret of the fact that they bored her, and threw them down petulantly. Una, who expected this to bring about the fall of the temple, was amazed to see that John took it all in her stride. These tantrums seemed to amuse her, draw her out of herself. For years John had been growing more self-absorbed, less confiding, and Una had put it down to artistic self-preoccupation, and had gone about on tiptoe, so to speak, in order that the muse should not be disturbed. Was it possible that her abstraction had been boredom? That she had not spoken because they had exhausted the topics between them?

But at least she could see, now that Evguenia was with them, that John was no longer working. To her that seemed a tragedy, but perhaps John knew that it wasn't. She had nothing to say, only love to offer, at this moment in her life.

Chapter Eighteen

It was the end of their home in England for the time being. Evguenia's health now governed their movements, and they packed up their things at The Forecastle, leaving the trustworthy Mabel Bourne in charge, to rent it when the opportunity offered, and shut it up when they couldn't; two ageing ladies swinging in space as though they were nebulae in the magnetic influence of a powerful star.

These two women had done great and courageous things together. They were pioneers in breaking down the hypocritical silence that had forbidden until then any open discussion of the sexual problems of women. As Catholics, they had had to defy the ruling of their church, yet insist on remaining in it, believing that one day those afflicted like themselves by this trick of nature, would have to be recognized and acknowledged as creatures maimed by God in the making, who should not have to stand outside His blessing.

And now, towards the end of this long march they had made to freedom, they were to be tripped up by those obstructions over which conventional marriages stumble, the straying eye, the sensual imagination, the lithe figure of a girl who showed herself available. Note that it was the conventional one, Una, who was affronted, she who had bravely adopted inversion and found happiness in it, not the congenital invert who felt no shame. To John, flirting with her own sex was a pleasure of life; a pleasure becoming less available as she grew older, and was more and more shut up in a privacy which had once added to her sensual joy, but which now, with a persistent invalid for company, seemed to threaten claustrophobia, as it had done twenty years before with the ailing Mabel Batten.

The qualities one most admires in Radclyffe Hall are her

courage and her unflinching honesty. Stephen Gordon in *The Well of Loneliness* is a perfect reflection of her creator. The solemn way in which she had dedicated herself to the writing of that book and had stood out bravely to defend it when everyone was trying to compromise, compares very favourably with the action of Virginia Woolf who, in the same year that *The Well* appeared and was promptly suppressed, published a brilliant historical fantasy, *Orlando*, which had female homosexuality as part of its theme. Virginia Woolf had identified the characters in her drama by including in the book photographs of Vita Sackville-West in the character of Orlando. We know from Nigel Nicolson's account that soon after the publication of *Orlando*, Virginia Woolf and Vita Sackville-West took a holiday alone together on the Continent. *Orlando* is, of course, a literary work, and *The Well of Loneliness* is a tract in the form of a novel. No comparison between the two books can be made on literary grounds. But a very distinct comparison, not to the advantage of Virginia Woolf, can be made in the authors' attitudes. Vita Sackville-West and Virginia Woolf were married women doing this on the sly. There is more honesty at least in Radclyffe's Hall brave appeal for understanding of this matter, and in Una's abandonment of the Admiral and her open surrender to lesbianism, than in the tittering jokes of Orlando and the secret passion indulged in hotels abroad.

But Una never got over the extreme conventionality of her upbringing. She expected eternal understanding and love, which John's congenitally inverted nature, instinctively in conflict with convention, could not supply. And so the diary never resumes. But nothing can shake Una free, although this, in the beginning of her romance with Evguenia, must have been what John longed for. Instead they travelled on together, now a *menage-à-trois* spending for the sake of Evguenia the summers in the North of France, and the winters in Italy, settling finally in Florence in 1936.

It was here that John fell ill. There were no symptoms by which the indisposition could be recognized, but that something serious had gone wrong was shown, as it so often is, by her failure to recover normally from an apparently minor accident. She had broken her ankle while they were in Rye for a brief stay in the summer of 1936, when *The Sixth Beatitude* was being published. The doctor there diagnosed it as a strain, and the break was allowed to set itself before it was discovered from X-rays in London that there had been a triple fracture, and the bone had to be rebroken and set. It was some months before she was completely mobile again. What was ominous was not so much the time it took her to recover, but the lassitude which seemed to have settled on her, which no effort of her own seemed able to shake.

Even in this depression they had jokes they managed to share. Father Ronald Pilkington, who was their chaplain in Florence, discovered as he thought something missing in their lives. In his own words:

> In May 1939 I came to know Miss Radclyffe Hall when she and Lady Troubridge asked me to call at their flat, after their parish priest of Luca had visited them and found that neither of them had been confirmed. I got them privately confirmed by the Auxiliary Bishop, Mgr Guiracchimo Bonardi. I remember they wanted to take new names and they chose two *male* saints, but of course when presenting them to the bishop, I translated them into the female gender.

The last years before the war, spent by them in Florence, were a time of beauty, shot through with sadness. John's weakness increased; she who had been the strong one while Una perpetually ailed, now sank into apathy from which she did not seem even to wish to escape. She tried to write, but nothing came of the effort, and her impotence in this regard was more ominous than the physical weakness.

Finally in 1939 they decided to return to England for a brief visit, sell The Forecastle, and then live permanently in Florence where they had taken and furnished a flat for themselves in the Via Bardia, and another for Evguenia nearby. There were already rumours of war in July of that year when they made the journey, but one cannot eternally wait on politicians, and so, pausing only to collect Evguenia who was in Paris, they went on to Rye, arriving there on 4th August.

Evguenia had come against her will. She had been involved in plans for starting a luxury shop in Paris with a friend, the nature of the luxury not being defined in the letters. But John had wearily insisted on her coming to England. Protesting, quarrelling, she had been carried off, and was now forced to live *à trois* with John and Una in Rye, which she loathed. John's eyes were causing her intense pain, and another operation – she had already had one in Rome – seemed necessary, but nothing could be decided at this moment. Every day the war news seemed worse. The subject was hardly mentioned in the small drawing-room of The Forecastle, being certain to create explosions of national temperament. Una, although Irish, had been brought up in the patriotic tradition. John, who was English to the core, discovered as the English do at moments of threat to their island, a love of it which in more peaceful times they never talk about. 'I am very homesick for England,' she had written from Florence to Souline before they came away. But Souline thought it the dullest, coldest, unfriendliest place in the world.

By the time they had disposed of The Forecastle, the sirens were already sounding their first warning, and their retreat was cut off. Worst of all, in John's view, Evguenia had been caught in the English climate. They quickly moved to the West country as offering the weather likely to be least harmful to her, and they put up, in their old-fashioned way, at one of those cottage hotels in Devon, filled with old ladies and old gentlemen loud with complaint. Evguenia could not bear what was bliss to Una and a habit with John. She fled to Exeter.

From then until the end it was a nightmare for them all. John's health steadily deteriorated. She suffered intense and almost continual pain. A further operation in Bath on her eyelids – the disease seemed to be ulcers growing on the inner lids – was unsuccessful, and she had to move to the Rembrandt Hotel in London to consult Sir Duke Elder and Sir Harold Gillies, the eminent specialists. A further operation was undertaken which gave some temporary relief, but the attack moved to other parts of her body. She had had a shattering cough for years, which was thought to have been a smoker's cough. She had made repeated but unsuccessful attempts to give up cigarettes, and now the X-rays revealed that her lungs were affected. They returned to Lynton, and Una took a house outside the town where John would be more comfortable than in the confined space of hotel rooms.

Then her whole physical system seemed to break down. She was taken back to London, X-rayed again, and this time an abdominal tumour had to be removed.

When she had recovered sufficiently after the second operation for the future to be discussed, and as Dr Amando Child, standing at the foot of her bed was wondering how to begin, she cut short the awkward silence with a typical John shaft of humour, tinged with impatience:

> I call it a shame; you have been left holding the baby. Do you stop swivelling your eyes and wondering how to tell me I've got inoperable cancer . . . of course I know it quite as well as you do.

It was a question only of time. They returned to Lynton on August 19, 1942. Souline was to spend her holidays there. She had been taking a shorthand course in Exeter, but had suddenly left and gone to live in Oxford. As she was a registered alien, she was not allowed to move without police permission, and re-registration with the police in the new district in which she settled. Souline's disregard of these regulations caused endless worry to John and trouble to the police. John was loyal to Souline, as she had been to Una and to every friend she had in life, and she was forced to accept this change and make the best of it. Souline was invited for Christmas, John pleading with her to come, the one whimper in this increasingly sad correspondence revealed in the phrase, 'I don't think I take up very much of your time these days.' In the end even this visit was cancelled by Souline, who wrote briefly a few days before Christmas to say that she had taken a secret and important job with the government, and could give them only a military address, c/o The West Central

Post Office in London. From an envelope of John's reply acknowledging this letter it is possible to identify from a pencilled post office superscription that she was in the Italian section, either of censorship or propaganda.

That was the end. They were never to see her again. The passionate affair was over. One partner was dying, the other had sickened of the bond, and silence, a grim, unbreakable silence, followed the thousands of loving words poured out between them in these nine years. Una broke her restraint at last. A letter survives, dated the 6th April, which starts simply 'Evguenia', tells her that Lord Dawson contemplates a further operation following the exploratory one that had identified the cancer, and that John has been very, very ill. The letter continues:

> He (Lord Dawson) is sending her to Lynton to recuperate for the further operation and if, in such circumstances, you decide to go away without keeping her informed of your address (and this at a time when the air raids are frequent), and if the strain breaks her down and she dies, it will be your doing, and on your conscience all your life – Una V. Troubridge.

There came no answer. Souline had disappeared. It was a difficult time for anyone who was homeless. How much more so for this temperamental young woman, made to bear the restrictions on movement and the constant surveillance of the police which was the lot of all aliens. Souline was proud of being a Russian, especially of being the daughter of a Russian general, and in 1942 and 1943, when John was dying, the noble triumph of the Russian resistance to the German Blitzkrieg had stirred deeply everyone's imagination. Souline was a passionate woman who had been awakened sexually by John. The first impression she had made was of an ugly woman, as we know seeing her through John' eyes:

> Souline, you are not a beautiful woman – I suppose I was right when I thought you ugly – but while I thought this I fell madly in love with you, and now I see no face but yours, no face seems beautiful to me but yours.

We know that plain people can appear beautiful, not only to the eyes of their lovers, but to everyone who sees them glowing with that beauty which passionate love animates. We also know that Souline was hard-hearted, selfish, grasping. But she must have had a heart to respond eventually to the passion which John aroused in her. We know how she fought against surrender to it as being unnatural and emotionally wrong. But then the animation of the spirit which physical love starts up overcame her scruples.

But one factor she could not measure because she had no experience of it, was the loyalty which is another form of love that can bind two people together who are no longer stirred by physical passion. Una was the immovable block between Souline and the command of the situation which, once aroused, she wanted. The years of fret about this turned her into an ugly woman again, while in a subtle way it bound the two old friends and former lovers more closely together. The situation is dramatized by John's grave and continuous illness and the temporary inertia of the Western front – part of a long-planned strategy of recovery and eventual triumph, which seemed to the young Russian girl, and to Stalin too for that matter, mere prudence at the expense of Russian blood. Souline disappears in a blind fury, and we cannot blame her as fiercely as Una does. John, the natural-born writer, remembered once a last glimpse of her when they were leaving from the Gare du Nord for England,

> . . . the look of your funny dear back with one shoulder hunched up as you walked away from me down the platform . . .

Souline had felt herself always the little wet cold dog, shivering on the doorstep. What made her fiery with pride was the glorious Russian achievement. She glowed again, turning her back on the two women who had always seemed to be in alliance against her.

Nineteen forty-three and the darkest, grimmest year of the war. London was dirty, dark and unkempt. The lights had gone out on the streets, and now they were darkening in this life.

Friends, not separated by the war, poured back, offering their sympathy. But there was really only one mourner, Una, who had been by her side for nearly thirty years.

She was moved from the Nursing Home to a convalescent home in Hampstead, so soulless a place that it made the more gloomy the parting that was coming between them. Then she was moved back to the London Clinic, and they managed to get a suite so that Una could sleep in the adjoining room and help with the nursing.

Her life, full of almost unbearable suffering, dragged on painfully and slowly. Finally Una took a flat in Dolphin Square, big enough to accommodate a day nurse and a night nurse.

But otherwise they were alone. Micky Jacobs, the novelist, who had been with them in their darkest hour at Sirmione, came to inquire after John. She asked if she might see her. Una said 'No, Mike dear,' 'You have no right,' stormed Micky. 'I have every right,' said Una. 'Now Mike, please go.' In the end she could make this assertion confidently. A few days later, release from a life that was no longer bearable, came gently as it nearly always does.

A week before her death she had made a new will appointing Una her sole executrix, and leaving to her all her fortune and property, 'trusting her to make such provision for our friend Evguenia Souline as in her absolute discretion she may consider right knowing my wishes for the said Evguenia Souline.'

What had her life been? A long round of self-indulgence, license, depravity? What continually surprises is the solemn conviction these women have that a great social wrong exists which must be righted. In this, women homosexuals have been much more militant than men, understandably enough as they have had to fight on two fronts, the sexual and the domestic, desiring equality in both.

John was born a poet, and an invert. Her lonely and unhappy life as a child deepened both instincts in her, and her inheritance of a considerable fortune on her father's death released her from the intolerable conditions of her mother's home. Because she had had to control the aggressive instincts of the invert, her growing-up was a painful time for her. Writing became a defence, a form of sublimation. But once she had got her independence she did not choose to sublimate the urge but to indulge it whenever she could. Yet she sought intellectual partners, for with them she was happiest.

With Una she had found a lover of the highest intelligence, a mentally stimulating companion, just at the moment when her literary powers were at their ripest, and when the moment seemed to have come in which a claim for the recognition of the fact of sexual inversion might be advanced. *The Well of Loneliness* was written in a missionary spirit, and the response to it was world-wide. It was one of those books which serve to undermine taboos, which clear away outworn conventions, which prepare the ground for legislation aimed at removing injustices perpetrated in the name of justice. Society makes laws for its good ordering, and as society is constantly changing, laws about morals have to be continually altered.

It was a life that had accomplished much, yet which in the end seemed to have been caught in toils of its own making. The figure of Souline represents the tragic element inseparable from the inverted nature. This love is barren. It is in that sense a finite love. And yet abounding faith does much to sustain it.

The day before she died, she murmured to the nurse who was doing something to alleviate her pain, What a life!' Seeing Una there she added, with that old look of courage, 'But, such as it is, I offer it to God.' After her death Una found a letter addressed to her. It was a last testament of the love that had held them together for 28 years. It said in part: 'God keep you until we meet again, and believe in my love which is much, much stronger than mere death.'

Thus in the end Una's goodness and love prevailed, and the remainder of her life was spent waiting until she could rejoin her lover and her friend. That moment came in 1963 in the circumstances I have described in the beginning of this book. She left instructions that were explicit; the night-clothes in which she was to be robed, the rings and bracelets she was to wear, the rosary and the crucifix in her hands, and on the coffin the inscription:

Una Vincenzo Troubridge
The Friend of Radclyffe Hall
Arrive at last the blessed goal –
When He that died in Holy Land
Would reach us out the shining hand,
And take us as a single soul.

Evguenia Souline married. She died some years ago. She was the catalyst in this drama. But what one remembers is not that fierce love, but the flame burning steadily and faithfully in the 'single soul'.

Index